THE STORY OF

PICKERING

by

John Rushton

Blackthorn Press, Blackthorn House
Middleton Rd, Pickering YO18 8AL
United Kingdom

www.blackthornpress.com

ISBN 9781906259280

© John Rushton 2011

Book Design by Simon Ellis
Email: simon@flexibubbleart.co.uk

CONTENTS

THE EARLY YEARS – FACT AND LEGEND

Pickering is a fine town, rich in community spirit, of busy appearance, dependant even now on a mixture of farming, industrial and service trades. There are grand landscapes in and around it. Residents and visitors alike can rejoice in a place full of history, but with a vigorous present and a hopeful future. Pickering was an ancient township, a parish and a hundred. The manor belonged to the Crown, latterly as part of the Duchy of Lancaster. The town gathers on the rising ground on each side of the Pickering beck. The township rises from the low level pastures of the vale up into the dales and hills of the North York Moors.

Remains of structures left by people of the Middle Stone Age have been found at the east end of Pickering Vale. The Neolithic or New Stone Age hunters and farmers also left long barrows, well made scrapers, arrows, spear heads and stone axes in their landscape. Metal working Bronze and Iron Age people added settlements, round barrows, dykes, tools and pottery fragments. Most have come to light as chance finds. Major Mitchelson in 1893, Dr. J.L.Kirk in 1925-28 and more recently R.H.Hayes explored many remarkable water-side timber pile dwellings, along the Costa beck, from the Iron Age and Roman times. Survey work now underway is expected to revise our old ideas and to reveal a countryside well used in all early periods.

Right
A Bronze Age round barrow west of Pickering

The Roman legions arrived in 71 a.d. to occupy the country of the Parisi tribe, on the Yorkshire Wolds and the limestone slopes of Pickering Vale. Their cart or chariot burials have been found at Thornton Moor and Cawthorn. Roman armies moved on northwards and westwards into Brigantia. They were here for three and a half centuries. Roman forts and towns at York, Malton, Stamford and Aldbrough were sustained by an active countryside, and good metalled roads. Roman buildings have been found at Newbridge and Newton Dale. Villa farmstead floors have been reported at Breckonborough and Burton riggs, and are suspected at Flamborough Rigg, Southbruff, Brough and several places with similar names. Roman coins have been found at Blansby, Carr Lane, Castlegate, Potter Hill, Whitby Road and Middleton Road.

A small fort and three camps can still be seen on the line of Wade's Causeway at Cawthorn north west of Pickering. This raised road crossed Ryedale from Aymotherby to Barugh and Riseborough, continued through Wrelton and Cawthorn camps to Julian Park, where an inscription was found, and to Lease Rigg where another fort stood across the road. It entered Pickering parish for a brief stretch. A fanciful legend told how the giant Wade and his huge wife Bell, made the road, to take Bell's cow to the moors, using a single hammer which they threw backwards and forwards, with great shouts. Bell carried stones in her apron, but when the strings broke, stone heaps were left on the ground. The couple built Mulgrave and Pickering Castles at each end of the road.

Left
Roman coins and artefacts discovered by Gary Kelly in and around Pickering

Cawthorn Roman Camp

Right
Wade's Causeway Roman
Road

HOW PICKERING GOT ITS NAME

The legend of how Pickering got its name has been variously dated to 220, B.C. before the Romans came and to the Dark Ages after they had gone, when a Peredurus was King at York. This old story claims that King Peredurus "builded the town of Pykering". He lost his ring in the river Costa, west of the town, but mistakenly accused his beautiful kitchen maid of stealing the jewel. The palace cook later discovered the ring in a pike's belly. The monarch was full of remorse. He married the girl and called his town Pike-ring, which became Pickering. Village tradition claimed that Black Howe at Newton on Rawcliff was the King's burial place and the legend lives on in the town's coat-of –arms which has a pike with a ring in its mouth.

Right
Pickering Coat-of-Arms

ANGLIANS, VIKINGS AND NORMANS

The Roman legions left Britain about 410.a.d, leaving independent British principalities occupying the partly Romanised countryside. Some Anglian people had been brought in from Europe, while the Romans were here, to defend the country against the Picts. More came in the 5th and 6th centuries, into early coastal settlements and onto the Wolds where an Anglian kingdom was separated out. This expanded, into districts once occupied by the Parisi tribe to become the Kingdom of Deira. Most of the townships, into which its landscape was organised, still carry Anglo Saxon names, ending with ing, ingham, ham or ton. An Anglo Saxon King Edwin, converted to Christianity in about 627, probably for political advantage. Mass baptisms followed. He was defended from assassination by his thegn Lilla, at a lost royal villa on the river Derwent, perhaps at Stamford Bridge. Lilla Howe was his reputed burial place. Deira, in time, was united with the kingdom of Bernicia further north, to become the greater kingdom of Northumbria.

Below
The church in the Anglian village of Pickering would have been similar to this one from Broadford-on-Avon. Remnants of the old church can be found in the later Norman buiding

The smallest unit of administration in Northumbria was the 'Hundred'. Pickering Hundred probably derived from some earlier Celtic or Roman administrative district. The Hundred stretched from Lastingham and Sinnington to the mark boundary near Ruston and Wykeham, and rose from the river Derwent up to the crest of the North York Moors, then called "Blackamoor." The boundaries were marked by streams, burial mounds, and standing stones. The large church parish of St Peter and St Paul Pickering may well once have been co-extensive with the Hundred. This parish still included Goathland, Kingthorpe, Marishes, Ebberston, Allerston, Wilton and Ellerburn in the 13th century. King Oswy of Deira established the Abbess Hilda's monastery further north at Streoneschalch, the Anglian place, which was later renamed Whitby. Others of the royal line founded monasteries at Hackness and at Lastingham around 653-5. Tradition claims that King Oswy and his son clashed at Oswy's dykes above Ebberston. A fine Anglo Saxon brooch was found at Keld Head west of Pickering in 1995.

Above This Anglian brooch was found in Pickering in 1995 and can now be seen in the Beck Isle Museum

Above A Viking trefoil brooch was found in Pickering

5

Viking raiders destroyed the early monasteries. A small Danish army led by Halfdan and Ivar the Boneless took York in 866-7. Danish leaders took over as lords of the greater country estates. Smaller townships were settled and given names ending in by and thorpe, such as Aislaby, Roxby, Farmanby and Kingthorpe. The old Pickering and Falsgrave hundreds were linked in the new wapentake of "Dic", probably named from its meeting place at one of the moorland dykes. After Erik Bloodaxe was killed in 954, the Viking Kingdom of York ended and Yorkshire came under Earls of Northumbria. The Christian Church was restored, enjoying a tenth or tithe of the produce of the land for its support. The Middleton, Sinnington and Ellerburn churches still show plentiful cross fragments in Scandinavian styles. Pickering has fewer pieces but a bronze trefoil brooch from around 900 with an animal on each lobe has been found.

Left
Detail of a cross in Middleton Church showing a viking warrior with his weapons

Morcar was made Earl of Northumbria in 1065. His most valuable Yorkshire estate was the Manor and soke of Pickering, valued at £88 a year. His hall was at the head of Hallgarth, next to the church of St Peter and Paul. There were four outlying demesne estates at Newton, Blansby, Barton and Easthorpe. The great meadow was half a league by half a league, a rich source of hay to sustain cattle through the winter. The commons were huge, sixteen leagues by four leagues, spread across the Hundred. The soke land, held by free men, included estates in eighteen places, among them Brompton, Thornton, Levisham and Middleton. The free sokemen owed military and court service to the Earl but could sublet, donate or will their own lands.

Below
Morcar's Hall in Hallgarth with its surrounding houses may have looked like this

The Norse King Harald Hardrada, defeated Morcar at the battle of Fulford near York. Hardrada was later killed at the Stamford Bridge fight. Meanwhile, William the Conqueror had landed with his Norman, Flemish and Breton followers. They won the battle of Hastings in 1066. Earl Morcar submitted to the new King William and briefly the north was ruled through its old lords. Direct rule followed after their rebellion and a siege of York. King William came north again. His "harrying of the north," drastically reduced the population and the farming assets of the Yorkshire lordships. The estates were distributed among the conquerors. Earl Morcar joined Hereward the Wake in Ely but was captured and given life imprisonment.

TOSTIG

In St Gregory's Minster in Kirkdale, a few miles to the west of Pickering, a sundial is set into the wall bearing the inscription, 'Orm, the son of Gamal, bought St Gregory's church when it was all broken and fallen, and caused it to be made anew from the ground for Christ and St Gregory in the days of King Edward, and in the days of Earl Tostig …'

This was the same Earl Tostig who was to die at the battle of Stamford Bridge, fighting against his brother Harold. Even by the harsh standards of the day, Tostig was brutal beyond reason. As the king's brother he was entrusted with the running of England north of the Humber with his base in York but his behaviour was so cruel, including the murder of Gamal, father of the restorer of St Gregory's Minster, that he was banished by the king in 1065. He promptly fled to Norway and offered his services to the Norwegian King Hardrada. He sailed with the Norwegian fleet which attacked York in 1066 and died at the battle of Stamford Bridge.

Above The crypt at Lastingham Church

ROYAL PICKERING IN A FEUDAL AGE

The Middle Ages in England can be considered as beginning with the arrival of Duke William of Normandy in 1066 and ending with the defeat of Richard III at the battle of Bosworth in 1485. This was a time of unsteady growth, punctuated by disease and wars and the little town of Pickering shared in these national trends.

The valuable Pickering manor was kept by King William and his heirs. Here was a centre for early recovery, as was Wrelton on the Roman road to the west. The Pickering Hall had its own plough team by 1086-7. Another twenty villein farms were also active but they were sharing only six plough teams. Instead of rendering £88, as of old, now they could only manage £1.0s 4d, a dramatic drop in value. The sokeland held another ten villeins with only two plough teams. Monks were briefly re-established at Whitby but were troubled by raiders and moved inland to Hackness and Lastingham, before 1078. Disturbed again, they left their remarkable newbuilt stone crypt below Lastingham church and moved to safer ground at York, to found St Mary's Abbey. Their estates at Spaunton, Normanby and Kirkby Misperton were also early centres of local recovery.

King Henry I secured Normandy and the throne of England, when he defeated his rival at the battle of Tinchebrai in 1106. His motte and double bailey castle was built on a hillside north of Pickering, with its high mound and great courtyards deeply dry ditched. Remnants of another earthwork castle on the west side of the beck at Beacon Hill may be earlier but this remains a mystery. The King came north to Pickering Castle. He established the Royal Forest of Pickering, as a game preserve for deer and wild boar, extended to include the Pickering and Falsgrave hundreds, on to the sea coast, a vast jurisdiction. His wife Maud settled a pauper hospital at Goathland, near the Roman road, far distant from the castle. Blansby and Dalby became "hays" or sanctuaries for the young deer. The Normans had settled the structure of Pickering, which still had twenty farmsteads seven hundred years later. The organisation of the "forest" of Pickering lasted until the mid 17th century.

King Henry gave the Pickering Church and his Hallgarth Hall to Archbishop Gerard, as a separate Rectory Manor, with its own three weekly courts and eight "oxgangs" of land. The Archbishop gave them, with Kilham and Pocklington churches, to the Deans of York Minster, subject to an obligation to feed fifty poor people with bread, ale, pottage, flesh or fish worth a penny, and to provide their shoes and vesture, at regular occasions. The Norman Kings granted away other manors and sokeland to several barons, new men "raised from the dust", like Robert de Brus, Walter Espec, the Fleming Turgis Brundos, Ivo de Vescy, Reginald Bushell and Nigel d'Albini, ancestor of the Mowbrays. The Vescy heirs had a castle at Malton and another at Castlegarth in Brompton. Turgis Brundos had a castle at Cropton looking up towards Rosedale. Their villages filled up again as land was brought back into cultivation. By 1163 Pickering had thirty-three families and its sokeland held thirty-one freeholders. Some were of Anglian and Viking descent, including Stephen son of Gamel at Pickering, and the heirs of Gospatric at Allerston.

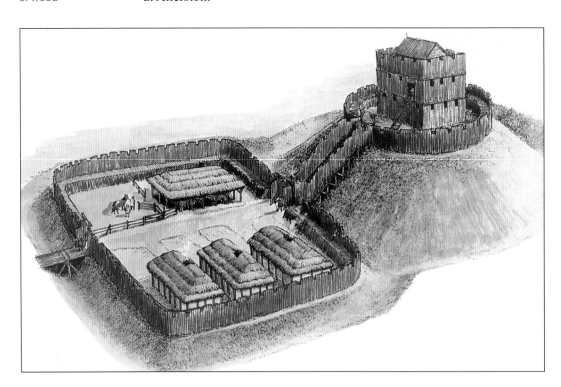

Scots raiders came deep into Yorkshire in 1138. While King Stephen was busy in the south, a northern Baron, William of Albemarle, lord of the great castle at Skipsea in Holderness, led the new northern barony to victory, against the Scots, at the battle of the Standard, fought at Cowton moor beyond Northallerton. He was made Earl of York, and custodian of the Crown lands. They said that he "ruled like a King in Yorkshire". He built himself a fine timber castle on Crown land at the Scarborough headland in Falsgrave hundred. A Borough town was laid out west of the great rock, and then a second New Borough further west and a port on the sands under the cliff. The next King, Henry II, persuaded him to hand them over, in exchange for Driffield. This King probably gave Pickering castle its inner stone curtain walls. Ansketil Malecake of Pickering supervised the conversion of Scarborough castle into a strong stone Crown fortress.

Both the King and the Barons had estates to spare. They gave lands to the new monasteries that they founded. First came the Benedictine and Augustinian houses and later the more ascetic Cistercians, who arrived at Rievaulx, in 1131-2. King Henry I had donated the tithe of his venison throughout Yorkshire to St Mary's Abbey, York. King Henry II gave all the Marishes from Kirkby Misperton to Ebberston to Rievaulx Abbey in 1158. Their lay brothers made the long Friar's Dyke and built several grange farmsteads. The Knight Templars were given manors at Foulbridge and Lockton. Small nunneries were founded at Little Marish, below Ebberston, at Rosedale and at Wykeham. The York Hospital of St Leonard's gained a rent of ten marks a year from an estate at Ellerburn. The Gilbertine monks of Malton received grange estates at Aislaby, Ebberston and Goathland. The St Nicholas Hospital was founded in Marton lane on the approach to Pickering from the Roman road. At an unknown date, an anchorite was given a dwelling in Westgate.

The Rosamund Tower
and curtain wall at
Pickering Castle

King Henry II had houses, within the Pickering castle walls, reached by bridges over the great ditches. A later stone tower bore the name of his mistress Rosamund Clifford, who may have used an earlier timber lodging on the site. King John came to stay at Pickering Castle in 1201, 1208 and 1210. During his visits the monarch hunted the wild boar and played backgammon. Alan Wastehose brought twenty-eight of his royal hounds another year. The King's grant of the market and the mill to the Pickering men, for a regular payment, probably marked the founding of the Borough of Pickering, initially concentrated in Boroughgate, and distinct from the older village. Burgesses paid four pence, house rent, twice yearly, while the villein farmers of the township paid other sums quarterly. Bryan the King's Usher garrisoned the castle with two sergeants and twenty-two men in 1203. The castle was strengthened during his quarrel with the northern barons. After granting Magna Carta, in 1215, he campaigned successfully against their Yorkshire castles.

Pickering and Galtres Forests remained valued hunting preserves and sources of meat for royal larders, especially after Ryedale and many other areas were disafforested. The King's fool arrived in 1227 to take twenty hinds and ten wild boars for the royal tables. Pickering timber was sent as far as York, Scarborough and Topcliffe castles for house building. The cutting of all main oaks was annually recorded and regulated by the foresters. Locals had limited rights, called "boots", to other wood, such as house bote, plough bote, hedge bote and cart bote. All large dogs had their claws cut. There were inquests on dead deer. Intaking of land was restrained. The several Forest courts met regularly to maintain the venison and the "vert", meaning the woods in which they flourished. A poacher of deer could be killed on sight.

The Church of St Peter and Paul was enlarged more than once but King Henry III had a separate castle chapel by 1227. The Deans of York kept the Rectory House at the head of Hallgarth, with its "Kirkham" manor. The lower part of the present Whitby Road was called Kirkham lane. Two of the Deans of York were from the Pickering family, and one of them founded a York hospital and a school. Another Dean abolished the ancient Dean's charity. A new Vicar was appointed to serve the parish church on the Dean's behalf in 1252, with ninety-six acres of glebe land. The outlying village chapels at Ellerburn, and Wilton, Ebberston and Allerston were given two shared vicars, at the same time. The castle chapel was given an endowed chantry priest to pray for the King's soul in 1255.

Right
The church of St Peter and St Paul was rebuilt from 1140 onwards

A MARKET BOROUGH WITHIN THE DUCHY OF LANCASTER

A major change was made in June 1267 when King Edward I gave the lordship of the Manor, Castle, Honour, Forest and Wapentake of Pickering, with other vast estates, to his son Edmund Crouchback. This brought the district within what would later be known as the Duchy of Lancaster. The father visited in 1280 and 1292 but the son, Edmund Earl of Lancaster, resided for longer periods. Thirty oaks were felled to warm Edmund and his wife for a six-day stay in 1281. He secured a new Castlegate fair in 1290 on the Eve, Day and Morrow of the Feast of Holy Cross. This survived as a popular feast until the early 20th century, during which the castle grounds were thrown open to all residents.

Below A royal banquet in the hall at Pickering Castle

Earl Edmund of Lancaster's demesne estate was administered from the castle. He held 194 acres of arable land, great meadows called "ings", two water mills let at £20, the markets and the tolls, fourteen cottages, and also the free burgages which paid him 15s.8d a year. His Bailiff was paid £12 a year, and his chaplain £3 while his old nurse Sophy received a £1 pension. Four headlands were set aside to maintain the castle porter's horses. The Constable had some acres in the Castle Ings. Fifteen hundred sheep and five score ewes came regularly to the castle for wool clipping. The villein farmers held the other "oxgangs" of land, as clusters of strips, scattered within the furlongs that made up the fields. They were obliged to repair the milldam, while the sokemen maintained the castle outworks. The Earl had regular manor, forest and wapentake courts, his own gallows, and he took fines for breaches of the assize of bread and ale.

For the first and only time, the Borough of Pickering was summoned to send two Members to Parliament, in 1295. A Dominican friar came in another year, from Scarborough, to preach a crusade at the market cross. Pickering held thirty-four free men in 1301. The substantial taxpayers included Sir Adam Bruce, John son of Hugh, William Malecake, and the Hospital of St Nicholas in Marton Lane. Tanners soaked their hides in tree bark. Borough merchants annually sent several sacks of wool to York, selling for as much as £7 a sack. Town houses were built from pairs of oak beams, rising to a ridge beam. A woodward guarded local interests in the vanishing woodland. Iron was worked in the hills above Levisham and Rosedale using charcoal for fuel. The sixty-two "bondmen" were farmers and craftsmen, including a baker, a cooper, fisherman, butcher, fuller, blacksmith, tailor, salter, dyer, shoemakers, a weaver and Clement the Potter. Elena had the first house in Willergate. A cow might be worth 5s, a sheep 1s and a small pig 6d. A quarter of oats could be obtained for 2s and a brass pot for 1s.8d. Not many had brass pots.

Right
A Dominican Friar
preaches at Pickering
Market Cross

Thomas, 2nd Earl of Lancaster led the baronial opposition to King Edward II and his favourite Piers Gaveston. When the King left his friend Piers in Scarborough castle in 1312, three hundred green clad Pickering men, led by John de Dalton of Kirkby Misperton attacked Scarborough Castle. Legend says that they took the high road, while a force from Scarborough came to Pickering on the low road. A large new stone Hall was built at Pickering Castle, in 1314, with a single upper private room, to serve as home for the Countess Alice Lacy, the very young wife of Earl Thomas. This building was remarkable and it cost £341. Eighty planks came for flooring a walkway. Only the footings and door ways remain of the broad hall, which must have had central columns to support the roof span. During a year's stay, Alice spent £285.13s 4½d.

Left
This cruck beam cottage would originally have been thatched and is typical of those found in Pickering

Robert the Bruce brought a Scots army, deep into Ryedale in 1322. The Kingthorpe manor house was damaged and the nuns fled from Rosedale Priory. The Pickering Lythe leadership, in the absence of the Earl, met to offer three hostages for a ransom of 200 marks, offered to avoid worse damage. The Scots pressed on to Malton castle and raided over the Wolds. Three years later, the hostages were still in Scotland and the ransom was unpaid. Earl Thomas was now suspected of collusion with the Scots. He was defeated by a royal force at the battle of Boroughbridge and was taken to Pontefract for beheading. Later people thought that he was a saint, because he had resisted the King. He did but he wasn't. His hat was thought to cure severe head aches.

Below

Pickering Castle with its curtain wall built by Edward II was completed in the 14th Century

Painting by Ivan Lapper

King Edward II re-possessed Pickering Castle and appointed new officers. His masons built a new gate with a drawbridge and spent £278 on a stone curtain wall with towers for the outer bailey. Lead sheets were delivered for roofing and a great springald was installed along with forty lances, eight crossbows and a hundred bolts. The old hall and the woolhouse were repaired. A new privy built near the new hall cost 4s.4½d. The King hunted the district for three weeks that year. He gave the Pickering poor a few pence and graciously allowed William the Dalby hermit pasture for a third cow in the Launde. King Edward III came in later years, giving food for 100 poor people, one Corpus Christi day. During the boom times of a royal visit, many townsmen and women served at the castle, and seventeen alehouse keepers welcomed his followers. Sir William Brus established a chantry for the souls of the respected Deans William and Robert of Pickering in 1337.

Left
The tomb of Sir David Roucliffe and his wife can be seen in Pickering Church

A SMALLER SOCIETY AFTER THE PLAGUE

The plague known as the Black Death struck many people throughout Britain in 1348-49, causing many deaths in Pickering Vale, and recurring from time to time. Richard Rolle, the famous religious writer from Thornton Dale died at Hampole near Doncaster. Henry the fourth Earl of Lancaster died in the plague of 1361. His daughter Blanche took the estates to her husband John of Gaunt. He became Duke of Lancaster. John repaired the castle in 1374. He gave the St Nicholas Hospital estate to his castle chantry priest and erected stabling for his horses in the outer bailey of the castle. His stock keeper at the castle in 1393 had 2696 sheep, which gave £37.12s.6d income from wool. Despite the general fall in population, the tax collectors still recorded 435 adults at Pickering in 1377.

When Henry of Bolingbroke, son of John of Gaunt, landed at Spurn in July 1399, he rode to Pickering Castle. With the support of the northern Percy and Neville families, he would continue south to claim the throne as King Henry IV, first monarch of the house of Lancaster. King Richard II was deposed and an old verse claims that he was briefly imprisoned at Pickering castle. John Marshall now held the old Bruce mansion called Eastgate Hall. Sir David Roucliffe, the local estate steward, who had welcomed Bolingbroke, was rewarded with life custody of the Castle. His great mansion house was in Old Walls close near Keld Head. He founded a chantry in the Parish church, in 1407 where fine effigies remain of him and of his wife in fashionable attire. The church was now a colourful place, richly adorned with wall paintings illustrating stories of the saints of the Christian church.

Right
Despite the ravages of the black death, there were 435 adults living in Pickering in 1377

The records of manor courts held in 15th century Pickering detail the character of local life. The demesnes were let to major landowners, a sort of middle class. The principal roads were Eastgate, Westgate, Castlegate, Boroughgate and Hungate, where the dogs once ran. Birdgate extended down into the Market place, and "Wolewardgate" was one of many back lanes. John Salter was charged with offering stinking fish at the market in 1422. Cottages had been built near the "stanbrig". Open areas remained, including "a waste near Hallgarth called Smithill", Hungate Green, Potter Hill and Tenter garth, where cloths were hung to bleach. We call it the car park, near the supermarket. There was a pannierman croft, a glover's limepit near the North Mill and a goose croft. Small plots south and west of the churchyard, and on the south side of the market place were carved out as sites for work shops, one eight yards by six, and another four "ells" by three "ells".

Below
Pickering Parish
church wall paintings

The Pickering hallmoot court annually appointed two constables, two market searchers, two yarn tellers, two field reeves, two ale tasters, two leather searchers, two water searchers and two pinders to impound stray animals. Each township had its own byelawmen to make good orders where the state had made no provision. One byelaw declared that every Pickering householder should "shut up nightly". Offenders frequently punished, included men for assaults and women for scolding. While King Henry VI reigned, Agnes Benson took hedging from William Day's garden, a lad went eavesdropping and six women refused to send for the aletasters to approve their ale. John Wright chased William Smith's mare. Another man kept his dunghill too long in the king's highway. The separate Pickering forest courts brought together a constable and four men from all the villages and hamlets from the coast to Wrelton. Those who walked in the Forest took oaths on St William's day not to break forest law. King Henry VII made efforts to restore deer stocks, appointing new men from outside the district to run his forest.

Below A wall painting in Pickering church showing the death of King Edmund and other scenes

Above
The Pickering
Hallmoot court
punished
breaches of the
peace

THE ROYAL PRISONER

King Richard II outraged his barons by his behaviour with his 'favourites' and he seemed more interested in the arts than in fighting. He was deposed in 1400 and his place taken by Henry Bolingbroke as Henry IV. How Richard died is not fully known but a verse written around 1450 by John Hardyng suggests he might have been in Pickering castle

The King then sent King Richard to Leeds
There to be kept surely and privately
From then after to Pickering went he needs
And to Knaresborough after led was he
But to Pontefract last where he did die.

Right
King Richard II

AN AGE OF RELIGIOUS DISAGREEMENT

The time of the Tudor monarchs, from 1485 to 1603 is remembered for the dominating characters of Henry VIII and Elizabeth I but also as a time of growing national consciousness and our separation from the Catholic Church which had dominated men's lives in the Middle Ages.

The traveller William Leland rode from Scarborough in 1540 finding his way to Pickering "by hille and dale meate plentifull of corn and grasse but little wood in sight". He said that "The toune of Pykering is large but not welle compact togither. The greatest part of it with the paroch chirch and the castel is on the south est part of the broke renning thorough the toune and standith on a great slaty hille. The other part of the toun is not so bigge as this; the brook rennith bytwixt them, that sumtyme ragith, but it suagith shortley again." "He saw the ruines of a manor place called Bruses Haul and a manor place of the Lascelles at Keldhead". Others tell us that Robert Hasting's house in Marketstead and Hallgarth had silver spoons, a mazer and a standing silver piece. Ralph Dodmer, a Pickering boy had gone to be Lord Mayor of London.

Left King Henry VIII

25

King Henry VIII and his ministers separated the English church from the Catholic church of Rome. The state dissolved the smaller monasteries, chiefly nunneries in 1536, in order to acquire their assets and estates. Rosedale Priory had held the Nun's garth at Middleton and three Pickering houses, which now passed into the hands of laymen. Pickering men joined the fruitless rebellion against taxation and change known as the "Pilgrimage of Grace". The dissolution of the greater monasteries followed in 1538. The extensive local estates of Malton and other Priories and Abbeys came onto the market. Sir Roger Cholmley the Recorder of London paid £665 to buy much of the Rievaulx abbey estate in the Marishes. The chantries in the parish churches were also abolished. The Guilds of the Virgin Mary at Pickering and Middleton churches ended in 1548 but their assets were diverted to maintain new Grammar Schools at each place.

Below
Pickering men joined 'The Pilgrimage of Grace' and may have been arrested when it failed

Queen Elizabeth's administration made the separate English church permanent. Attendance was compulsory for a time. A Pickering parish register was started in 1559 and there were new pews in the church. The bible and the services were now in English. There was controversy between lingering Catholicism and new Protestantism. Rows in the church were not uncommon. Robert Lemyng once shut the good book on the parish clerk's hands in the church in 1594. Robert Pratt abused the churchwardens in 1601. Vicar Edward Mills was deprived of office after local protests in 1615 that he had shown little attention to preaching the gospel. Long sermons were the order of the day, but the youngsters would nip out of the back door for the usual games in the churchyard.

Right Pickering's Parish register was begun in 1539 to record christenings, marriages and deaths

Midsummer Day meetings were held for Pickering youth with a piper. There were about a dozen marriages and up to fifty baptisms in a year. One vicar owned a warming pan and a feather bed. He had bacon flitches hung in one room, and a weaver's loom in another.

A TROUBLESOME KNIGHT

The first Tudor monarchs had difficulty controlling their more powerful subjects who often took the law into their own hands. There were constant quarrels about land and money between Sir Roger Hastings of Roxby and Sir Richard Cholmley a local magnate. Followers of the two men roamed the countryside with 'bows, arrows and long spears in manner and form of war', setting ambushes and accosting each other's families. Sir Roger Hastings with twelve of his men broke into Pickering Castle to release one of his servants, John Harwood. By the time of Henry VIII, such occurrences had become rare.

Above
Artist's impression of Sir Roger Hastings

CIVIL WAR

Seventeenth century England was a time of civil war and religious turmoil. Charles I was executed and England was for a time a republic. The old ways were restored when Oliver Cromwell died and Charles II was put back on the throne. It was clear the king now acted with Parliament and not as a supreme ruler.

John Ripley and Robert Rogers ran the Elizabethan tanneries in Pickering. There were eleven maltsters by 1608. There were novelties. Roger Parke built a Brass kiln near Keld Head, sixty feet by twenty-three feet. Edward Barker erected a new forge, near the stone bridge at the bottom of Potter Hill. A new House of Correction was opened in 1611 to alter the ways of those of an idle or independent disposition. Tradition claims that it was in the Undercliff. Several coppices, locally known as haggs, were established for sustaining wood supplies, between Blansby Park and the town. Henry Lord Danvers as Castle Steward had rights to hunt for minerals and some coal mines were opened on the commons. Newton dale well gained a medicinal reputation and even had a house built for bathing.

Left
Artist's impression of new forge that was established on Potter Hill

The Civil War between the forces of the Crown and those of the Parliament, began when King Charles I moved from York to raise his standard at Nottingham in 1642. A Royalist force occupied Thornton Dale the next year but was attacked by three Parliamentary units and was forced to surrender 120 men. Another five hundred were not far away but it was said that they "had not the spirit to assist their fellows". Sir William Constable's Parliamentary cavalry took Pickering castle in 1644, sweeping on to Whitby. Troops were said to have used the church, where the font was broken and a prayer book torn. Helmsley castle saw a short siege and Scarborough castle a prolonged battering. During these troubled times, Pickering Forest was disafforested and Blansby ceased to be a royal deer park. Sir Henry Osborne lived at the old Hallgarth Rectory house in 1643.

Religious nonconformity surfaced strongly during Oliver Cromwell's Protectorate. Some wished to reform the Church of England. Others sought separation from it. George Fox, the founder of the Society of Friends, or Quakers, preached in the church schoolhouse, once the chantry chapel, in 1652. His followers quietly "waited on the Lord", instead of attending conventional services. They also refused to pay church tithes. Several were imprisoned in Pickering castle for disobedience to authority. They bought a house to convert into a Meeting House in 1680. A few Roman Catholics met secretly with Father Nicholas Postgate. The more numerous Protestant dissenters were driven into secret cottage meetings, only to emerge decades later, after the Toleration Act of 1689. A Meeting House was licensed for Protestant Dissenters in 1702 and a chapel built in 1720.

Right Pickering Castle
was attacked in 1644

29

A prospering body of gentry rebuilt their houses on a larger scale in the late 17th century. George Conyers had a seven-hearth house in Burgate and Mr. Strangeways, a descendant of the Robinsons of Thornton Risebrough, held the only nine hearth house in the town. Stone walling was more often used in more elaborate buildings. The keeper of the Castle prison was sworn to stop locals pulling down the castle walls to build their houses. The Rectory house at the head of Hallgarth was rebuilt as a good gentry house, just north of the tithe barn, in 1698. Sir John Temple leased Blansby Park in 1699. Ebberston Hall was built for the Master of the Mint, to the "Palladian design" of architecture by Colin Campbell in 1718. More statutes were being passed by Parliament and some of the local gentry, serving as "justices of the peace" were the main channel of local government and local justice.

Left Quakers were imprisoned in Pickering Castle for refusing to pay tithes

The new linen industry employed many men and women. Flax was woven and spun in the houses of the moorland dales, the villages and the town. You could convert a byre into a weaving chamber. Dyer George Staines was accused of polluting the river in 1685. The Kirkby Moorside clothier Simeon Sturdy took the house next to the beck on the north side of the road six years later. Paper making from linen waste began at Ellerburn about 1679 and was worked later at Pickering low mill. Woollen cloth was also produced for local use. Fulling mills were on the Costa and Pickering becks. The town had fifty-five weavers, eleven flax dressers, twelve bleachers and two dyers by the late 18th century, when a linen market was established in the Black Swan yard. The notorious Mary Campion supplied linen drapers from Hull to London in the 1780's.

Right
The Old Rectory in Hallgarth was built in 1698. The bay windows were added in the late nineteenth century

The Duchy surveyor reported that the Pickering common fields and meadows together made 2516 acres of cultivated land in 1676. Newton on Rawcliffe had another 400 acres of common fields. Two oxpastures numbering 202 acres gave good fodder for the plough beasts. The Crown sold off its demesne arable to Robert Harding and Thomas Hutchinson. Piecemeal field enclosures had already begun at Thornton Dale and spread slowly among the numerous freeholders of Pickering. The exchange of the freeholders' strips brought lands into compact blocks, which were eventually enclosed with fences or hedges. The huge commons stretching beyond the fields remained un-inclosed but some saw new use by conversion of fringe moorland into rabbit warrens. A court of sewers met to ensure river weeds were cut and to improve lowland drainage. Pickering beck had to be five yards broad at the bottom from Vivers to the Ing dikes.

Left
There were fifty-five weavers in Pickering in the late 18th Century

Above
Keld Head House
has its origins in the
late seventeenth
century

ROBERT HUGGETT AND THE POOR OF PICKERING

Wills are a useful source of information. They tell us what people owned and about their family ties. In 1658 Robert Huggett of Great Edston left a will in which he left his mother in law, Elizabeth Huggett, his cottage in Pickering and all its contents and when she died it was to pass to James Coates of Little Barugh. James Coates was to give twelve shillings a year at Martinmas to the poor of Pickering but this appears to have been quietly forgotten.

THE GEORGIAN REVOLUTION IN FARMING

For a rural town like Pickering, the eighteenth century was to see many changes. The agricultural revolution swept away ways of doing things on the land and some lost their hold on the land to become labourers. Transport improved and new opportunities at home and abroad were seized by the more enterprising.

Below
Pickering in 1787

Traffic had made its way to and from York via the old Roman Road. The Keld Head Inn was built for John Park, facing the Marton lane in 1731. Thomas Lowther the Pickering carrier was drowned watering his horses at York in 1740. Now changes came thick and fast. The Malton river navigation, made effective in the second quarter of the century, attracted farm exports from all Pickering Vale, the north Wolds and Ryedale. The York, Malton, and Scarborough turnpike road was opened in 1751 to carry genteel visitors, in both private and public coaches to the seaside watering place known as Scarborough spa. The road from Lockton lane end to Whitby was turnpiked in 1764 and the Pickering to Malton road in 1786. The tolls charged allowed some improvement and a profit. Stage coaches appeared and the post went into them. John Baines' New Globe at Pickering was renamed the Black Swan Inn and became the principal coaching house. The "England Rejoice" coach later called at the White Swan Inn. Canal schemes planned in the nineties to link Pickering with Whitby, Scarborough and Malton all came to nothing.

Better off folk were living in new ways. Richard Simpson a weaver of 1746 was worth £111. His house had two parlours and a chamber. John Conyers had his new "capital messuage" north of Eastgate. Anthony Oates built a large mansion near the Castle by 1777. James Harrison, the Boroughgate glazier installed the larger sash windows into the bigger houses and John Mathers installed new plumbing in the eighties. Bricks were made at Black

Below Profits from whaling allowed a more extravagant life style

Bull, Westgate Carr, Tofts and Middleton. Curved red pantiles became the general roofing material in place of thatch. Coal was coming from Malton water-side and on donkey trains from Goathland. New possessions altered the life style. William Pennock in 1704 sold a few groceries, deals, salt, hemp and whalebone. John Noble three decades later owned a pepper pot, cheeseplates, tin dish covers, a coffee pot, Delf plates and a looking glass. Gentleman John Piper had a long case clock and the fashionable striped hangings on his four poster bed in 1758. Mr. Walker set up as an apothecary, and there were soon two surgeons who also acted as man-midwives. Simeon King bought the smith's shop at the corner of Boroughgate and Market Place for conversion into a grocer's shop.

The Yorkshire coast exerted a lure on inland places, offering fresh opportunities, as England became a maritime nation. Pickering's William Hay was on the hired ship "Loyal Merchant" in 1695 and Richard Strangewayes sailed on H.M.S. Newark in 1703. Sam Harding was a mariner in 1742 and John Marshall by mid century. John Frank was drowned at sea. These men were from well-known Pickering families. Captain Nicholas Piper sailed to Copenhagen in 1761. Fourteen years later, he joined partners to buy the 251 ton "Henrietta", built at Whitby in 1764.The vessel was adapted for whaling, and made profits sufficient to rebuild several Pickering gentry houses. The crew secured 499 whales during forty-four voyages. William Scoresby, born at Nutholm near Cropton, became a highly successful master of Piper's whaling ship, while Captains Bean and Kearsley from Pickering Lythe were as famous in their day. James Machel wrote home in 1805 from a transport off Portugal. He had lost his hat overboard in a gale of wind. Letters from Captains Bird and Dobson in 1818 have one wrecked near Yarmouth, and the other ashore in Sweden. George Grundy had just enlisted in the East India service.

Left
The White Swan Inn was one of Pickering's first coaching inns

A few Pickering men achieved fame in the national capital or across the seas. Population was growing with births annually exceeding burials and the pressure to succeed elsewhere was strong. Ryedale migrants went to Nova Scotia in 1775. Joseph Pilmoor was a Wesleyan missionary to New Jersey in 1769, James Calvert missioned Fiji, while much later George Piercey went to China and Thomas Crosby to British Columbia. William Marshall wrote his farming classic "The Rural Economy of Yorkshire" in 1788 and in 1799 wrote proposals for a rural institute. He died in 1818 having converted his Beck Isle house into the first English farm college. Memorials in the parish church recall father and son Nicholas and Robert King, who played a major part in planning the city of Washington DC in the United States of America and in mapping the interior.

The Napoleonic Wars economy favoured farming expansion and the inclosure of common lands. An Act of Parliament of 1785 arranged for the inclosure of a great part of the Pickering uplands. Parts of the West Moor, Littledale Rigg, Haugh Rigg, Yatts and the High Moor were allotted to individuals in place of their common rights. The Town Greens, and the Low Carrs were divided and enclosed in their entirety but although 10,129 acres were allotted, some of the higher ground was not worth the cost of fencing and hedging. The Duchy of Lancaster secured awards near to the town, where new roads, dry stone walling and a few new farmsteads soon appeared. Much drainage was attempted in the lower grounds. Only a few marl pits and stone quarries remained for common use. Many new common roadways were defined between the enclosed lands.

Right
William Marshall's House became England's first farm college. It is now the Beck Isle Museum

Parish church communion services were attended by a hundred parishioners drawn from five hundred Pickering families in 1745. Religious revival came in the next decades but chiefly benefited the nonconformists. John Manners formed a Methodist society at Pickering in 1764. Several visits by John Wesley led to the formation of village societies, with active cottage meetings, united in a lively circuit. Nor was this all. An Independent or Congregational chapel was built in Hungate in 1789. A new Quaker meeting house arose in Castlegate in 1793 .The Wesleyan Methodist chapel was built in Hungate, a Primitive Methodist chapel in Bridge Street, and a Swedenborgian church formed in 1834. An Allelujah Hall was in Westgate. The Primitive Methodists, popularly called "Ranters", dipped deepest into local society. At their 1821 camp meetings Jane Ansdale and eight other preachers, with five praying companies "wrestled for the souls of sinners", while women sang Gospel songs. Many people were very familiar with Bible teachings.

Local democracy was nourished by Methodism. The spirit and the methods of self government spread to secular voluntary societies formed to fulfil specific aims. The age of voluntary action opened with the setting up of the self help friendly societies, the Pickering Unanimous Society formed in 1778 and the Pickering Benevolent Society a year later. The Poor Man's Friendly Society had to wait till 1836. Thomas Seavers opened the first town printing press in 1792 and Boak's printing house was started in Birdgate in 1815. They spurred the Pickering Bible and Tract societies, which sought to spread the printed Christian word.

Below An extract from the 1785 Act of Parliament which enclosed Pickering's common land

Rechabite groups urged an improvement in the condition of women. Temperance and Abstinence societies promoted their causes. Official encouragement was given to the Pickering Lythe Rifle Volunteers launched in 1786 and reformed in 1803 to resist Napoleon.

And whereas *Anthony Oates,* Esquire, *William Watson, Thomas Atkinson, Richard Simpson* the Elder, *Richard Todd* the Elder, *Samuel Skelton,* Gentlemen, and divers other Persons, are Owners of the several other ancient Messuages and Cottages, and Scites of Messuages and Cottages, in the Town of *Pickering* aforesaid, and are, or claim to be, by virtue thereof, entitled to a Right of Common upon the Whole of the said Commons and Waste Lands, subject to such Right of Depasturage as the Owners of certain other ancient Messuages and Cottages, and Scites of Messuages and Cottages, situate within the said Townships, are respectively entitled :

And whereas the said several Commons and Waste Lands are capable of being improved, and rendered of much greater Benefit and Advantage, as well to the Crown and its Lessees, as to the several Persons entitled to Right of Common thereon, than the same are at present, if the said Commons and Waste Lands were divided,

An older, traditional way of life survived the new religious and social pressures. The Pickering port stakes, horse race weeks were high points of the years in the late 18th century. Cock fights and stage plays were held in the Black Swan yard. The pantomime "Bluebeard" was performed in Pickering in 1813. A race was run from Pickering to Helmsley on "dandy horses". Weddings were followed by races for the "bride's garter", eventually replaced by a ribbon. Three annual fairs occupied the Mondays near Candlemas Day, Old May Day and Martinmas Day. Shrove Tuesday ball games and Martinmas Week visits to home and hirings continued as before. As late as 1811, there was a "crutches rearing", a feast to mark erection of timber crucks for a house. There were Mischief Nights, April fools, May Goslings and "Stephening" by the young. Ale houses were numerous and "Market Mondays" through the year saw some heavy drinking. The Beer Act of 1830 sought to reduce gin drinking, but rapidly increased the number of beer houses. The Friendly societies had their feast days.

THE FATHER OF BRITISH WATER COLOUR PAINTING

Francis Nicholson was born in Pickering in 1753 the son of a weaver. He had some education at local schools but his talent was in painting rather than weaving. He painted local scenes in Yorkshire but left for London in 1803 to better his career. Throughout his life he painted in watercolour and published a manual of water colour techniques in 1820. He was elected President of the 'Society of Painters in Watercolour' and was called, 'The father of British water colour painting'. He died in London in 1844.

Left
Francis Nicholson

SQUIRES AND LABOURERS. RICH AND POOR

The nineteenth century saw a growing population, industrial revolution and a century of peace from 1815 to 1914 which allowed economic growth and social improvements.

George Stephenson surveyed the valleys in 1832 for the proposed Whitby-Pickering horse and carriage railway. This opened in 1836 to bring "coal to the interior". The first passenger arrivals were welcomed by five bands and cannon fire. The first ever cheap railway tickets were introduced on the line in 1839. The railway was sold to George Hudson's York and North Midland Company in 1844. He replaced horses, by steam engines, joined the railway to the new York-Scarborough line and turned Whitby into a holiday resort. Pickering gained a new station and a link to the emerging national railway network. The first railway excursion left the Pickering station for Grosmont Bazaar in 1848. Farming products went out by rail and fertilizers came in but the great expansion of farm output was largely achieved by hard labour from a growing workforce. After mid century, locally made winnowing, and threshing machines made their appearance.

Left Pickering's first railway was horse-drawn

Eastgate, Pickering

Small-scale local industry flourished for some decades in the Victorian market town. Gas was made at Pickering in 1847. The Albert Foundry began in Champleys yard two years later. Fletcher's Park Street foundry was remembered for its frying pans. Woods opened a new freestone quarry ten years later, with stone water troughs among their products. The town still had five public waterpumps. The linen industry migrated to the West Riding and the tanneries to the ports but the town brickworks worked into the nineties. Windles adapted one old mill for bone crushing for fertilizers. The Hungate bone mill gained a fine steam engine and a new steam corn mill opened in 1865. Breweries remained active in Eastgate, Potter hill and at the White Swan. Yard and furnace brooms were made in small workshops. giving the town the nickname of "Besomshire". Shops multiplied, some making a few of the products that they sold. English the chemist claimed that his sheep dip had guarded thousands of animals against the tic, lice and fly. Pape made aerated waters and a mixture good for the face-ache. Mr. H.F. Place made teeth.

The Victorians sought an expansion in basic education. A new Grammar School had been built behind the teachers Hallgarth house in 1828 to replace the schoolroom within the church. This only took 32 pupils. There were a handful of dame schools but Nonconformist Sunday Schools pioneered the expansion of elementary education, partly to encourage bible reading. A Wesleyan Methodist School was built at Pickering in 1856 extending teaching to many who previously hadn't known any. The National or Church of England School was formed the next year in Hallgarth, the building designed by architect John Gibson. The Sunday Schools had far more pupils than day schools until late in the century. Education was not seen universally as a great advantage. Most employment was in farm labouring. The more fortunate entered craft apprenticeships. James Marfitt's apprentice indentures of 1822 required him to abstain from dice, tables, bowls, alehouses and matrimony.

Local newspapers arrived with the Pickering and Thornton Dale Mercury published in 1857. The readers paid a penny every Saturday, for "twenty columns of closely printed information". The publisher was W. Bellerby of Park Street. and the printer William Heselton of Market Place. Early papers were much read in barber's shops and village reading rooms. Rival newspapers during June 1859 spoke of "mean and unprincipled falsehoods in the Pickering Mercury last Saturday concerning the Kirby Moorside and Helmsley Brass Band". The correspondent, was told to sink into "the ranks of folly and depravity". An advertisement sought "a comfortable home for an intemperate female". Later years brought the Gazettes and Heralds, as readership spread. The "news" became a permanent feature of local and national life.

Left
Dame Schools provided some education until the churches took on provision

Magnetic iron ore with high yields was discovered and first worked at Rosedale west side in 1851. Initially, the rock was brought to Pickering in carts. The discovery quickly made rustic Rosedale into a hub of industry on a scale not previously known in the district. The Rosedale east iron mines began working in 1859. Lovel's horses pulled the boilers to Rosedale incline, built for raising quarried ore to the moor top. The Rosedale Railway was built in 1861 to take iron ore northwards to Battersby incline and hence to Cleveland. The population of the dale rapidly grew offering good wages and virile community life, with some resulting stimulus to the nearest market towns.

The Pickering population had doubled through the 19th century from 2000 in 1801 to 4000 in 1881 but the numbers fell away as the rural demand for farm labourers waned and small industries migrated to industrial districts. Local railways supplemented the national network. A Pickering-Gilling Railway was constructed in 1882. The Pickering to Seamer and Scarborough railway opened four years later. There was hardship at home. Winter soup kitchens operated for several years in the nineties. Nine hundred families received free soup in 1892. Many migrated from the town seeking employment in the new industries, the British Empire and the United states. Edward Windle was a sergeant in the Punjab. John Eden went to join the North West Canadian Mounted Police. There were hundreds who quietly moved away. William Fletcher in Market Place offered assisted passages for farm labourers to Canada, for £3, and for infants at 10s. Two pillar boxes were erected by the Post Office for posting letters in 1890.

Right
The Rosedale Iron mines were a stimulus to Pickering's economy

New local government boards had replaced fading manor courts. A Pickering Board of Health was elected in 1863, with squire James Mitchelson as chairman. Under the Public Health Act, the Board could make byelaws, remove nuisances and improve public housing, drainage and cleanliness. The iron bridge was built in Hungate, to give access to the coal depot. The Board took over the markets from the Duchy in 1878. A Pickering Gas and Water Company bought the gas works from the Railway and set up water works at Keld Head. A new police station, lockup and court house was built at lower Hallgarth. A new cattle market opened in Eastgate, ending the stock markets in the streets. A foundry site was converted to a Market Hall for selling produce. The Board of Health was replaced by an Urban District Council with greater powers in 1894. The nine members were annually elected until 1907, after which they served for three years. A School Board was formed in 1896 to extend compulsory education.

Left
Poverty forced many to leave Pickering and the population fell

A wealth of new Pickering societies were started in late Victorian and Edwardian days. Most of their members were drawn from the better off but some provided services for others. The Pickering Glee and Elocution society could offer a production of "Jessie the belle of the bar" in 1876. A Stape Band joined the existing Pickering Band. A Victoria Lawn Tennis club played in the castle grounds. The Pickering Association Football club, a Golf club, a Bowls Club and the Pickering Fishery Association, were joined by a Cycling Club, with a bugler who rode in the vanguard. The Conservative Club saw competition from the Liberal Club opened on Smiddy Hill in 1908. Other Societies had a charitable purpose, including the Pickering Co-operative Society, the Charity Organisation Society, a branch of the R.S.P.CA, the Pickering District Nursing Association, the Clothing Clubs and a branch of the Red Cross.

The Church Commissioners bought the old Rectory House in 1858 and Mr. Cockburn was the first vicar to live there. He was energetic for parish improvement, putting gas light into the church, founding the Marishes red brick chapel, a penny bank, a reading room and coal distributions for the poorest. His successors gave church and chapel attendance a close connection with "respectability" which lasted for decades. The Parish church building was restored in 1877 with new foundations inserted under the tower. The 15th century wall paintings were once again revealed to view. Vicar Lightfoot from 1881 to 1902 restored the status of the parish church, adding an infant schoolroom, boilers, ventilators, a parish magazine and even a St Peter's football club. The Newbridge mission room was opened for quarry families in 1883. The Nonconformist chapels were just as busy. Potter Hill Primitive Methodist chapel was built to hold a congregation of 700 worshippers in 1885. A new Wesleyan Chapel opened in Hungate in 1890. St Joseph's Roman Catholic church was opened in 1912. The Salvation Army staged a lively campaign in the town.

Below
The Primitive Methodist Chapel was built in 1885

GEORGE COCKBURN

Victorian Pickering was scandalised by the alleged affair of its married Vicar, George Cockburn, with one of his parishioners, Jenny Wardell. There had been gossip in the town about the vicar's visits to Miss Wardells' house at irregular hours and had he been seen holding her ankle when she climbed a ladder? The vicar was hissed in the streets and the congregation at the Parish church fell to a handful. Cockburn was brought before the Church of England's own court in York to answer the charges of adultery in 1864. He was suspended from his living and left Pickering although the charges brought against him were not proved. It has been said that Cockburn's fault was not that of seeing another woman but crossing the class divide and seeing a woman who was 'beneath him'.

Left
George Cockburn and Jenny Wardell photographed together in Scarborough

INTO A WIDER WORLD

The pace of change in the twentieth century has been staggering. The Wright brothers first flew their flimsy biplane in 1903 but there was a man on the moon in 1969. It was a century of total warfare which struck every family in the land but also a time of increasing prosperity and welfare.

The nation was engaged in the world war from 1914 to 1919. Volunteers and later conscripts marched away to fight on the "western front" against Germany. Many were killed in the trench warfare. The enormous losses are even now recalled in town and village war memorials. Others returned wounded or shell shocked, and many were maimed for life. Some passed through a Red Cross Hospital in Hallgarth. Local letters tell of a great sadness across the lives of many families. Food shortages were severe due to the submarine blockade, so that more land was brought into cultivation. German airships were seen over the town and Scarborough saw battle cruiser and submarine bombardments. The peace was celebrated on July 19th 1919 with a bonfire on Beacon Hill. Pickering British Legion Branch was formed for ex service men in 1922. The War Memorial Hall was opened and a memorial was unveiled in the Parish church to the United States of America Ambassador, Walter Hines Page, widely viewed as largely responsible for bringing that country into the war against Germany.

Right
Pickering Market Place around 1900. It is gas lit. The only sounds would be the human voice, the wheels of wagons and the whistle of the train

The twenties and thirties were not easy times in agriculture or the local industries, although there were developments with nurseries and horse breeding. The Rosedale mines closed and local unemployment rose. The Forestry Commission plantations were started at Dalby in 1921 to renew national timber resources. A Dalby Forest camp was formed in 1933 for retraining the long-term unemployed from the industrial West Riding. A fish hatchery was established at Keld Head. Castle Restoration was begun after the ruins were transferred from the town to the Ministry of Works. The Town Council promoted some work schemes as well as local improvements, including the sewerage scheme and the first council houses in Goslipgate.

War with Germany, Italy, and Japan dominated the years 1939-1945. German armoured forces smashed through the French and British defence lines in Belgium. The army was evacuated from Dunkirk but lost equipment and many men. This was a national disaster and invasion was expected. Pickering Home Guards were formed and Air Raid Wardens, who practised dealing with incendiary bombs using shovel, sand bucket and stirrup pump. Windows were "blacked out". Gas masks and identity cards were carried. An army camp was made near the castle and tank barriers built on roads. Heavy air attacks on British ports and airfields in 1940 seemed to herald a channel crossing. The barrier presented by the Royal Navy and the fierce defence by fighter pilots in Hurricane and Spitfire aircraft prevented that invasion.

Left
The Territorials march through Pickering on their way to the front in 1914

Young men and women joined the army, navy and air forces, or worked in farming and essential industry. Marginal land was taken in as submarine attacks on convoys of shipping brought shortages. Food and clothes were rigidly rationed. War Agricultural Committees pressed farmers to maximise output. A "British Restaurant" at the Memorial Hall provided many with simple nourishing meals. "Dig for victory" campaigns expanded gardening and there were drives to raise money in gifts and loans to buy aircraft, to adopt ships and to send parcels to prisoners of war. Many children were evacuated to Pickering from Middlesbrough and Hull which were heavily bombed by the German air force. The British Bomber command carried air attacks into Germany but with heavy losses.

Above
Evacuees came to Pickering from Middlesbrough and Hull

Above
War Memorial

Above
The Memorial Hall was opened in 1922

Local men and women served in all parts of the world, including the Middle East, North Africa, Italy, and Burma. Over a thousand captured Italians were brought to a large prisoner of war camp established near Malton in 1942. From 1943 many troops were stationed locally, for training on the moors and wolds. The Northumberland Fusiliers, Sherwood Foresters, the 27th Lancers, the Welsh Guards, Polish Regiments, Canadian and United States servicemen eventually left for the invasion of Normandy and the conquest of Europe. The war ended in 1945 in an austerity peace. Victory in Europe celebrations took place in heavy rain. The atomic bombs dropped at Hiroshima and Nagasaki soon brought the war with Japan to a close. People felt they had helped each other more in the war years and there was a determination to make more social advances. The National Health Service, expanded education and social insurance were among the results.

Pickering recorded 4193 people at the 1951 Census. The numbers shrank a little over the next decade, despite a hundred new houses being built. Families were smaller now and living standards were rising. A welfare clinic opened in Train Lane in 1955. A confident Council, with women among its members, and with powers to build houses, started Council estates at St Nicholas Way in 1956. The widening of approach roads and a traffic roundabout altered the town's main road junction in 1960. A new fire station, court house and police station were built nearby and a library opened in Market Place. The old Eastgate cattle market was made into a large car park. Changing technology in the wider world had influence too. There was talk of birth control clinics. The telephone exchange became automatic. Banks put in accounting machines and a launderette made new washing machines familiar.

Left
Pickering's first Council Houses were built in Goslipgate

Middleton Road in 1911 (above) **and 2011** (below)

The road has been tarmaced and widened and the car has replaced the horse but externally, little seems to have changed. Inside the houses there has been a revolution of comfort, convenience and technology.

Pickering Market

Right
The floods of 2007
were particularly
damaging

Right
New housing has filled
out the town

Education was dramatically expanded in these years. The Pickering Grammar School had merged into the younger Lady Lumley's School in 1905, in a new building for seventy pupils. Parents had to be able to pay the fees, as there were only a handful of scholarships. A new Education Act of Parliament in 1944 ended the fees. If you passed the examination you could go. By 1951 there were 320 in a school built to hold 200. Headmaster David Baxandall in 1958 moved the scholars into a new Lady Lumley's School at Swainsea Lane. This was made comprehensive for all children from eleven years and soon held over 600 pupils. The school opened up undreamt of channels for local sons and daughters to "do well" and came to frame the young lives of the whole town and district. The County Junior School expanded into the Middleton Road building. University Education became available for some decades, to those able to qualify for it and a broadening stream went from Pickering. The only loss was the Yorkshire dialect.

Farming yields rose but farm employment contracted as machinery and other innovations came in. Farms became rare within the town boundary. Tractors replaced horses and steam engines. Lorries took distribution from the railways. Markets were becoming regional and Pickering cattle market closed in 1965. Farmland and forestry plantations extended as the moor was deep ploughed with new machinery. A village for Forestry Workers was constructed at Dalby. The town gained an Agricultural Education Centre. Water cress cultivation at Keld Head and expanded nurseries flourished. Intensive chicken rearing and egg production enjoyed decades of prosperity. Every community wanted light industries to provide employment for a growing body of working women and to replace farm work for men. Joseph Mays clothing factory opened in Eastgate in 1951. Regular bus and train services allowed some to travel to work at Kirkby, Malton, Scarborough and even York. The Derwent Plastics factory opened in Carr Lane in 1970, adding valuable permanent employment.

In ways, large and small, novelty stalked the land. Old technologies were fading as new ones appeared. The railway line from Pickering to Scarborough closed for passengers in 1951. The Malton-Pickering-Whitby Railway was stopped as uneconomic in 1965 and the track to Malton was lifted. Many now travelled regularly by the United, Ryedale and West Yorkshire bus services. Car ownership spread rapidly. New tourist visitors were attracted to caravan camps. Moorlands were selling the new ballpoint pens in 1959. An automatic telephone exchange came into operation. After Russia launched Sputnik 1 into space in 1957, a missile early warning station was built on Lockton High Moor, to deter airborne attack by giving sufficient warning to allow a massive response. This became operational in 1963, offering very new kinds of employment.

Above
At first the cinema,
then the radio and
later television brought
a wider world to
Pickering

Leisure was transformed by the motor car, and even more by the advent of cinema and then television. Films had first been shown in the Temperance Hall, but for several decades the Castle and Central cinemas offered a magical escape for many regular viewers. Television Sets were hired and shared to watch the Queen's Coronation in 1953. Soon they were in every home, commanding hours of evening and weekend leisure. The same decades saw a flourishing of new societies taking people out of their houses. The Recreation Ground committee, the Working Men's Club, the Over Sixties All Day Club and the Ryedale Sports club developed their premises. A Business and Professional Women's club was formed. In the sixties, the Volunteer Fire Service, the Red Cross, Toch H, new Play Groups and the W.R.V.S. united volunteers in the service of others. Rotary and Lion's groups, later joined by a Round Table, combined social activity and charitable work. Sports clubs supported angling, badminton, billiards, bridge, cricket, football, gunnery, hockey, motoring, swimming and tennis. Other societies promoted allotments, brass bands, cage birds, drama, freemasonry, pigeons, music, temperance, trade unions, youth and the United Nations.

Right Sport has long
been an important
part of Pickering life.
Here the Town's
1933 football team

Above
Lady Lumley's School was built in 1905. It is now the County Junior School

Right
The North York Moors Railway has become a vital part of Pickering's tourist economy

For a decade or two, national government became localised with branch offices in the town managing agricultural subsidies and advice, a labour exchange, a youth employment bureau, a forestry commission office and the milk marketing board. The Urban and Rural District Councils also had town offices and workshops. Malton Road had its County Court house and police station. The trend was soon reversed. The government offices moved away. The Ryedale Water Board gave way to a more distant Water Authority. The Pickering Urban and Rural District Councils were abolished in 1974. Many of their powers passed to a Ryedale District Council centred at Malton and covering a vast area. The town was left with a Town Council with more limited functions.

Cheap air traffic made hotter climates attractive and challenged the command of the seaside resorts. The motor car and motor coaches opened up the Yorkshire countryside for tourist visitors. A North York Moors National Park declared in 1952 was chiefly occupied in countryside conservation. Pentland Hick in 1962 created the Flamingo Park Zoo at Kirkby Misperton. He saw a need for a day tripper attraction closer to the populated centres than Scarborough. As Flamingoland it became a major attraction. The Railway from Pickering to Grosmont, managed and run by volunteers of the North York Moors Railway Preservation Society, was re-opened. It would both encourage and benefit from countryside tourism. This was to play a major part in making Pickering a busy destination for both visiting and tripper tourists. Volunteers opened the Beck Isle Museum in 1967.

Pickering was expanding again. The 4186 people of 1961 in ten years rose to 4545 and to 6846 in 2010. Newcomers found the market town an attractive place of retirement. but there were young families too. Amid many changes, the town centre managed to maintain its character. Children's playgrounds were opened near new housing at Ruffa lane and Firthland Road. An Older People's home was built on the old Workhouse site in Whitby Road. Ropery Road was made to link Market Place and Hungate across an old derelict railway good yard.

The Musical Society opened the Kirk Theatre in Hungate. A supermarket opened in the lower rear of Pickering Market Place, challenging smaller shops. A new Library was built on the Ropery. The Isabella Court Day and Residential Centre for those with learning difficulties was opened at Keld Head by the Wilf Ward foundation. Ryedale Swimming Pool was opened off the Malton Road in Pickering.

Pickering has always enjoyed a big event. Queen Victoria's Golden Jubilee celebrations in 1887 included the traditional Smiddy Hill ox-roast. A Grand Historical Pageant in the castle in 1910 attracted visitors over four days. Almost everyone from the town either saw it or was in it. The Coronation celebrations for King George V ended with the usual Beacon Hill bonfire. The Pickering Sports Committee organised the first Traction Engine Derby in 1953, a race between four engines, which attracted six thousand visitors. This prepared the way for decades of annual traction engine rallies at the town. A 1964 rally claimed thirty thousand visitors. Pickering Carnivals were annual from 1949 with long processions of decorated floats. John Pearson produced Castle and Street Pageants in the seventies and Ryedale Round Table ran Market Place Pickering Feasts and pram road races.

Individuals still made a difference. Reg Harvey realised that Pickering had a town scene capable of enhancement. He annually planted daffodils on the grass verges and decades later, they remain with us. Faced with plans for an inner town car park on old railway land, John Paul led volunteers to add a riverside walk. Lady cricketer Polly Marshall, townsmen Alan Pickup, Keith Snowden, Ron Scales and Gordon Clitheroe, each recorded real local history in their memoirs of life in and beyond Pickering. Joe Passey launched the Jazz Festival in 1988 which continues annually with great success.

Below
The War weekend has become a popular annual event

Ivon Baker of the North York Moors Railway organised the first Wartime Weekend in 1992 featuring evacuees at Pickering station. This grew into an annual event attracting thousands. Simon Boak ran many Traction Engine and Trucking rallies before building an Exhibition Centre in 2005.

Many of the most dramatic changes of recent decades altered life behind the scene. Much of this real progress was shared with the rest of the nation, in lengthening life, better education and better health. A dramatic rise in living standards took washing machines from launderettes into houses, better heating into homes, electrical and gas cookers and then microwave ovens into kitchens. Refrigerators and freezers allowed healthier food storage. Cars became a common place, causing congestion in the town center and trials banning them from the Market Place on Mondays. Television and video made a remarkable change in leisure time activity. The computer with its access to the internet, surprised many by finding a way into every house and each generation.

The newer building estates filled out the town, behind the back lanes, which had bounded the precinct for so long. Older building character was retained by modernising housing in the market place and in the older streets. Pickering developed two small industrial parks, where workshops and warehouses could flourish. Local supermarkets and distant retail warehouses at the bigger towns altered the balance of market place shops. Some were developed for a growing tourist trade. An antiques bazaar was a notable success. Gaps were taken up by a few charity shops. A new style of eating place appeared, with food styles not previously known, many from other nations. Some out of town corner shops and even village public houses succumbed to competition. A new Health Centre was established in 1995 at South Gate. There was a new sports centre, a swimming pool and a tourist information centre.

Few could have predicted the success of Pickering as a destination for touring visitors. A main factor was the retention of an attractive town centre, a sloping market place which could house weekly Monday markets as easily as annual crowds at Traction Engine Rallies and October Wartime Weekends. Along the many attractive byways, you reached the historic Parish Church and chapels, the museum, the castle, trout farms, and a restored railway station with a new roof in 2011.

The North York Moors Railway offered nostalgic rides in steam trains to the moors, to Grosmont and Whitby. The television film "Heartbeat" made Goathland famous and it is repeatedly shown. Thousands come each year. As well as day trippers, others stay in caravan camps, farms, forest cabins and hotels to explore a National Park, embracing both moors and coast. Not far afield, Flamingo land and the Eden Camp War Museum were joined by the Dalby Forest Outdoor Pursuits Centre.

Recent decades have seen a strengthening of community life. New Pickering societies have been formed in every decade, for sport, charitable and social work, and for every hobby and social activity. Several societies gained permanent quarters, or extended and improved what they had including the Kirk Theatre, the Recreation club, the WRVS centre, Ryedale Sports Club and the Working Men's Club. The cinemas closed but a forty seat Studio Theatre was opened in the Friends Meeting House which also hosts live plays. The Pickering Memorial Hall Trust was established as a charity and the hall was refurbished in 2001 as a social centre. A community newsletter launched in 1998 developed into the Pickering Beacon magazine, which is delivered to every home in Pickering. The Pickering Civic Society and the Pickering Town Council strive to improve community life. Pickering is fortunate to have such a many sided heritage.

A LIFE IN PICKERING IN THE TWENTIETH CENTURY

Ron Scales was born in Pickering in 1921. He attended the Church School in Hall Garth and later Lady Lumley's School on Middleton Road. He remembers playing in the middle of the road when the loudest noise was the sound of horses' hooves. When he left school he worked in an architect and surveyor's office until 1940 when, at the age of nineteen he joined the Royal Air Force. Ron flew as a gunner for 138 squadron making low level drops of supplies and agents into occupied Europe. On his twenty-second birthday he was shot down and captured. There followed imprisonment in Russia and Germany and finally, as the Russian Army advanced, a six hundred mile forced march into Germany, a march on which many prisoners of war died. Ron escaped and returned to Pickering, as he recalls, 'weighing five stone and covered in lice.' He married Margaret, whom he had met before the war and in 1961 took up a post with the Ministry of Agriculture, visiting farms throughout North Yorkshire. Ron and Margaret had one daughter, Jill, who tragically died in an accident in 1977. Ron retired in 1984 and he and Margaret have travelled widely and are now enjoying retirement in their home in Pickering.

Right Ron Scales
Photo. Gordon Clitheroe

Acknowledgements

The Blackthorn Press acknowledges and thanks the following for their kind assistance in providing photographs and illustrations:

Beck Isle Museum, Gordon Clitheroe, Dorothy Cohoe, The Dalton Estate, Mr and Mrs Harrison, David Ireland, Garry Kelly, Pickering Town Council.

All photographs are by the Blackthorn Press.

The Blackthorn Press has attempted to contact copyright owners of artwork reproduced in this book and it welcomes queries from those not acknowledged above.

Cambridge Introductions to Music
Electronic Music

This accessible *Introduction* explores both mainstream and experimental manifestations of electronic music. From early recording equipment to the most recent multimedia performances, the history of electronic music is full of interesting characters, fascinating and unusual music, and radical technology. Covering many different eras, genres, and media, analyses of works appear alongside critical discussion of central ideas and themes, making this an essential guide for anyone approaching the subject for the first time. Chapters include key topics from synth pop to sound art, from electronic dance music to electrical instruments, and from the expression of pure sound to audiovisuals. Highly illustrated and with a wide selection of examples, the book provides many suggestions for further reading and listening to encourage students to begin their own experiments in this exciting field.

NICK COLLINS is Reader in Composition at Durham University.

MARGARET SCHEDEL is Assistant Professor of Music at Stony Brook University.

SCOTT WILSON is Senior Lecturer in Composition and Live Electroacoustic Music at the University of Birmingham.

A complete list of books in the series is featured at the back of this book.

Cambridge Introductions to Music

Electronic Music

NICK COLLINS,

MARGARET SCHEDEL, and

SCOTT WILSON

CAMBRIDGE
UNIVERSITY PRESS

CAMBRIDGE UNIVERSITY PRESS
Cambridge, New York, Melbourne, Madrid, Cape Town,
Singapore, São Paulo, Delhi, Mexico City

Cambridge University Press
The Edinburgh Building, Cambridge CB2 8RU, UK

Published in the United States of America by Cambridge University Press, New York

www.cambridge.org
Information on this title: www.cambridge.org/9781107010932

First published 2013

Printed and bound by CPI Group (UK) Ltd, Croydon CR0 4YY

A catalogue record for this publication is available from the British Library

Library of Congress Cataloguing in Publication data
Collins, Nick (Nicholas)
Electronic music / Nick Collins, Margaret Schedel, and Scott Wilson.
     pages   cm
Includes bibliographical references and index.
ISBN 978-1-107-01093-2 (hardback)
1. Electronic music – History and criticism.   I. Schedel, Margaret.
II. Wilson, Scott, 1969 Nov. 26–   III. Title.
ML1380.C623   2013
786.7 – dc23   2012050086

ISBN 978-1-107-01093-2 Hardback
ISBN 978-1-107-64817-3 Paperback

Contents

Illustrations

Tables

Acknowledgments

With huge thanks to everyone; just too many to list. Some of you are named in the text, and others just helped regardless.

Scott would particularly like to praise Daria for putting up with him, Jonty Harrison for expert input, and Gayle Young for help in tracking down images. Margaret would like to thank her electronic music teachers, in order from high school through doctoral degree: Howard Fredrics, Geoffrey Wright, McGregor Boyle, Ichiro Fujinaga, Cort Lippe, Pauline Oliveros, and Mara Helmuth for their inspiration, support, and dogged determination to make circuitry musical. For varied assistance which may or may not have ended up in the final book, Nick would like to send out additional thank yous to Heiko Hoffmann, Chris Goddard, Brian Kane, Laurie Spiegel, Mick Grierson, Thor Magnusson, Leif Shackelford, Bill Thompson, Leonie Edwards-Jones, and Fredrik Olofsson. Public gratitude is also due to Vicki Cooper, Rebecca Taylor, Fleur Jones, Beata Mako, Gaia Poggiogalli, and Jon Lloyd at Cambridge University Press.

We would all like to thank our students for their unwavering curiosity, probing questions and acceptance of new sounds.

Chapter 1

Introduction

Welcome to an exploration of electronic music, in many places and many guises. In societies tracking technological developments, the role of electricity in music has had a great impact on musical production and consumption, a musical influence as worldwide as the network of telecommunications. It has changed the balance of the instruments most commonly practiced, for example, toward electric guitars, turntables, and arguably the computer itself, and promoted an emphasis on recordings as the driver of mass musical contact. Yet the transformation has not been total, for traditional activities like live performance have continued in strength, albeit somewhat transfigured by such electronic factors as amplification and the Internet. Participation is not always subservient to passive reception, but is actively encouraged in such instances as musical video games and generative software for mobiles. Acoustic instruments have lost none of their charm and history, though some new history has been written by the interaction of acoustic means and the electrical transformation of sound. There always remains the option of turning off the power, but, unsurprisingly, we won't advocate that step in this book.

The term *electronic* formally denotes applications of the transistor, a specific electrical component popularized from the mid-twentieth century onward that enables the substantial miniaturization of circuits. Joel Chadabe titles his book on the history of electronic music *Electric Music* and the best terminology is sometimes contentious. You may see reference to *electroacoustic* music as an overall term: In the broadest sense, it simply means sound reproduced using electronic means, such as loudspeakers, but can be employed in a more constrained sense of highly designed electronic art music for close listening with an emphasis on space and timbre (more on this later). The connection of electronic music to *computer music* is also strong, since computers are the most general purpose and powerful electronic devices we come into contact with; however, computers themselves as everyday objects arose much later than many other electrical devices of note and aren't required in many forms of electronic music making.

Music and technology

The intricate design of acoustic musical instruments involves a practical mastery of physics as much as the newer pursuit of creating devices which exploit the principles of electromagnetism. But it is particularly the far-reaching musical consequences of the electromagnetic force that engage us in this book.[1]

Whilst static electricity – a build-up of electrical charge which is suddenly drained, the large-scale version being lightning – was known in antiquity, the full harnessing of electromagnetism was left until the scientific era. At the turn of and in the early nineteenth century, scientists were active who often went on to lend their names to the fundamental units: Volta (inventor of the battery, circa 1800), Ampère (elucidator of the relation between current and magnetism), Ohm (eponymous in the famous law relating voltage and current through resistance), and Faraday (pioneer of electromagnetic induction amongst many other experimental breakthroughs), to name four.

In the next two chapters, we will investigate recording and broadcast technologies, in the main electrical, and then early electrical musical instruments. We will encounter technologies both for the recording and manipulation of pre-existing sound, and for the direct electrical generation of new sound. In one common formulation, these two options are known as sampling and synthesis; there has sometimes been tension between these two approaches, though these days we are much more comfortable with their unification as available techniques. The chronology of these developments follows the explosion of practical applications of electricity in the second half of the nineteenth century. Table 1.1 gives a timeline of some important points in the history of telecommunications and electrical engineering technology pertaining to the book as a whole.

For now, we should note, and try to allay, some potential tensions between conceptions of music making as direct, natural, expressive, emotional, and social, and the mediations that technology can impose. It is easy to find examples of electronic music devices whose performance practice is substantially different from the traditional acoustic coupling of human body and instrument. Think of a sequencer interface as controlling musical pattern playback rather than individual events.[2] Amplification enables disproportionate human effort,[3] where a light touch of a button can have a massive stadium-filling effect;[4] indeed, in network music, this could be triggered across multiple stadia where the musician is not even physically present. Yet, however high the technology, the human hand has a presence, having established the conditions of its use, designed and programmed the system, and made musical decisions intended for human appreciation. The fast speed of technological advance is a constant tension,[5] but we trade off the stress of keeping up with the continually exciting potential of creating new art.

Table 1.1 *Timeline of some selected technological advances*

Year[a]	Technology
1822	Charles Babbage anticipates (mechanical) computing. Designs for a fully programmable Analytical Engine date from 1837, and the nongeneral purpose Jacquard Loom of 1801 used punched cards for programmability
1837	Morse telegraph patented
1876	Telephone patented (closely contested at the patent office)
1906	First public radio broadcast. The first wireless experiments date to the 1890s, and the first regular wireless service was in 1920
1926	First public television demonstration, though mass adoption of television really occurs after the Second World War
1940s	First electronic computers; some controversy over exactly which computer was the first fully programmable general purpose device
1969	Men walk on the moon and broadcast from there
1977	First mass production of pre-built home computers. There are earlier 1970s kits, and electronic music pioneer Erkki Kurenniemi released a microcomputer in Finland in 1973![b]
1989	World Wide Web protocol devised
2002	Point at which the world's archived data became more than 50 percent digital rather than analog[c]

[a] Dates in this book have been cross-checked from multiple sources, both conventional encyclopedias and specialist textbooks; there may remain a few errors, due to disagreement in sources and ambiguities in historical texts based on such factors as dates of conception versus the granting of a patent or first performance. Some existing timelines for electronic music appear in Holmes, *Electronic and Experimental Music*, and Collins and d'Escriván (eds.), *The Cambridge Companion to Electronic Music*, as well as Mark Ballora's course notes (www.personal.psu.edu/meb26/INART55/timeline.html) and Paul Doornbusch's "A chronology/history of electronic and computer music and related events 1906–2011" (www.doornbusch.net/chronology).

[b] See the film *The Future Is Not What It Used to Be* (2002), directed by Mika Taanila; and Mikko Ojanen, Jari Suominen, Titti Kallio, and Kai Lassfolk (2007) "Design principles and user interfaces of Erkki Kurenniemi's electronic musical instruments of the 1960s and 1970s," *Proceedings of the 2007 Conference on New Interfaces for Musical Expression* (NIME07), New York.

[c] Martin Hilbert and Priscila López (2011) "The world's technological capacity to store, communicate, and compute information," *Science*, 332(6025): 60–5.

The reference to astronauts on the moon in Table 1.1 above was deliberate and was meant to illustrate the connection of new technology to the public imagination. The unfamiliarity of electronically created sound when first introduced was often used in film music as an illustration of psychological disturbance or the supernatural. Yet in the popular excitement of the space age after the Second World War (and an accompanying boom in science fiction), it perhaps found its most enduring connection. Famous examples might range from the soundtrack by Bebe and Louis

Barron of *Forbidden Planet* (1956) to the afro-futurism of Sun Ra and Parliament Funkadelic.[6] The German band Kraftwerk's main output is a series of concept albums on technological themes, and the very name "techno" espouses the technology link-up (the future as an escape compared to the troubles of everyday life can be highly attractive).[7] The annals of electronic music history are full of pieces themed around outer space or high technology; for instance, whilst Kraftwerk's *The Robots* (1978) is well known, there are a large number of precedents, including Frank Coe and Forrest J. Ackerman's *Music for Robots* (1961), Erik Nordgren's piece *Crazy Robots* (1964), and Paul Boisselet's *Le Robot* (1965).[8]

The relationship of musicians with technology continues to be an active area of theorizing and necessarily practical decision making.

Definitions and categories

We have already noted the existence of alternative overall terms in the field of electronic music. Going further, why have a separate topic of *electronic* music at all? We need to pause for a moment and consider the utility, and the danger, of categories.[9] Labels can be helpful, because they let us break down knowledge into manageable components for discussion. At the same time, they may corrupt the true picture and set up artificial boundaries where there don't have to be any.

Electronic music is not somehow expected to be self-contained. A guitarist might play an acoustic as much as an electric guitar and a composer might work with all manner of ensembles from orchestras to laptop groups. The respected computer music composer Paul Lansky decided to no longer write any music for computer in 2008 and is currently happily composing for acoustic instruments with traditional scores. A rock band might incorporate a turntablist, yet not consider themselves to be creating electronic dance music. Artists trained in the visual arts have turned to sound art, and musicians have become involved in digital art. We'll see many of these cross-currents in later chapters of this book.

One of the core terms in use in musical discourse, popular music, allows for many definitions, and leads to many confusions and tensions based on people's differing expectations. As Roy Shuker observes, we might emphasize one or more of sheer popularity, economic commercialization, the central status of recordings, and particular music theories.[10] Electronic music itself shows vestiges of these tensions, particularly between experimental artists pursuing "high art" and those who follow more commercial goals, with a generous area of ambiguity in between. For example, think of art rock projects, of commercially successful music with radical twists which popularize experimental discoveries.

So, like many authors, at least we've raised these issues, even if we cannot resolve them. Instead, we'll proceed, on the agreement that we understand the implications of choosing categories. At points, we'll confront this again, in particular in discussing the profusion of styles of electronic dance music, a situation where the producers, journalists, and fans are themselves highly active in coining labels and trying to make niches where none might have existed a week before.

Historiographic issues

Much of the history of electronic music is contemporary, still resolving around us, or happened relatively recently, within a few human lifetimes. This can help the historian of electronic music; there is the chance to interview some pioneer practitioners and capture details of scenes as they emerge. At the same time, knowing what to document suffers bias based on an investigator's cultural background and geographical locale, and interviewees don't typically have a neutral opinion of themselves! New movements are exciting, but undeveloped, and their take-up and long-term significance is uncertain. The pressure to discover, whether a journalist needing a new story or an academic another article, may prematurely label phenomena and falsely exaggerate differences at the expense of connections to other developments. In biology, speciation events are not immediately recognized, but can take time to resolve; the same goes for mimetic events like the spawning of musical genres, even if the timescale of cultural replicators is much faster than genetics.[11] Choosing which narrative to follow amongst many alternatives, whether tracing the availability of technology, the role of individual personalities, or the small-scale or large-scale social and economic background, is a standard dilemma of the historical musicologist.

In understanding the historical context of developments, it is worth keeping in mind general historical events and sociological concerns. The Second World War (1939–45) in particular accelerated the development of many technologies, just as it provoked many life-changing personal experiences for those growing up to be the post-war generation of musicians. Tensions between France and Germany after the war are often linked to elements of the rivalry between the schools of musique concrète and elektronische Musik, particularly in the early 1950s; the leader of musique concrète, Pierre Schaeffer, had been in the French Resistance. The post-war years of relative peace in the more prosperous countries saw economic booms and busts in the rise of new technologies, shifts in the post-colonial world order, and radical development in societal convention. We might mention 1960s liberation, protest and civil rights movements, or the transition from tie and suit-wearing electronic music composers in the 1950s to electronic music nudists or tattoo and piercing-covered noise musicians.

Revision is part of the process of historical and scientific investigation, where theories once held are disproved. Scholarship in recent years has turned up many interesting precedents that older electronic music textbooks had not admitted, such as the wire recorder, gramophone, and optical film soundtrack experiments substantially pre-dating musique concrète. There are no doubt "facts" in this textbook that will need to be re-appraised in time, however honorable and rigorous our intentions.

Analysis

Finding a common basis for analysis that works across such a diverse set of musics as in this book is cause for concern. Even if we can agree on a set of standard musical descriptors, different works require different weights for each. Nonetheless, we need to proceed pragmatically here if we are to start investigating, and in this spirit, four fundamental candidate properties in music are as follows:

- *Rhythm*: The placement of musical events in time, usually at or near human physical gestural rates (though electronics also allow faster rates).
- *Pitch*: Resonances/oscillations in sound at identifiable auditory periodicities.
- *Timbre*: The "sound" of sound, its essential character, including many attributes such as the time-varying loudness and spectral make-up, roughness of tone, or brightness.
- *Space*: The location of sound sources, as well as the real or virtual acoustic environment.

Sonic details can be revealed over different timescales, as for example in the contrast of immediate rhythmic timings against longer-scale formal structure. Musical processes can also exhibit interactions between simultaneous actions (such as vertical correspondences at one time, local aggregates such as a harmony, and parallel streams as in counterpoint and layering) and successive events (melody within one line and events within a distinct stream).

For the benefit of succinctness, we are resolving on a common-sense view of musical attributes that may leverage the reader's existing intuitions. Nonetheless, the complexity of these musical facets can fill whole books in their own right, and music theories in electronic music bring their own concepts to bear. In particular, the notion of a *sound object* as a superset and extension of the concept of a note often appears. Imagine a sound continuously evolving, rather than a singular simple strike or ring. Such morphing and transformation can be found in acoustic sources (change the shape of your mouth while continually singing at stable pitch, for instance, shifting between vowels), but is present to a high degree of design in much electronic music.

Representations in electronic music deviate substantially from Western classical scores or pop/jazz lead sheets. Electronic music composers have found new ways to notate music as they have explored new techniques to create it; for example, time in some 1950s scores might appear measured in inches of passing magnetic tape, and sound objects have affiliated parameter trails showing, for example, their amplitude envelope (time-varying loudness).

The most general representations must deal with raw sound itself (and hopefully show something of its perceptual effect) rather than assume music is composed of a bunch of discrete note instructions.[12] Spectrograms and other time-frequency representations often appear in analyses of electronic works,[13] and will appear in this book too. Figure 1.1 is an example (or, rather, four examples); each sub-graph has time proceeding left to right and demonstrates the energy content of the signal over a range of component frequencies increasing up the vertical axis. This breakdown of sound into a large number of simultaneous channels, a filter bank, is very useful in going beyond a simple time domain view of amplitude fluctuation. It allows us to see the activity level of sound in different areas, much like a graphic equalizer display, and the physiological process of your inner ear.

Some controversies in electronic music

As a field which has in many ways mirrored social and economic developments, and which, out of necessity, has at times raised issues of access vs. institutionalization, open platforms vs. commercialization, and artistic freedom vs. standardization, it should be no surprise that the history of electronic music is full of debates and controversies. We present here two examples of themes that have arisen in the theoretical discussion of electronic music and that may help to indicate the sorts of debate you may encounter both in this book and further afield.

Mass participation

Professional musicians, critics, and other stakeholders in musical life sometimes have an uneasy relationship with amateur musicians whose sole income is not derived from music. Yet electronic music is replete with examples of prominent figures who had multiple careers, whose experimental work was a noncommercial sideline, or who simply enjoy the act of creation, whether or not it leads to any wider recognition. The early days of electronic music studios saw restricted access, given limited facilities and high expense. Although some private individuals did set up their own facilities (such as the Barrons), the 1950s was mainly a time of privileged clubs clustered around particular facilities, with many "name" composers

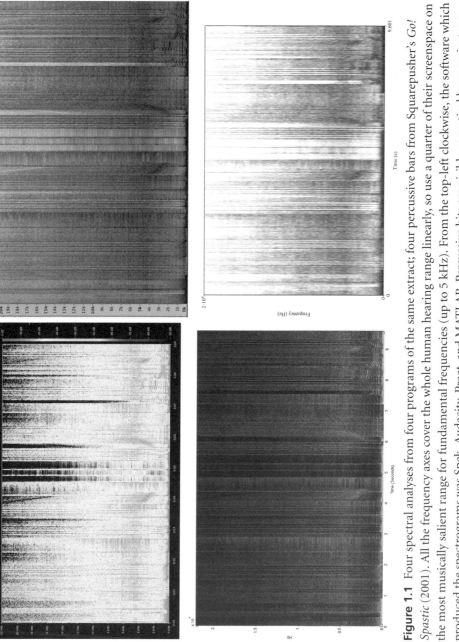

Figure 1.1 Four spectral analyses from four programs of the same extract; four percussive bars from Squarepusher's *Go! Spastic* (2001). All the frequency axes cover the whole human hearing range linearly, so use a quarter of their screenspace on the most musically salient range for fundamental frequencies (up to 5 kHz). From the top-left clockwise, the software which produced the spectrograms was Spek, Audacity, Praat, and MATLAB. Percussive hits are visible as vertical bars; an instance of speech near the end appears as the horizontally co-fluctuating formant curves in the lower part of the plot.

from the instrumental field being those invited to take part in electronic exploration. Fortunately, this situation eased as prices came down; analog synthesizers became affordable for musicians in the 1970s, and digital hardware and cheap computing made electronic music highly accessible (at least in wealthy countries) from the 1980s onward.

In the current era, innumerable artists and releases across multiple media compete for bandwidth, and the impression is of a joyously unstoppable mob of activity. For example, 1,000 dubstep tracks are uploaded to SoundCloud per day, Last.fm lists 65 million songs, and listening to all the music released each week would take a music critic a lifetime longer than he or she would have available to write reviews. So the filters of advertising budget and trusted information sources tend to dominate still, despite some opportunities to go viral.

This makes the study of electronic music joyful and challenging. When more music is released each week than you could comfortably listen to in a year,[14] in studying electronic music, you will continually encounter artists you have never heard of before. Two human beings can always find different parts of the information network to share with one another, so two scholars will always have slightly different personal perspectives on the musical field.

DIY record releases are not new, and accelerated particularly in the post-punk period from 1978 or so onward, aided by organizations such as Rough Trade, with many independent labels being established.[15] Although the recording industry these days is often attributed to a few big record labels that have eaten up many smaller concerns, independent releasing still goes on, particularly now in the digital domain through net labels, digital distribution-only packages, and music services enabling anyone to release work for sale (CDBaby, Tunecore, and the like).

Gender and international involvement

Ideally, human activities would always show a fair mix of practitioners reflecting the statistical make-up of human populations. Unfortunately, electronic music has often seen a greater concentration of male adherents, particularly in previous decades. It is not that there aren't plenty of examples of important female artists active in the 1950s and 1960s, such as Elaine Radigue, Else Marie Pade, Alice Shields, Bebe Barron, Pauline Oliveros, and more. The BBC Radiophonic Workshop was set up by 1958 (not without initial resistance!) after a great deal of lobbying from Daphne Oram. Following the precedent of British wartime employment practices, it had a fairer mix of female sound designers including the much-feted Delia Derbyshire, but still bucked the trend of mainly male employment elsewhere in the BBC reclaiming jobs after the war.[16] In recent years, women have actively challenged all stereotypes of male musical thrust; Björk Guðmundsdóttir in particular has provided a clear and leading international role model. Despite significant liberations, it remains important to acknowledge the existence of such issues in order to avoid future discrimination. There are various initiatives in progress to celebrate female contributions to electronic music; an interesting, if US-centric, starting point is the book *Pink Noises*, which collects perspectives from many creators.[17]

International involvement in electronic music is also a concern. Fortunately, there have been many historical worldwide connections (Theremin's Russia and Halim El-Dabh's Egypt, for example), and the spread of the technology is relatively wide. Admittedly, some developments are concentrated in particular nations where technology is first honed: The US in particular was home to much early computer music research, though Australia and Britain, with their own contributions to early computing, sneaked in some 1951 computer music of their own.

In later chapters, we shall encounter many further themes and issues, including the extended compositional worlds opened up by electronics, the concerns of intellectual property, or what it means to perform live. There is a huge amount to investigate in electronic music and there is a mass of musical activity ongoing; there are also dangers, like the obsolescence and maintenance issues with fast-paced technology development. We hope that this dynamism will come across in the pages ahead and that your own appetite for investigation will be suitably whetted by what you read.[18]

Further listening

Each chapter implicitly suggests listening in featuring the work of many diverse artists; we can only suggest starting points, given that there is much more great music to discover than space. There are books specifically dedicated to annotated discographies of electronic music, for example, Dave Henderson's *Journey to a Plugged In State of Mind*.[19]

Online sources are a great way to discover music these days, including many rare releases (Jean Michel Jarre's *Music for Supermarkets* (1983) is an LP with a limited edition of one copy, but, having been played once on Radio Luxembourg, has made its way to YouTube ...). Depending on availability in your Internet locality, Spotify, Pandora, Last.fm, Deezer, Grooveshark and more offer legal streaming services. Charity shops and thrift stores may be good sources for original LPs and cassettes if you own the necessary earlier analog equipment. In many cases, music has been re-released on CD, is available for download, or, for more recent music, was inherently a digital release in the first place. There are a host of online record labels (net labels) to explore, and many releases have begun to deviate from fixed recordings entirely, in the guise of interactive software for many different devices. Some parties have sought to make historic resources available, despite legal issues over orphan works, such as Ubu Web (www.ubu.com) and the Creel Pone re-issues series for lesser-known electronic music works.[20]

For course tutors or the interested collector, two helpful starting points for a historic electronic music collection are the following:

Various Artists (2000) *OHM+ The Early Gurus of Electronic Music 1948–1980.* Ellipsis Arts: CD3690.

Various Artists (2005) *Acousmatrix: The History of Electronic Music.* BVHAAST: CD 0206.

Further reading

At the end of each chapter, lists of recommended further reading will appear.

Braun, Hans-Joachim (ed.) (2002) *Music and Technology in the Twentieth Century* (Baltimore, MD: Johns Hopkins University Press).

Chadabe, Joel (1997) *Electric Sound: The Past and Promise of Electronic Music* (Upper Saddle River, NJ: Prentice Hall).

Collins, Nick and d'Escriván, Julio (eds.) (2007) *The Cambridge Companion to Electronic Music* (Cambridge University Press).

Cox, Christoph and Warner, Daniel (eds.) (2004) *Audio Culture: Readings in Modern Music* (London; New York: Continuum).

Holmes, Thom (2012) *Electronic and Experimental Music*, 4th edn. (New York: Routledge).

Manning, Peter (2004) *Electronic and Computer Music* (Oxford University Press).

Théberge, Paul (1997) *Any Sound You Can Imagine: Making Music/Consuming Technology* (Hanover, NH: Wesleyan University Press).

Chapter 2

Recording technologies and music

Recording has captured people as well as sound; Glenn Gould famously retreated to a basement recording studio rather than give another imperfect concert, though the trace of his singing remains indelible on the discs he created there.[1] The relationship of musicians with studios has changed from suspicion and sideline to a central embrace. A few have rejected recording, particularly in scenes of improvised music where location-specific uniqueness is held as key, but even most improvisers have been tempted to record their work for broadcast or release at some stage. Recordings have become a central part of the music business, an international publicity engine for artists as well as a mechanism of archiving. Communication and storage technology means that musical information is easily transferable between cultures and different eras. As the history of electronic music intersects well with the history of recording, most historical electronic music survives documented in recorded form.[2]

Recording technologies

There are precedents to pure audio recording machines. Examples might be found in musical scores, which work like extended memory representations even if they do not hold every detail of reproduction, and the mechanical scores implicit in music boxes, carillons, or the nineteenth-century fad for street organs. More exotic early automata include the floating quartet of robot musicians by the great engineer Al-Jazari, created to entertain a royal drinking party in 1206, and the celebrated flautist and tabor and pipe mechanical players of Jacques Vaucanson (the first from 1738).[3] The home use of player pianos[4] from around 1900 to 1929 in part reflected initial inadequacies of recording quality. Yet a transition occurred from strong bourgeois traditions of home music making to listening mediated by recordings or broadcast (itself increasingly based around recordings): The main part of the twentieth century focused in on a more passive mode of reception for many.

Although one speculative theory holds that sound may have been captured through vibrations of the potter's wheel in the casting of pots or other manufacturing processes,[5] and melodies and speech were mimicked by champion budgies and other parroting birds,[6] the earliest recording technologies for raw sound itself in a modern sense date from the nineteenth century. Leon-Scott's phonautograph (1857) allowed scientific plotting, though not playback[7]; Edison's[8] phonograph from 1877 established the more conventional record and playback functionality. The phonograph was a fully acoustic recording system which worked with the horn-collected incident signal pressed via a stylus onto tin foil wrapped around a cylinder drum. The invention had low fidelity, short recording times, and a business plan which emphasized speech above music. It took some time for recording as a medium to take off beyond the invention of the gramophone by Berliner in 1887. The phonograph records vertically by "hill and dale" through helices on the outside of a drum, where depth of incision stores instantaneous amplitude, whereas the gramophone records horizontal displacements in spiral tracks on a flat disc with amplitude represented by deviation from the groove center, which proved to be the longer-lasting convention for records.

The history of recording spans different eras of technology.[9] Developments might be broken down into regions of acoustic recording (from 1857), analog (electrical) recording (from 1898) and digital (from around 1957 for the earliest computer music, though with telecommunications precedents). The peaks of popularity of these technologies do not match their earliest appearance, of course. Acoustic recording has some of the most charming images, with musicians clustered around the horn of the recording device. In many early sessions, louder instruments like brass were often substituted for quieter strings merely in order to get adequate power of vibration to the incising needle. The notion of "acoustic recording" was gradually superseded by electrical in a number of stages, including electric motors to drive the turning of the player (rather than manual winding) and electrical amplification as a stage in disc cutting. We should also keep an eye on the spread of broadcast technologies, which challenged (and continue to challenge in the present day) self-ownership of recordings and playback devices. The rise of wireless radio from 1920 helped to restrict gramophone sales, at the same time as the two in combination killed off player pianos.[10]

Valdemar Poulsen's wire recorder of 1898 was the first true analog electrical recording medium and was initially marketed for office dictation and telephony purposes. It took some decades for electrical recording to supplant acoustic recording after the invention of effective amplification with the vacuum tube. Microphones themselves as transducers from acoustic to electrical signal date from the use of carbon microphones in the telephone (1876).[11] By the 1920s, the carbon microphone was being superseded by new models more familiar from later recording practices,

Figure 2.1 German magnetic tape recorders photographed in 1941.
Bundesarchiv, Bild 183–2007-1026–500 / CC-BY-SA

such as the dynamic and capacitor mics, particularly due to the newly flourishing radio broadcast industry.[12] Electrical recording became an essential part of the signal chain for higher-quality recordings, where amplification could overcome the difficulties of direct acoustic inscription, if impeding sales of the Stroh violin (an expensive alternative violin with a special amplifying acoustic horn). The conductor Stokowski in particular was a great enthusiast for new recording technologies and often put his Philadelphia Orchestra at the disposal of engineers for tests.

The recording process before the Second World War, but for a few early experiments via disc cutting and optical film sound, required single-take recording. More extreme editing quickly took off with the wide adoption of magnetic tape recorders after the war, as technology from Germany was returned to the US shorn of patent restrictions. Radio performers could pre-record their shows, and editing sleight of hand became a production norm across the vast majority of music styles, including classical. Multitracking quickly followed, where multiple tracks exist in parallel on a tape without requiring a mixdown to a single channel, and the number of available tracks expanded with each succeeding decade. The post-war economic boom also supplied an enthusiastic market for recordings amongst new hifi buffs and teenagers with disposable income.

The second half of the twentieth century saw a fast succession of consumer formats, led by robust 45″ and 33 1/3″ records, but diversifying through audio standards for automobiles and portability such as cartridges and cassettes. From the early 1980s, consumer digital formats such as the CD (and, to a much lesser extent, MiniDisc and Digital Audio Tape) began their own takeover, and we now exist in a world where digital download release is the key market. Although stakeholders have tried to hold the market static at particular formats, change has continued apace; vinyl records have retained a little functional and nostalgic value in DJing (though digital systems undermine the crates of records approach) and charity and thrift store collecting, but cannot claim any significant market penetration.

One inexorable correlate of technological change has been a push to greater flexibility of editing. The number of tracks is only limited by processor speed and memory in computer-based systems, and nondestructive click-and-drag editing is an expected standard for digital audio workstations. Types of recording machine vary in their inherent artifacts and sonic characteristics; the clean signal of CDs is to some a characterless sterility. Although the quality of recording media has tended to rise in terms of dynamic range and frequency response, there have been consumer-led factors at play as well as engineering advances, such as the rush to compressed MP3 files in the 1990s popularized through much shorter download times. To be fair, such psychoacoustic compression has been refined to the point of providing a fully convincing perceptual experience if the bit rate is sufficient, as evidenced in many double-blind trials.[13]

With digital systems in particular, we rely on highly refined manufacturing. Whilst the principles of a record are visible in its grooves, and a rough sound can be created even by manual scratching with the stylus, the fine laser reflection measurements underlying CD playback, or other workings of computer technology, are reliant on hugely complicated industrial processes. Digital archiving is a tricky subject, with no stable long-term solution. Although CDs have built-in error correction bits, they can still be damaged to the point of breakdown.[14] There are no perfect long-term recording solutions, but merely a succession of holding formats.

It is worth noting that recording has grown and exists side by side with broadcast, and early electronic music was often associated with facilities run by broadcasting networks. The two are intertwined; radio programs can be pre-recorded for broadcast (as Bing Crosby found to his delight with the arrival of magnetic tape in the US) and advances in recording technology supplying live broadcast, such as microphones, impact on recording studio technology. The advance of public radio in the 1920s seriously dented both gramophone and piano sales, though the Great Depression of the 1930s must also take its share of the blame for the downturns. In the current era, we see such hybrid forms as personalized streaming services, where the user can choose the substance of the music stream he or she draws from

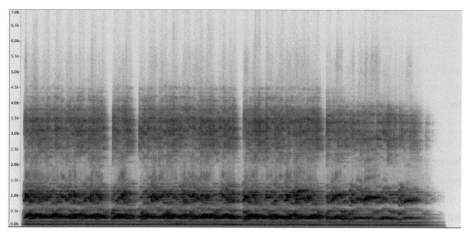

Figure 2.2 Spectrogram of Halim El-Dabh's *Wire Recorder Piece* (1944)

a provider such as Pandora, Spotify, or Last.fm.[15] Podcasting is a democratized broadcast solution. Traditional radio and television broadcast remains resistant to full online integration, though digital radio broadcast is now replacing analog services in some countries as the electromagnetic broadcast spectrum is continually re-negotiated following technological change.

Pioneers of recorded sound composition

Our contemporary freedoms in sound capture and transformation took some time to establish themselves as standards of musical composition, even after the supporting technological capacity arose. But although the full flowering of editing potential is a post-Second World War phenomenon, closely linked to the international commercial rise of magnetic tape, there are precedents in unorthodox experiments with record players, film soundtracks, and even an inspired co-option of a wire recorder (see below).

Halim El-Dabh

In 1944, Halim El-Dabh borrowed a heavy wire recorder from Middle East Radio in Cairo and took it to record the choir at a religious ceremony.[16] He then processed the recordings in the studio, using filtering to remove the fundamentals of the voices and keep the higher harmonics; he was fascinated by the beating of the higher partials and wanted his transformative piece to reflect that. He also had access to acoustic chambers for manipulating reverberation, and could perturb the acoustic of the original recording by adding resonance and echoes. The final work, an Egyptian coup preceding the first

French musique concrète by four years, was premiered at an art gallery as the 20-minute or so piece *The Expression of Zaar* (1944). A fragment is still available now as his *Wire Recorder Piece* (Figure 2.2) shows a spectrogram of this extract (audio sourced from *An Anthology of Noise & Electronic Music / Fourth A-Chronology 1937–2005*. Sub Rosa: SR250). The pitched resonances are seen as the strong horizontal lines of sustained energy in concentrated bands.

German and Russian experimental film makers, as well as mainstream film sound designers, created many early examples of recorded sonic art; edited sound became available as a matter of course much earlier in the film industry, through optical film sound equipment in particular.[17] The first combined sound and vision experiments pre-date the twentieth century, with the Edison company roughly synchronizing a photograph and a kinetoscope with a common drive belt in 1894 (Dickson's Kinetophone).[18] A number of further attempts were made to combine phonographs with film projection before the mid-1920s, uniformly failing through such issues as poor sync and low sound amplification. Although the eventual commercial turn to the talkies from 1927 was initially based around a sound-on-disc system (Vitaphone) rather than sound on film, by 1930, the superior editing ease, synchronization, and quality of the optical film soundtrack had made it the primary option. One notable early work anticipating later post-war sound experiments is the 1930 radio piece *Weekend* by Walter Ruttmann, created through optical film sound techniques and evoking a weekend of life in Berlin through manipulated soundscape recordings.

While we consider film, we should acknowledge that sound design in film for some time had the lead on sound synthesis as well as editing techniques;[19] Rouben Mamoulian's film *Dr. Jekyll and Mr. Hyde* (1931) uses exciting high pitched abstract sound in its soundtrack for the transformation scenes.[20] Experimentalists such as Arseny Avraamov in Russia and Rudolph Pfenninger in Germany explored directly inscribing patterns on the optical film soundtrack as a method of sound synthesis in the 1920s and 1930s.[21] Famous realizations include early 1930s work by Oskar Fischinger on "Sounding Ornaments" with publicity documents of the time showing (mocked-up) factory production methods for (over-sized) shapes to lay on the optical track.[22] Later drawn sound synthesizers include Evgeny Murzin's ANS or Daphne Oram's Oramics project, and a powerful illustration of optical techniques is Norman McLaren's *Synchromy* (1971), mirroring visual and audio drawing.[23]

These creative experiments in film were paralleled by an increasing consciousness of the potential of the phonograph as a new experimental tool. Artists often pre-empted traditional composers in adoption. László Moholy-Nagy, amongst others, anticipated the repercussions the phonograph would have; Dada performers in 1920 were playing records in reverse and manipulating pitch.[24] But the composers would soon catch on; in 1924, Respighi suggested using the call of the nightingale in his *Pines of Rome* via a specific gramophone record. In 1930, Paul Hindemith and Ernst Toth held a concert of "Grammophonmusik," music created through manipulating records of instrumentalists, presented live through the use of multiple turntables.[25] The young John Cage on a European exchange witnessed this Berlin concert presentation and was to use turntables for his own *Imaginary Landscape No. 1* (1939), which with piano and percussion employed records of tones, re-pitched live through the expedient of a variable speed turntable.

Such art experiments would inevitably also appear in a more commercial context. An important transitional figure here is the inventive guitarist Les Paul. In 1947, overdubbing multiple layers through generations of mono discs in his garage, Paul made 500 test versions of *Lover (When You're Near Me)* (eventually released on Capitol in 1947), an eight-part rendition of the jazz standard. Once he obtained one of the newly commercialized tape machines, there was no stopping him; he later adapted his machine for multitracking, allowing simultaneous tracks on a single tape, though also making good use of his existing overdubbing expertise.[26] Some of the most glorious recordings in the new age of editing are those created by Les Paul with Mary Ford, who had a string of hits in the early 1950s showing off the glorious possibilities of layering voice and guitar. Often recorded on the road while on tour, Les and Mary introduced many virtuosic techniques, from the importance of perfect takes at each iteration of recording (they couldn't go back once they bounced down) to such effects as recording at half speed to obtain double speed playing up an octave at normal playback rate.[27] Overdub recording might be said to have come of age with their 1951 US No. 1 record *How High the Moon*. Where film editing machines were out of the reach of anyone but professional cinema trade sound engineers, new tape machines were accessible to dedicated engineer-musicians.

Despite many precedents in art music, radio art, and cinema sound, electronic music history texts tend to focus on the school of musique concrète established by Pierre Schaeffer. Working in Paris at Radiodiffusion-Télévision Française (RTF) since the early 1940s, Schaeffer had his breakthrough year in 1948, using turntables as a compositional medium. The depth of theorizing that accompanied this venture is what has established it in the minds of many academics as a primary force, though the popularization of editing should truthfully be credited much more to such studio pioneers as Les Paul or Walter Legge. Schaeffer, beginning his work with record players (since tape was only taken up at his studios in 1951), would have envied the complex disc editing facilities developed by Warner Brothers for its Vitaphone sound film system of the late 1920s. To cut the attacks from sounds, he would laboriously drop the needle at exactly the right point whilst dubbing to a new acetate on a disc-cutting lathe. Nonetheless, by April 1948, Schaeffer had created the first concrete study, *Étude aux chemins de fer (Railroad Study)*, manipulating sounds obtained from recording six different trains at railway sidings. Many more studies followed, with an early broadcast on radio in 1948 and a turntable concert performance in 1950.[28]

The "concrète" part of the name refers to the rejection of any abstract intermediary product of composition like a musical score, favoring instead direct manipulation of sound materials themselves. To Schaeffer and his school, listening was paramount, and he extensively theorized on the perception and classification of sound over the coming decades as many composers worked at his studio laboratories. The difficulties of listening were confronted by trainee composers serving long listening apprenticeships, and Schaeffer's idealized state of "reduced listening" free of association is a concentrated experience which the first study continues to present as a challenge; can you hear the sounds in and of themselves without the evocation of everyday environmental signification? This focus on sound over external meaning would prove influential amongst certain groups of artists, as well as creating fertile ground for challenges when "soundscape composition" arose later in the century. The very term "musique concrète" was introduced by Schaeffer in 1949 and had fallen out of his favor by 1957,[29] but persists as a historical encapsulation of this experimentally significant work (which we will discuss further in Chapter 4).

Around about the same time that musique concrète was beginning, the high-fidelity movement in America saw the release of sound effects records. Emory Cook's *Rail Dynamics*, a simulation of passing trains, dates from 1949, only one year after Schaeffer's study, though more angled to the joy of trainspotting than concerns of musical development. Admittedly not the sound object composition of Schaefferian reduced listening ideology, it did bring nonmusical instrument sounds to many living rooms: Hifi obsessives often preferred to test their systems with sound effects rather than music.[30] But openness to timbral presentation was an important facet of gradual acceptance running through twentieth-century music.

Art music facilitated through magnetic tape, *tape music*, quickly became an international pursuit. Cage and his collaborators' "Project of Music for Magnetic Tape" saw a laborious six-month tape-splicing project around the precise realization of the chance score of *Williams Mix* (eventually premiered in 1953 as the first eight-channel work). We will continue the story of the opening up of tape composition in academic, private, and commercial studios in later chapters, alongside the availability of other new musical technologies.

Compositional possibilities

Rather than make do with music existing at one time and place, recording technology opens up meetings of musical material from many eras and locales, and rewards the kinds of patient studio transformation that cannot be achieved in the pressure of the live moment. Ease of editing of the captured sound goes hand in hand with ease of transfiguration and re-purposing, and an armada of effects processes can take the artist a long way from simple playback. Perfectionism is encouraged, and commercial recordings, classical or otherwise, can be the product of a massive array of splices. Milner calls this the "ProToolification of the world," Pro Tools being but one of many current digital audio workstation products. He selects a rock album, Def Leppard's *Hysteria* (1987), as a demonstration of a recording you wouldn't expect to be so painstakingly constructed, but which is actually an utter studio fabrication.[31]

Some editing techniques

Precision editing: Splicing together from multiple takes, with all glitches hidden behind fades. Cutting out bad parts, pasting in good, splicing to taste.

Multitracking: Isolating parts in separately recorded tracks, allowing gradual recording of the final result stage by stage, and potentially preserving isolation of parts right through to the final mix.

Overdubbing: Recording one part on top of another, keeping the mixture of both though losing their separation. No longer required at all in high memory, high CPU digital editing environments, though of substantial historical importance in the formation of many recordings.

Mixing: Choosing the relative emphases of all parts in moving toward a finished product, with elements of control typically over each track's equalization, dynamics, volume envelope, and effects unit automation.

However, we shouldn't make the mistake of thinking that the most interesting recordings are always associated with the newest or most powerful equipment; constraints can always prove creatively stimulating and ideas are often followed through regardless of the time involved. Abbey Road got an 8-track tape machine in 1967, only after the Beatles had finished recording *Sgt. Pepper's Lonely Hearts Club Band*! Public Enemy's Bombsquad production team in the late 1980s worked with samplers with very small memories, deliberately recording at low sample rates or taking the sample from higher-speed record playback to fit more in, whilst giving charismatic rough edges to the sound.[32] The exciting experiments in remix culture fostered by dub pioneers in Jamaica such as King Tubby and Lee Scratch Perry were hardly carried out in the most well-equipped studios in the world at the time, though they were certainly musically cutting edge. Furthermore, "deficiencies" in equipment can in the right aesthetic circumstances make for productive inspiration. The charm of the artifacts of particular recording media have recurred as deliberate effects, for example, in the infatuation with authentic vinyl crackle in 1990s Bristolean trip hop.

We'll discuss in Chapter 10 the artistic engagement with recording side-effects and accidents in the genre of glitch music.

A strong trend of recent decades, especially since the mix-tapes and extended dance versions of 1970s disco, the beat sourcing of hip hop, and the dub plates of Jamaican music, is the re-use of recorded audio by third parties, whether privy to the original multitrack masters or just the final aggregate release. Of course, covering of musical materials is a long-standing tradition which was not invented solely for disco medleys like *Stars on 45*: For example, when Mozart's *Marriage of Figaro* was presented in Prague in 1786, local buskers quickly produced their own arrangements of the popular arias. But recording processes make available the audio itself as the subject of new arrangements.[33] There are a host of examples of audio re-purposing, from Caruso's 1907 recordings re-mastered with a new orchestral backing (c. 1930), through Elvis re-made for art in James Tenney's *Collage #1 ("Blue Suede")* (1961), *The Adventures of Grandmaster Flash on the Wheels of Steel* (1981), Martin Rushent's obsessive remixing project for *The Human League Unlimited Orchestra* (1982) (2,200 main edits and 400 small edits for repetition effects),[34] or Jive Bunny's grossly commercial samplings.

Covers and remixes teach us that any well-known track might have come out very differently, given some slight shift in studio circumstances. The sequence of actions that lead to a "definitive" mix may well have gone in another direction, and remixes help to illustrate some of the wider space of transformational possibilities given raw signal starting points. When analog recording dealt with the irrecoverable bouncing of tracks, choices were final, but digital equipment's unstoppable memory expansion allows for effectively unlimited undos and unlimited combinations, with editing of absolute precision. The average home user can now produce a polished transition rather than a pause-button cassette mix-tape. Indeed, many home users remix the content they would otherwise more passively consume, and without any need to stop at remixing a single piece, the mash-up lets them explore two or more at once in novel combination.[35]

Controversies of recorded music

Recorded sound has had profound consequences for musical practice, sometimes extending the range of possibility, sometimes undermining traditional practice and perturbing musical actions. On the positive side, we might claim studio perfection beyond the vagaries of human performance, empowering previously impossible soundscapes and temporal and geographic dispersion of recordings without the physical presence of the originating musician. The minuses are more contentious across aesthetic and economic factors; nested business interests might not complain, whilst many musicians have had to change their playing style to accommodate the requirements of recording technology and its audiences.

The three-minute pop song in part owes its existence to the maximum side length of 10″ 78 rpm records; where some early twentieth-century dance bands would have naturally played much more extended pieces in their live sets, recordings forced them to curtail the apparent length.[36] Radio friendliness to the three-minute work had ossified the format before long-playing albums could recover the ground, even though much dance music (from disco and on into electronic dance music) continued to favor extended workouts in the club versions. From the 1920s, microphone technique advanced the careers of intimate crooners like Rudy Vallée at the expense of music and opera hall acoustic performance. Aside from technological constraints and biases, stylistic change was driven at a great rate due to the new availability of information. Musicologists of recording have noted the paranoia of jazz artists worried about committing their personal techniques to recordings,[37] changes in vibrato use in singing,[38] the increasing demand for perfection in live performance caused by a false impression of "perfect" (edited) recordings,[39] and many more.

The challenge to attitudes, clashing new possibilities with threats to established musical status, is revealed in a single quote from Stokowski on the possibility for lip-syncing new opera performance. In a 3 May 1932 editorial for the *New York Times*, "Stokowski Testing Singerless Opera," the conductor observes that the soprano "may sing like a nightingale, but she looks like an elephant . . . Electricity will change her. We can take her voice and record it on a disk. Then we can select a beautiful lady who really may be accepted by the audience for a Venus. Then we can synchronise voice and action and create a perfect illusion."[40] Lip-syncing and other dishonesties have come home to bite many times since, from the Monkees to Milli Vanilli, and now into the age of Auto-Tune. For the latter, the very unreality of the effect at its most extreme has been in turn a much-desired musical effect and a self-conscious recognition of the trickery of the recorded world.

If there is one topic in recording that stirs up the greatest hoo-ha, it is the issue of intellectual property. The music industry relies upon certain protections for recordings, both mechanical rights over the recordings themselves and publishing rights over the musical materials abstracted from any one recorded instantiation.[41] These rights have been particularly challenged by the sheer fecundity of digital technology, which allows so much ease of copying and so much encouragement to get involved in content creation and remixing. The legal situation is complicated, compounded by the worldwide distribution situation and varying copyright laws across territories.

Sampling challenges intellectual property in new ways beyond old-style plagiarism of the elements of a song; it allows the complete re-purposing of an existing sound recording. Although mechanical copyright has been invoked at various junctures in the history of recording in bids to rein in re-duplication or control radio broadcast content, the digital sampler as a device made sampling so straightforward a practice as to spawn many new musical mannerisms and antagonize rights holders en bloc. The late 1980s in particular, a period associated with frenetic musical developments in hip hop, saw things come to a head, and the musical fecundity of "sampladelic" production by such artists as Public Enemy or De La Soul was substantially reined in by the 1990s. Jesse Kriss has made a beautifully informative website (http://jklabs.net/projects/samplinghistory) showing original sources and those who sampled them between 1952 and 2004; whilst sources peak in the 1970s, sampling albums peak around 1990, though without significantly tailing off after that point. After a raft of out-of-court settlements and some rarer legal judgments, sample clearance practices are firmly in place as a matter of business course and the popularity of sample-based works is established as one cultural preference.[42]

Finding positives in sampling, we might point to the importance of such practices as signifyin' in African-American culture, the need to have a right of cultural reference to comment on culture and history.[43] Against a fast turnover of recording careers, careers have also been renewed by re-purposing. In a poignant scene in the film *Scratch*,[44] DJ Shadow surveys a basement stacked with records: "almost all of these artists no longer have a career." Yet, through him and other sample-friendly artists, they have a further chance to live on, and some licensing deals for samples operate on the basis that the earlier artist gains a fresh record contract. Sampling itself is just a literal manifestation of processes that occur in creativity; it can be a fine line between plagiarism and innovation, for human creativity proceeds not teleologically to a known end, but by a rich process of trial and error founded on prior art.[45] Policing the line between rip-off and novelty is an involved struggle, a constantly ongoing study in cultural attitudes. Artists themselves have taken up the subject productively; the Kopyright Liberation Front's various projects in pop subversion from 1987 to 1992[46] and John Oswald's plunderphonics work[47] are two notorious examples amongst many. Both saw the imposed destruction of one of their record releases, which, however, continue to be available to this day online.

Further reading

Bayley, Amanda (ed.) (2009) *Recorded Music: Performance, Culture and Technology* (Cambridge University Press).

Cook, Nicholas, Clarke, Eric, Leech-Wilkinson, Daniel, and John Rink (eds.) (2009) *The Cambridge Companion to Recorded Music* (Cambridge University Press).

Eisenberg, Evan (2005) *The Recording Angel: Music, Records and Culture from Aristotle to Zappa*, 2nd edn. (New Haven, CT: Yale University Press).

Elborough, Travis (2009) *The Long-Player Goodbye: The Album from Vinyl to iPod and Back Again* (London: Sceptre).

Frith, Simon and Goodwin, Andrew (eds.) (1990) *On Record: Rock, Pop, and the Written Word* (London: Routledge).

Katz, Mark (2004) *Capturing Sound: How Technology Has Changed Music* (Berkeley, CA: University of California Press).

Milner, Greg (2009) *Perfecting Sound Forever: The Story of Recorded Music* (London: Granta Publications).

Chapter 3

New sounds and new instruments: Electronic music up until 1948

Having considered the general history of recording, we'll now examine the development of electronic music more intensively up until just before the middle of the twentieth century. Selecting dividing points in historical surveys always involves a degree of arbitrariness, but for our purposes, 1948 provides a useful line, corresponding as it does not only with Schaeffer's first musique concrète studies, but also to signs of the forthcoming post-war economic boom, following a wartime technology push in such areas as communications and computing. The year 1947 had seen the beginning of practical transistor technology, and the first commercial magnetic tape recorders in the US appeared after Bing Crosby's broadcast from tape in November 1947.

In looking at this early period, we'll explore the creation of new instruments and new sounds through nascent electrical technology, jumping around slightly in history to explore different ideas and lines of development. Artistic and commercial measures of success will at times work together and at other times be in conflict. The history of electronic instrument development is an extremely diverse one, presenting many different *interfaces*: For our purposes, we can consider the interface to be the mechanism(s) via which a performer controls an instrument. We might make a useful distinction between those instruments that make use of, mimic or augment traditional instrumental interfaces (most notably, but not exclusively, the keyboard) and those which explore entirely new ones. The latter category includes some exotic developments indeed[1] and there has been an ongoing debate about questions of accessibility, virtuosity, and expressivity with new interfaces for musical performance. Traditional interfaces (at least potentially) allow for performers to take advantage of existing skills, but at the same time may limit the potential of an instrument by constricting the range of control and expressivity. As we will see below, the decoupling from a physical (i.e., acoustic) means of sound production resulted in both new possibilities and new problems.

Electronic instrument pre-history

Strictly speaking, the earliest known electric instrument was the Denis d'or (the "golden Dionysius"), which was invented and constructed by the Czech theologian Václav Prokop Diviš (1698–1765), probably in about 1748.[2] Diviš was an interesting character, having also invented the lightning rod at the same time as, but independently of, Benjamin Franklin (see panel below). The Denis d'or reportedly consisted of about 790 iron strings, which were struck like a clavichord, rather than plucked, and made use of an ingenious and complex system of stops. These latter were said (in various combinations) to allow it to imitate an astonishing array of instruments, including, it was claimed, aerophones. Diviš devised a novel method of temporarily charging the strings with electricity in order to "enhance" the sound. What effect this had is unclear (unfortunately only one instrument was made and this did not survive), but it apparently also allowed Diviš to deliver an electric shock to the performer whenever he desired, a feature which might well explain the Denis d'or's lack of longevity.

Benjamin Franklin's lightning bells

One of Franklin's lesser-known inventions was his lightning bells, which date from 1752. In fact an early form of electrostatic device, these consisted of two bells on insulated supports, one connected to a lightning rod and the other to the ground. Between them, a metallic ball was suspended. When enough charge had built up in the bell connected to the lightning rod, the ball would be attracted to it. Upon contact, it would become charged to the same potential and would then be repelled, hitting the other bell and transferring its charge, at which point the process would repeat.[3]

"In September 1752, I erected an Iron Rod to draw the Lightning down into my House, in order to make some Experiments on it, with two Bells to give Notice when the Rod should be electrified. A contrivance obvious to every Electrician.

I found the Bells rang sometimes when there was no Lightning or Thunder, but only a dark Cloud over the Rod; that sometimes after a Flash of Lightning they would suddenly stop; and at other times, when they had not rang before, they would, after a Flash, suddenly begin to ring; that the Electricity was sometimes very faint, so that when a small Spark was obtained, another could not be got for sometime after; at other times the Sparks would follow extremely quick, and once I had a continual Stream from Bell to Bell, the size of a Crow-Quill."[4]

In fact, Franklin is erroneously credited for inventing these; something he perhaps alludes to with the phrase "A contrivance obvious to every Electrician." The electric chimes as they were called (though not really an instrument) were in fact invented in the 1740s by Andrew Gordon, a Scottish Benedictine monk working as a professor in Erfurt, Germany, who also invented the first electric motor.[5]

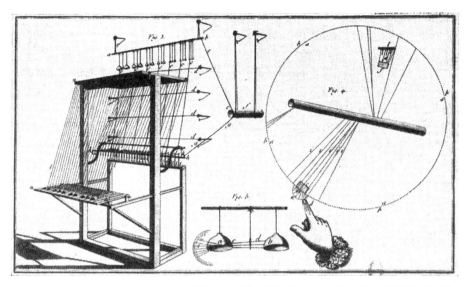

Figure 3.1 Jean-Baptiste Thillaie Delaborde's Clavecin électrique (1759). Public domain, from http://commons.wikimedia.org/wiki/File:Clavessin_electrique.jpg

A similar development to the Denis d'or came about ten years later with Jean-Baptiste Thillaie Delaborde's Clavecin électrique. It was invented in 1759 and is the earliest electric instrument to survive to the present day. Despite the instrument's name, it was not in fact a harpsichord, but rather a sort of electrically controlled carillon. (Delaborde felt that it deserved the name as a reflection of the instrument's quality.) Like the electric chimes (see panel above), it used an electrostatic charge to cause a clapper to alternate between two bells (a pair for each of seven pitches). According to Delaborde, when the instrument was played in a darkened room, each note resulted in a visible spark. Charge was provided through the use of a Leyden jar: Invented by Pieter van Musschenbroek in 1746, this was the first form of capacitor.[6]

In 1836 the scientist Charles Grafton Page demonstrated a way to electrically produce sound. He discovered that by placing a magnet close to a coil connected to a battery, the magnet would vibrate, producing an audible pitch. Page called this "galvanic music," although it wasn't really an instrument.[7]

In the mid-1800s, the Prussian physicist Hermann von Helmholtz designed what is usually recognized as the first sound synthesizer, as described in his landmark book *On the Sensation of Tone as a Physiological Basis for the Theory of Music*, published in 1863. The instrument was built by his student Rudolph Koenig and consisted of a number of tuning forks which were kept in constant vibration using a series of electromagnets. Each of these was coupled with a brass resonator, which had a shutter that could be variably opened via a keyboard mechanism. Helmholtz was really interested in demonstrating his theory of timbre rather than creating a new musical instrument, and notes were tuned to the first ten harmonics of a base frequency. By varying their strength, he could create sounds on this pitch with different timbres, most notably vowel sounds. Nevertheless, although it was not intended as a practical instrument, his Klang Synthesizer provided an important demonstration of the principle of *additive synthesis*, that is, constructing a sound out of its component frequencies, a technique which would see further use in later developments.[8]

Music through the air: The impact of communications technology

One of the more revolutionary areas of invention in the nineteenth century was that of long-distance communication, arriving first with the telegraph – made practical by Samuel Morse by the middle of the century – and later the telephone. The precise details of the invention of the latter are somewhat disputed, although it is usually credited to Alexander Graham Bell, who was in any case the first person to be granted a patent for it. Elisha Gray, an American engineer, is another strong contender: Having created a telephone prototype in 1876, he filed for a patent a mere two hours after Bell. Advocates of Gray's claim to inventing the device stress that while Bell filed first, it later emerged that the device Gray patented actually worked, whereas Bell's did not.[9]

Similarly, the early twentieth century saw a bewildering development in new technologies for sound transmission. As we shall see, the drive to develop wireless transmission techniques, e.g., radio, resulted in numerous technological developments that had additional musical applications.

Nicola Tesla had already conducted experiments in wireless transmission in the late nineteenth century. Building upon the work of Tesla and others, the inventor Guglielmo Marconi made long-distance transmission practical, achieving what is generally considered to be the first transatlantic wireless transmission on December 12, 1901 between Cornwall and Newfoundland, a distance of some 3,500 kilometres. The success of this demonstration is somewhat disputed (the signal was reportedly very weak, and Tesla and others claimed that Marconi had violated their patents), but repeat demonstrations established wireless transmission as a viable approach, opening the door for first wireless telegraph and eventually broadcast radio.

Indeed, what was effectively the first AM radio program broadcast was made just a few years later by Reginald Fessenden from Ocean Bluff-Brant Rock, Massachusetts, on Christmas Eve, 1906. Using a primitive transmitter, Fassenden broadcast himself playing *O Holy Night* on the violin and reading from the Bible to ships out at sea.[10] However, it took until 1920 for radio to really start to take off in a bigger way, with the first news broadcast (by station 8MK in Detroit), the first college radio station (at Union College in Schenectady, New York), and the first licensed commercial broadcasting station (KDKA in Pittsburgh) all arriving around that year. Also in 1920, the Sociedad Radio Argentina aired a broadcast of Wagner's *Parsifal* in Buenos Aires (although there were only about twenty homes with receivers in the city) and in 1922 the Marconi Research Centre in England began regular entertainment broadcasts. The British Broadcasting Company Ltd., the pre-cursor to today's BBC, was also established in 1922, providing a model for public broadcasters in other nations, including the RAI in Italy and the Reichs-Rundfunk-Gesellschaft in Germany. Later, public broadcasters in Europe would establish experimental radio laboratories, which would also serve as places of experimentation for musicians exploring the emerging possibilities of electrically generated sound (we will explore this further in Chapter 4).

Technological spinoffs: Adding up sounds and taking them away

In 1906, the inventor Lee De Forest patented a definitive breakthrough in vacuum tube technology, the Audion, and the forerunner of triode valves.[11] This was a crucial development for radio, as it allowed tuning circuitry to operate with far greater accuracy than ever before. It also proved to be significant for musical purposes. In 1915, De Forest himself filed a patent detailing how the Audion could be used as an oscillator for producing musical tones. He employed a technique called heterodyning, which involved combining two high-frequency tones in such a way that a new audible frequency – the difference between the two combined frequencies – resulted. In the same year, De Forrest created an instrument called the Audion Piano, which had one Audion per octave.[12] This was the first instrument to use heterodyning oscillators, an approach which would continue to be used in electronic instruments until the development of the transistor. Real-world sounds such as the notes of musical instruments generally consist of energy at many frequencies, and the development of practical oscillators (both vacuum tube based and others) made Helmholtz's idea of building up sounds out of component frequencies both powerful and practical.

Approaches opposite to additive synthesis are generally termed *subtractive* techniques, since they involve taking away energy at one or more frequencies. In the mid-nineteenth century, experimenters working with Leyden jars (see above) noted that they exhibited resonant properties when discharging, i.e., the current oscillated at a certain frequency. Acoustic resonance was already understood as a physical phenomenon in which an oscillating body (e.g., a string, the sounding chamber of a violin, or a room and the air within it) would reinforce certain frequencies and diminish or cancel out others. A way of describing what happens to sound within a resonant system is to say that its spectrum (the make-up of energy at various frequencies) is *filtered* by the sound. By the late nineteenth century, electrical filtering technology had developed to the point of allowing applications in telegraphy, and later telephony and radio. For example, in combination with heterodyning techniques, several signals could be "multiplexed" together, allowing for more efficient transmission. Again, there turned out to be significant musical applications for filtering technology, and many electronic musical instruments make use of both additive and subtractive approaches to create and vary their sounds.

Long-distance music

As well as rivaling Bell as the inventor of the telephone, Elisha Gray was also notable for a contribution to the field of musical invention. In 1874, he gave the first demonstration of his Musical Telegraph, the first instrument designed to transmit musical sounds via electric (then telegraph) wires.[13] He discovered that by using electromagnets, he could cause steel reeds to vibrate (a kind of simple electromagnetically driven oscillator) and that the resulting signal could be transmitted. The device was capable of playing notes over two octaves, and later models included a tone control and a simple loudspeaker.[14]

Early electrical lighting systems provided another possible means for musical transmission. Prior to the invention of the light bulb, electrical lighting using carbon arc lamps was in use throughout Europe. These produced light by means of an electrical spark leaping between two carbon electrodes, which were thus heated to the point of incandescence. One issue with this approach to generating light was that it was noisy, and the British physicist and engineer William Du Bois Duddell conducted a number of experiments at the end of the century to see if this noise could be reduced. In the process of trying to do this, he discovered that by varying the voltage sent to the lamps, he could create resonances in the audible frequency range. By attaching a keyboard, he could control the frequency of the oscillations, with the arc lamp acting as a sort of loudspeaker. During a demonstration of the Singing Arc in London, the audience noticed that other arc lamps on the same circuit also "sang," suggesting the possibility that lighting circuits might be used to disseminate music (a notion which foreshadows more recent developments in power-line networking). Duddell toured Britain with his invention, but it was never adopted generally and he didn't even file a patent for it.[15]

However, the idea of music from a distance found its first really practical realisation in Thadeus Cahill's Telharmonium, which in some senses anticipated broadcast radio, Internet streaming, Muzak, and network music.[16] Cahill's notion was to create a keyboard instrument, capable of producing a variety of sounds, which could broadcast music via dedicated telephone lines to homes and businesses. Although it could, using a mechanical attachment, be operated automatically like a player piano, the primary intention was for it to be played live in order to allow real human expressivity in the performances. Cahill built three versions of the instrument, each of them immense – the first weighed seven tons and the second and third almost 200. Cahill himself preferred the name Dynamophone or (according to at least one source) Electric Music Plant.[17] Together with his partner Oscar Crosby, he created the New England Electric Music Company and later the New York Electric Music Company (NYEMC) (both ironically incorporated in New Jersey) to raise funds and produce the instrument. In 1905, they negotiated an agreement with the New York Telephone Company to lay special lines for transmitting the Telharmonium's music, and in 1906, a special hall for the instrument was created (later named Telharmonic Hall) in a building at Broadway and 39th Street in Manhattan.

There is some mystery surrounding the details of the keyboards used with the instrument. It seems that Cahill experimented with different designs, with the aim of solving the age-old problem of being able to play in just intonation while still being able to modulate to any key. Although all three instruments bore a superficial resemblance to an organ, with a number of manuals and a pedalboard, the second Telharmonium's keyboards were unusual to say the least. Descriptions vary, but there is general agreement that they consisted of alternating white and black keys, with no gaps in between, and were capable of producing unusual tunings. Extant photographs of the keyboards of the second instrument, taken in 1907, seem to show two manuals, each consisting of four terraced banks of 84 keys, alternating black and white as described above. Selecting the same note on different banks allowed for adjustment of intonation (most significantly the ability to play just intoned thirds), choosing between an equal tempered note, a slightly sharp version, and a slightly flat version. The fourth bank allowed pitches to be tuned as a harmonic seventh relative to the fundamental ten semi-tones lower, i.e., almost a quarter-tone flatter than equal tempered minor sevenths. This would have resulted in 48 pitches per octave, but the instrument was incomplete, so some pitches would not sound. According to one account, special symbols were used in the notation to indicate alterations in tuning, so it seems probable that whole pieces had to be transcribed.[18]

Examination of the various patent documents shows only standard keyboard designs, and the third Telharmonium reportedly had normal keyboards (albeit with some remaining potential for playing just intoned thirds), so it seems likely that Cahill was never completely satisfied with the results. This possibly reflected the difficulty of playing these four bank designs. The diagrams accompanying the fourth patent application (issued in 1917) show three normal manuals and a pedalboard in the traditional arrangement, with the strictly alternating black-and-white design limited to what was referred to as the dynamic manual. The latter was one of Cahill's earlier innovations, first realized in a modified organ in 1887 and included in all three Telharmonia. The keys on this manual corresponded to graduated steps from quiet to loud, and allowed for near-instantaneous changes in dynamics. When a performer's hands were not free to play this directly, a weight could be used to hold down the desired key.

In any case, the instruments must have been extremely difficult to play, and not only because of the keyboards in the second version. On the version shown in Cahill's fourth patent, the three normal keyboard manuals and the pedalboard were augmented by four "swell" foot pedals, which allowed for the level of the notes played on each manual to be smoothly changed. A series of timbre control switches varied the strength of different partials, allowing for each manual to produce a different timbre. Cahill suggested that the first of "preferably" two players operate the four pitch manuals, the second the timbre switches and the dynamic manual, and each of them should control two of the four swell pedals. In addition, players might have to make adjustments in the instrument's master tuning rheostat (a device used to manually vary resistance in an electric circuit) in order to compensate for drift in the master motor's speed, and thus the instrument's tuning.

This latter aspect was crucial, as the Telharmonium's sounds were generated using rheotomes, which were the earliest form of tonewheels, driven by the motor mentioned above. These consisted of a metal disk which rotated end-on to a wire brush, which served as an electric pickup. The disks had bumps along the rim which would contact the brush as it turned, and the number of bumps combined with the speed of rotation determined the frequency of the resulting sound. The output of these was essentially sinusoidal (i.e., consisting of energy at a single frequency), but Cahill added additional tonewheels to allow for the production of harmonics (again a form of additive synthesis; Cahill had extensively studied Helmholtz's work). This, in conjunction with the instrument's various expression devices, allowed for a number of different timbres to be produced, and listeners reported that the Telharmonium was capable of imitating a variety of traditional instruments, particularly orchestral woodwinds.

A clever arrangement allowed for individual tonewheels to serve as different harmonics for different notes. To be effective, however, the instrument needed to be able to produce sinusoids at frequencies in between tempered pitch. As noted above, even in the second version, the keys did not map precisely onto the available

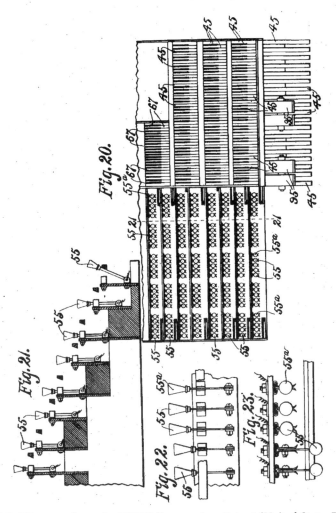

Figure 3.2 Diagrams from the 1917 Telharmonium Patent (United States Patent and Trademark Office, public domain). The dynamic manual is labeled "67"

tonewheels, since the instrument was never completed and some were lacking. As such, some notes were created using "phantom" fundamentals, making use of a well-known psychoacoustic phenomenon whereby listeners will hear a missing fundamental, provided that enough of a note's other harmonics are present.

The idea of the Telharmonium was well received, with commentators as notable as Mark Twain (a subscriber and financial backer of the project) singing its praises: "Every time I see or hear a new wonder like this I have to postpone my death right off. I couldn't possibly leave the world until I have heard this again and again."[19] Referring to the possibility of combining the Telharmonium with an arc lamp distribution system like the one that Duddell's work suggested, he said: "If a great Princess marries, what is to hinder all the lamps along the streets on her wedding night playing that march together? Or, if a great man should die – I, for example – they could all be tuned up for a dirge."[20]

In the July 1906 issue of *McClure's Magazine*, the journalist Ray Stannard Baker wrote an article entitled "New music for an old world" in which he praised Cahill and his invention.[21] He was particularly impressed with its potential to democratize music in the same way that free libraries and galleries had opened up access to literature and visual art. The best music would no longer be accessible only to wealthy urbanites. (Baker was probably somewhat optimistic in this regard, given the need for dedicated lines and the fact that telephone adoption in rural areas of the US remained relatively low until the 1920s, by which time the Telharmonium Company had collapsed.)

In a sort of pre-cursor to later debates about the negative effects of synthesizers on traditional music making and of recent controversies over MP3s and music streaming, Baker also speculated on the effects the device might have on musicians. He felt that the instrument would reduce the frequency and likelihood of strikes, since a few musicians could cater to listeners over a wide area. Again perhaps somewhat presciently, he noted that the Telharmonium's "peculiar and beautiful tones may in their very sweetness and perfection fail to please everyone. As artists and architects know, there is a certain appeal to the senses in that which is imperfect and irregular."[22]

In contrast to Baker's skepticism about the Telharmonium's sound quality, his article attracted the attention of the virtuoso pianist Ferruccio Busoni, who foresaw the potential of such instruments to produce new sounds. In his 1907 *Sketch of a New Esthetic of Music*, he wrote of the utopian possibilities the Telharmonium suggested, saying: "Let us take thought, how music may be restored to its primitive, natural essence; let us free it from architectonic, acoustic and aesthetic dogmas; let it be pure invention and sentiment, in harmonies, in forms, in tone-colours (for invention and sentiment are not the prerogative of melody alone).'[23] Busoni thus articulates what would later become a form of electronic music dogma, which has often been articulated with a similar lack of critical reflection: That electronic means would open up music to the possibility of any sound.[24]

Unfortunately, serious technical problems arose which plagued the project. Although the Telharmonium used dedicated lines, they ran alongside those for voice. Because of the limits of shielding technology of the day, this resulted in crosstalk, whereby the signal transmitted on one line becomes audible on another through a process of electromagnetic induction. This meant that people's phone conversations were interrupted by Telharmonium music. This led to numerous complaints by users of the telephone system. According to an article called "Music on wires" published in the *New York Globe and Commercial Advertiser* in January 1907, at least one marital dispute arose because of this, when a woman refused to believe that her husband was working late because she could hear the *William Tell Overture* playing in the background.[25]

The New York Telephone Company, already nervous about its regulatory status and under fire for what was described as terrible service in general, decided that it couldn't afford the bad publicity and cancelled the deal. In 1907, Lee De Forest (see above) conducted some experiments on wireless broadcasting of Telharmonium music, but the Brooklyn Naval Yard complained that it was interfering with the Yard's signals, so the NYEMC decided to wait until wireless technology was more reliable.

The company continued on under Cahill for a number of years, but by 1914 finally filed for bankruptcy. Sadly, none of the three instruments survived to the present day. Cahill's brother Arthur stored the prototype until 1962, when it was finally scrapped, due to the apparent lack of any interest in preserving it.

Heavenly voices

A somewhat similar instrument to the Telharmonium was the Choralcelo ("heavenly voices") invented by the Boston engineer and musician Melvin Severy with the assistance of his brother-in-law, George B. Sinclair, between 1888 and 1909. Unlike the Telharmonium, the Choralcelo was intended for domestic use, albeit with the majority of the rather large instrument concealed in the basement of the house which housed it. The instruments had two keyboards, an upper 64 note one and a lower 88 key one, along with a pedalboard. A pianola-style paper roll mechanism allowed the Choralcelo to play automatically.

The heart of the Choralcelo was what was called the "interruptor," which consisted of a number of brass cylinders cut with grooves, which spun at different speeds and were driven by an electric motor; in other words, a collection of tonewheels similar in principle to those used in Cahill's instruments. In addition, there were a wide variety of "auxilliary units" which actually generated the sound. The "piano unit" involved a set of piano strings which could be both struck by hammers in the standard fashion and made to vibrate using a set of electromagnets. This was accomplished by feeding each magnet a series of pulses of DC current generated by the interruptor at a frequency which (theoretically at least) would coincide with the fundamental of the corresponding string. Other auxiliary units coupled electromagnets to a wide variety of sound producers and resonators involving pieces of metal, wood, and glass, buggy springs and chimes, along with resonator tubes made from different materials, and a performer could select different combinations via an organ-like system of stops. However, matching the frequency of the various sound producers precisely was not a straightforward problem to solve, especially given the rather inconsistent quality of electric current during the period, which may have been one reason for the instrument's long period of development.

A number of Choralcelos were manufactured for various wealthy clients (possibly as many as 100, including at least one installed on a yacht) and at least two have survived in working condition to the present day.[26]

Playing the Ether

In addition to keyboard-based instruments like the Telharmonium and the Choralcelo, the early twentieth century also saw some novel interfaces and instrumental forms, ranging from the expressive to the fantastic. Nikolai Obukhov's Ether, which dates from 1918, was perhaps the most extreme. Obukhov was an experimental composer whose music was known for its embrace of mysticism (he signed his name "Nicolas l'illuminé") and its use of unusual notation. The Ether was in essence an electronically powered wind machine. While it was described as "inaudible" by some sources, Obukhov maintained that it produced sounds from five octaves above to five octaves below the range of human hearing, supposedly having a subliminal effect on the listener.[27]

A more practical instrument (and one which remains in use to this day) was invented two years later, which sensed movements of a performer in the air around it. Originally called the Aetherphone, it is usually referred to by the surname of its inventor, Theremin.[28] Born Lev Termen in Russia, the researcher Leon Theremin devised a novel interface consisting of two antennae which protruded from a box containing sound-producing electronics. The first antenna, a vertical one, controlled pitch, while a horizontal loop controlled the instrument's volume. By moving one's hands in proximity to these, a performer could control the sound in quite detailed ways through the principle of capacitance. The continuity of pitch (glissandi are trivial to play) and the nature of the resulting tones led many to describe the sound as "vocal" in character, and it is possible to play the instrument with great expressiveness.

The theremin's most notable exponent was the American performer Clara Rockmore, who developed a virtuoso technique using fingering patterns for fast passages. Visually, theremin performance can be quite impressive, and Theremin said that he wanted it to be like "the conductor of an orchestra." That said, it can certainly be a very difficult instrument to play well, due to the lack of haptic feedback (e.g., vibration transferred via touch) or any physical guides for pitch and amplitude levels.

Theremin found his way to the US in 1927 and, after demonstrating the instrument in New York City, negotiated a licensing agreement with RCA to mass produce it. Only about 200 were made before the corporation decided it was unprofitable, and in 1938 Theremin returned to the Soviet Union. In his book on Theremin, Albert Glinsky explains that he was abducted by NKVD agents (the forerunners of the KGB), and it was later revealed that Theremin had been a spy himself. While one might be tempted to think that his return was due to the high regard that Soviet officials had for electronic music, Theremin was put to work there inventing espionage devices, including one of the first listening devices, which was called "The Thing."

Somewhat similar to the theremin, and more practical than the Ether, was Obukhov's Croix Sonore ("sonorous cross"), which he used in more than twenty different compositions. It took the form of a brass cross 175 cm high, with an ornate star at the cross point, protruding from a globe with a flattened base. By moving one's hand closer or farther from the star, a performer could vary the pitch. Unlike the theremin, volume was controlled by a device concealed in the performer's other hand rather than by an additional antenna.[29]

In keeping with his broader artistic aesthetic, Obukhov seems to have designed the instrument with the visual effect clearly in mind. In all known public performances the player was female, who seems to have been intended to appear as a sort of priestess involved in a religious rite. A *New York Times* review of a 1934 performance of Obukhov's *Book of Life* described the Croix Sonore performer as drawing out "notes that throbbed like twenty violins or at times sang like a human voice."[30]

The instrument fell into disrepair following Obukhov's death, but did survive to the present day. It's currently on display at the Musée de la musique in Paris.

In between the keys

German inventors also made contributions to new instrument design. Jörg Mager, a primary school teacher and organist, had a revelatory experience during the hot summer of 1911 when some of the upper notes on his organ became detuned, leading to an interest in microtonal tuning systems. Also inspired by a passage in the composer Arnold Schoenberg's *Harmonielehre*, in which Schoenberg expresses with regret his view that experiments in microtonal composition are probably somewhat pointless while so few instruments exist that are capable of playing them, Mager constructed a quarter-tone harmonium in the same year and went on to publish a theory of quarter-tone music in 1915.[31]

Mager realized that electronic instruments afforded greater possibilities for variations in tuning and set about developing a related family of instruments. Working with the electronics firm Lorenz A.G. – which supplied him with tone-generating circuitry that used heterodyning oscillators and was capable of producing seventy-two tones to the octave – Mager produced his first electronic instrument in 1921, dubbed the Elektrophon (and later the Sphärophon as a reference to the ancient philosophical concept of the Music of the Spheres). The instrument used a semi-circular dial to control pitch in a continuous glissando, but had no conventional keyboard. An improved version, the Kurbelsphärophon, was completed in 1923 and was given its debut at the Donaueschingen Festival in southwest Germany. This instrument made it possible to play discrete pitches using an interface consisting of two switchable handles and a double foot pedal to control the volume, and added some filters to vary the timbre. Although it was not particularly successful, the Russian composer Georgi Mikhailovic Rimsky-Korsakov (grandson of Nikolai) did compose some quarter-tone pieces for the instrument.

With the assistance of the physicist Oskar Vierling and support from the city of Darmstadt, Mager then went on to develop the Klaviatursphärophon in 1928, a version which replaced the handles with two short-keyed monophonic keyboards, cleverly arranged to allow the performer to play on both keyboards at once with the same hand, creating interesting duophonic tones. Although this was perhaps an acknowledgment of the advantage of using an established interface, the keyboards did support microtonal tuning. The next development in Mager's family of instruments was the Partiturophon, a four (later five) manual and voice version of the Klaviatursphärophon, first completed in 1930. His final instrument, the Kaleidophon, is somewhat more mysterious. Completed in 1939 (the year of Mager's death), it was said to have been monophonic, with a more piano-like keyboard, and was capable of "kaleidoscopic" tone mixtures, influenced by the ideas of Schoenberg and Busoni.

Although Mager's instruments saw significant use, mostly in theatrical productions, he struggled to produce a production-ready instrument, in part due to his somewhat limited technical skills. None of his instruments are thought to have survived the Second World War, and Mager himself died impoverished of heart failure in Aschaffenburg, a few months before the outbreak of hostilities.

During this time, the Hochschule für Musik in Berlin had established a Rund-funkversuchstelle, a kind of laboratory for experiments in music, sound, and radio. Friederich Trautwein invented his Trautonium in about 1928 while working there. He was joined soon after by his student, the physicist and composer Oskar Sala.[32]

The Trautonium was a monophonic instrument, but one designed with a specific emphasis on expressivity. Instead of playing a keyboard, the performer placed a finger along a wire to control pitch, allowing for microtonal variation. A bar beneath the wire allowed for articulation and volume control. This interface allowed for rapid figuration and quick changes of pitch. In the first versions, the sounds were produced by neon-tube relaxation oscillators, which produced a sawtooth-like waveform. These were sent through two resonant filters, and the performer could control the volume ratio of these using a footpedal.

The instrument had some success and Paul Hindemith composed a number of trios for three Trautoniums in different tunings. It was used to imitate bell and gong sounds in the premiere of Richard Strauss' *Japanese Festival Music* in 1942 and in performances of Wagner's *Parsifal* in Berlin in the 1950s. Albert Einstein referred to it as a "harbinger of future scientific importance," although he was not entirely convinced of its musical worth. Sala later developed a two-manual version, the Mixturtrautonium, which he used to compose music for several soundtracks, most notably Alfred Hitchcock's *The Birds*. The wire interface idea was further developed in other forms, such as MIDI ribbon controllers, and Sala continued development of the Trautonium up until his death in 2002.

Another popular instrument was developed about the same time in France by Maurice Martenot, a cellist who worked as a radio telegrapher during the First World War. Like Trautwein and Sala, Martenot was inspired to try to increase the range of expressivity possible with electronic instruments, in particular, thinking of the pitch variation possible with string instruments. In the initial version, a performer pulled a ring attached to a ribbon left or right in order to vary the pitch, leaving the other hand free to manipulate various controls which affected the dynamics and timbre. Martenot continued developing the instrument for decades, adding a six-octave keyboard (again perhaps a concession to established instrumental technique, but which unusually allowed lateral movement to vary the pitch) and a lever on the bottom which allowed a performer to vary the timbre. Latter versions had a number of different "stops," with names such as Onde, Nasillard, and Souffle, offering a variety of different sounds varying from sine waves to pink noise. They also included four different loudspeakers, which produced different effects, including one which had a small gong as a diaphragm and one which included strings for sympathetic resonance.[33,34]

The instrument was and remains very popular (Radiohead's Jonny Greenwood is a notable fan). Numerous classical music composers made use of it, including Olivier Messiaen (most notably in his *Turangalîla-Symphonie*), Pierre Boulez, Giacinto Scelsi, Arthur Honegger, and Darius Milhaud, as well as Frank Zappa. The instrument ceased production in 1988, but several conservatories in France still teach it. In 1997, the *Ondéa* project started working to produce new instruments with the same characteristics as the ondes Martenot.[35]

Also in France, the engineer René Bertrand developed his Dynaphone (distinct from Cahill's Dynamophone/Telharmonium) in around 1927. Like the Sphärophon, it was a monophonic instrument which used a dial to control pitch over a range of seven octaves. A button was used to articulate notes, while the other hand could control timbre and volume. Although the instrument was championed by the composer Edgard Varèse, it was not significantly different from its competitors, and Bertrand and Varèse were unable to secure funding to further develop it in the 1930s.

Seeing the light

Optical sound was discussed briefly in the previous chapter on recording. Again it was Lee De Forrest who patented a technique in 1919 which allowed for synchronised optical sound on film.[36] Unsurprisingly, there were a number of musical instruments in the first part of the twentieth century that made use of photoelectric cells to convert light into sound.

The Russian Futurist painter Vladimir Baranoff Rossiné invented a novel instrument called the Optophonic Piano in 1916.[37] It used a number of revolving glass disks that Rossiné had painted, in combination with a number of filters, mirrors, and lenses controlled by the instrument's keyboard, to create varying images, which were both projected onto nearby walls and used to generate sound. The latter was accomplished via a photoelectric sensor, which converted the variations in intensity of light into a signal to control the pitch of a single oscillator.

A similar but more generally useful instrument was the Celluphone ("Cellule Photo-électrique"; any resemblance to cellular phone is completely coincidental!) invented in 1927 by the French engineer Pierre Toulon. Resembling an electric organ, a series of rotating disks with slits in them alternately masked and passed a light. As with the Optophonic Piano, a photoelectric cell picked up these variations and used them to control vacuum tube oscillators (one per octave).

A variety of similar instruments were developed in Europe through the rest of the 1920s and 1930s, including the Superpiano (1929),[38] the "Radio Organ of a Trillion Tones" (1931)[39] and its successor the Polytone Organ (1934),[40] the Syntronic Organ (1934), the Photona (1935), and the Welte Licht-Ton Orgel (1936).[41] In principle, most of these could be understood as early implementations of what came later to be known as *wavetable synthesis*, since the disks effectively encoded a waveform which formed the basis of the synthesized sound.

More generally interesting were the Hardy-Goldthwaithe Organ (1930)[42] and the Singing Keyboard, developed by Frederick Sammis in 1936. Both these instruments qualify as some of the earliest *samplers*, synthesizers which use recorded sounds as the basis of the notes they create (though neither was capable of recording sounds themselves). The former used the by-now familiar glass disk approach, storing some seventy-one sampled notes on one disk. The latter more directly adapted technology from film sound, storing samples on pieces of 35 mm film.[43]

Meanwhile, and more radically, the Soviet artist Arseny Avraamov created the first "hand-drawn" soundtracks in 1930 by shooting still photos of waveforms drawn on paper.[44] A variety of artists and film makers (for example, the Canadian film maker Norman McLaren, the British composer Daphne Oram, and the Greek composer and architect Iannis Xenakis) explored similar ideas throughout the twentieth century. Some of these will be discussed in later chapters.[45]

Hammond time

Many of the instruments discussed in this chapter were revolutionary in terms of sounds, interface, and construction. Commercial success was a relatively rare commodity. One notable exception was the 1935 invention of Laurens Hammond. The Hammond organ has come to be recognized as a classic design and one of the most popular electronic instruments of all time. It was the first practical electric organ and was mass produced for use in churches and people's homes, where it rapidly replaced the older reed organs, such as pedal-pumped harmoniums, then in use. Throughout the 1960s and 1970s, the sound of the Hammond organ became ubiquitous in a wide range of popular music, including blues, gospel, jazz, and progressive rock, with Hammond virtuosi like Ethel Smith and Jimmy Smith. It was also used to a lesser extent by some avant-garde classical composers, such as Karlheinz Stockhausen.[46]

Building on Cahill's work with the Telharmonium – but on a much smaller scale – Hammond's original design used ninety-six tonewheels, which rotated in front of electromagnetic pickups, rather than coming in contact with metal brushes. Five of these tonewheels were included only for mechanical balancing purposes, so a total of ninety-one different frequencies could be produced. As in the Telharmonium, these are not precisely correct and compromises in tuning were accepted. A series of sliding drawbars, labeled to match organ stops, allowed the performer to vary the strength of each harmonic.[47] Like many electronic instruments, the Hammond organ was advertised as being capable of an "infinite" number of tone variations. The US Federal Trade Commission took issue with this, however, and in 1938 ruled that although the Hammond Company could call its product an organ, it had to drop the "infinite" claim, since it was only capable of 253,000,000 possible combinations.[48] Eventually the Hammond Company replaced the tonewheel construction with fully electronic sound generation, but it is a testament to the success of the design that tonewheel models were still made into the 1970s.[49]

The many different variants and models of instruments produced by the Hammond Company and others are too numerous to discuss in detail here, but one "add on" worth mentioning is the Leslie speaker, or Vibratone, first created by Don Leslie in 1941. Really a combination of amplifier and speaker, this used two rotating elements (one for the treble and one for the bass) to create tremolo and Doppler effects. The speed could be varied to achieve a variety of different results. Although not produced by the Hammond Company, the Leslie speaker became closely associated with the "Hammond sound."

Laurens Hammond invented another notable instrument in 1939, along with John Hanert and C. N. Williams.[50] The Novachord was never as successful as the Hammond organ (only 1,069 models were ever made), but it is notable as the first commercially produced polyphonic synthesizer. Unlike Hammond's organs, the Novachord used vacuum tubes to produce tones. A clever design allowed multiple octaves of notes to be derived from twelve top octave oscillators and for all seventy-two notes of the keyboard to be played polyphonically. It also had a number of resonant filters, a six-channel vibrato unit, and an early ADSR (attack/decay/sustain/release) envelope unit to control the way in which the amplitude of notes changed. The instrument suffered from a lack of stability, but did see some commercial use in soundtracks, particularly for horror and science fiction films, as well as in popular music. Notably, the British singer Vera Lynn used it in her 1939 recording of the song *We'll Meet Again* by Ross Parker and Hughie Charles.

The Hammond organ was one of the earliest keyboard instruments to reach the masses, but many others came after. One example, the Clavioline, was invented in 1947 and consisted of a keyboard and a separate amplification unit. It was notable for the wide range of sounds it was capable of producing and its high-quality vibrato.[51]

New sounds, new controversies

Throughout the early development of electronic music, we can see a variety of attitudes toward the sounds new instruments produced. Some inventors, such as Cahill and Hammond, attempted to mimic, or at least approximate, existing instruments. Others were more interested in new sonic possibilities and, as noted above, there were numerous claims of having accessed "infinite" sonic possibilities (even from Hammond regarding his "organ"). However, the possibility of musical instruments that can produce "any" sound raises the question of what exactly makes a sound musical and led many to wonder whether there need be any real limit to this.

The notion that any sound could be music is often (and famously) ascribed to the American composer John Cage. Indeed, in his 1937 essay *The Future of Music: Credo*, Cage exhorts instrument designers and composers to embrace an expanded sonic palette, including notably electronically produced sounds, and pointedly disapproves of new instruments which attempt to "imitate" those of the past, comparing the work of their inventors to that of early automobile manufacturers who copied aspects of horse-drawn carriage design.

In truth, this trend of new sounds for music goes back much further,[52] as we can see for example in the gradually expanding percussion section in classical orchestral music throughout the nineteenth century, or in the Intonarumori (musical noise generators) of the futurist writer Luigi Russolo, whose *Art of Noises* was published in 1913. We shouldn't be surprised by precedents: Even Cage's famous silent piece of 1952, *4′33″*, had pre-cursors in Alphonse Allais' 1897 *Funeral March*, and in an entirely rest-based movement within Erwin Schulhoff's 1919 *Fünf Pittoresken for Piano*.

In contrast to Baker and Twain's praise for the Telharmonium, the latest musical developments were not always popular, regardless of whether they aspired to continue existing lines of musical development or not. A 1931 article in the *New York Times*, with the flattering title of "ELECTRICITY, ETHER AND INSTRUMENTS: Some considerations, reflections, and inferences on the modern cult of vitamine-less art and the synthetic aesthetic," referred with disdain to "pipeless organs" and "remote, jejune, and desiccate approximations of living music," rebuke enough to send any self-respecting instrument inventor running into the arms of the avant garde. (The same article refers to jazz as "sterile," so one might be forgiven for questioning its validity.)[53]

Of course, this contrast between the avant garde and the traditional, the experimental and the commercial, should not be viewed as a simple dichotomy, but it does provide a useful distinction to bear in mind as we look forward to the 1950s and beyond in subsequent chapters.

Further reading

Davies, Hugh (2002) "Electronic instruments: Classification and mechanisms" in Hans-Joachim Braun (ed.), *Music and Technology in the Twentieth Century* (Baltimore, MD: Johns Hopkins University Press), pp. 43–58.

Glinsky, Albert (2000). *Theremin: Ether Music and Espionage* (Urbana, IL: University of Illinois Press).

Helmholtz, Herman (1948, original 1863) *On the Sensations of Tone as a Physiological Basis for the Theory of Music* (London: Longmans, Green, and Co.) (trans. Alexander J Ellis, translated from the 4th German edn.).

Holmes, Thom (2012) "Appendix 1: The evolution of analog synthesizers," in *Electronic and Experimental Music*, 4th edn. (New York: Routledge), pp. 472–81.

Holzer, Derek (2010) "A brief history of optical synthesis," *Tonewheels: Audiovisual Performance*, www.umatic.nl/tonewheels_historical.html.

Hugill, Andrew (2007) "The origins of electronic music," in Nick Collins and Julio d'Escriván (eds.), *The Cambridge Companion to Electronic Music* (Cambridge University Press), pp. 7–23.

Roads, Curtis (1996) "Early electronic music instruments: Time line 1899–1950," *Computer Music Journal*, 20(3): 20–3.

Weidenaar, Reynold (1995) *Magic Music from the Telharmonium* (London: Scarecrow Press, Inc.).

Chapter 4

The post-war sonic boom

After the previous chapter, which spanned some centuries of gradually accelerating activity, we'll slow down our pace and take a look at some developments after the end of the Second World War. This makes sense, as looking forward into the 1950s we see an astonishing number of separate strands develop, each at a fevered pace. The explosion of prosperity and technology after the war created many new possibilities, and the development of electronic music during this period (sometimes referred to as a "golden age") reflects this.

A world of disparate centers

From the vantage point of today, it is difficult to imagine the world of the 1950s. Although post-war peace efforts such as the establishment of the United Nations (UN) in 1945 were representative of a broad trend toward internationalization, the world remained relatively unconnected by today's standards of instant communication and easy transmission of data. The widespread development of post-office mechanization didn't begin until the mid-1950s. While easier than it had hitherto been and naturally less restricted than during the war, travel was more expensive and less frequent than it is today. For example, although there were domestic flights throughout the US by the 1950s, they would cost around $100 – about $800–$1,000 in 2012 money – and were thus just barely within the reach of ordinary people. Jet travel only became practical in the late 1950s. It was only 1956 that the first transatlantic telephone cable was laid, replacing the previous unreliable and extremely expensive radio telephone service.[1]

Given this state of affairs, while there was certainly much crossover, discussion, and visitation going on, it is not surprising that a certain amount of parallel development took place. Given the expense (and often size) of the equipment, a major aspect of this period was institutional support; much of the work that was done was dependent on public or private funding in order to be viable. Nevertheless, some of the first private studios were also established in this period, bringing with them an explosion of idiosyncratic custom development.

Surrounding all of this was a spirit of exploration and innovation, buoyed perhaps by the optimism of the post-war period. This is the time in which many of the basic techniques and technologies of electronic music originated. As noted in the previous chapter, national broadcasters served as an incubator for much development in electronic music, in many cases providing equipment, facilities, funding, and technical support for projects that might not have been commercially viable. We'll start the chapter with a look at some of the most significant radio studios.

Stressed concrete (or how I learned to stop worrying and love the sounds)

We first encountered Pierre Schaeffer, an engineer and announcer for Radiodiffusion Française (later the ORTF) in Chapter 2. Schaeffer had established an initial experimental studio, called Studio d'Essai ("Test Studio," later Club d'Essai), at its facilities in Paris in 1942. In 1948, he was struck by a seemingly strange but revolutionary idea: to produce a "concert of locomotives."[2]

The result of this flash of inspiration was his short composition *Étude aux chemins de fer* (literally *Study on the Paths of Iron*, but more properly translated as *Railroad Study*), which consisted of the sounds of locomotive wheels and whistles, arranged in rhythmic patterns. This is generally recognized as the first example of what Schaeffer called *musique concrète*.

Étude aux chemins de fer was the first in a series of five musique concrète studies that Schaeffer composed in that year, using cut phonograph records for recording and assembly. The others made use of a variety of real-world sounds, including toys, instrumental and vocal sounds, canal boats, saucepans, etc. Collectively, these were referred to as the *Cinq études de bruits* and were presented in a radio broadcast called *Concert de bruits* (*Concert of Noises*) on October 5, 1948.[3] A year later, Schaeffer was joined by the composer Pierre Henry, and together they presented a public concert of their musique concrète works in 1950.

The basic idea of musique concrète was to use real-world sounds as sources and (via various forms of manipulation, editing, and processing) find the musical potential within them. This was in many senses a new way of working, or at least a relatively unique combination of ideas that had been explored in other ways in the past. The emphasis on exploratory "play" (*jeu*) was also important. Aspects such as form tended to emerge semi-organically from the musical implications of the material. This was in essence a very pragmatic way of working, since the materials were only partially constructed, and those using them had to account for the nature of the original (not entirely pliable) sounds.[4]

In 1951, the *Groupe de Recherche de Musique Concrète* (GRMC) was formally established within the RTF, along with a purpose-built electronic music studio (finally including tape machines rather than disc-cutting equipment). Numerous composers came to work at the studio, including Edgard Varèse, Olivier Messiaen, Pierre Boulez, Iannis Xenakis, Karlheinz Stockhausen, and Arthur Honegger.

From 1952 to 1956, Schaeffer was busy with other projects in the RTF and left the group's management to Henry and Philippe Arthuys. When he returned in 1957, he was unhappy with the direction the group had taken. As fallout from the disagreements that followed, Henry and Arthuys resigned. Schaeffer established a new collective within the RTF to replace the GRMC, the *Groupe de Recherches Musicales* (GRM), which also included the composers Luc Ferrari, Iannis Xenakis, Bernard Parmegiani, and later François Bayle, who would become its most significant director from 1966 to 1997.

The members of the GRM continued to refine Schaeffer's techniques as well as the intellectual and aesthetic underpinnings of their work; Schaeffer himself was obsessed with theorizing the new music. As early as 1955, he and others had begun to use the term *musique acousmatique* to describe what they were doing, replacing the older musique concrète term.[5]

The term *acousmatic music* alluded to the teaching practice of the Greek philosopher Pythagoras, who reportedly initiated probationary students (the akousmatikoi, meaning listeners) into his school by teaching from behind a curtain for the first five years of their study.[6] In Schaefferian terms, the notion is one of hearing a sound without seeing or being aware of its cause.[7]

In 1966, Schaeffer published the *Traité des objets musicaux* (*Treatise on Musical Objects*), outlining his theory, and a related set of recordings with documentation entitled *Le solfège de l'objet sonore* (*The Solfege of the Sound Object*).

Listening to Schaeffer's sound objects

Schaeffer's *Traité* represents one of the earlier attempts to theorize the ways in which electronic music functioned and was perceived. His ideas are more concisely laid out in Michel Chion's *Guide des objets sonores, Pierre Schaeffer et la recherche musicale.*[8]

Broadly speaking, Schaeffer made clear distinctions between a physical sound source and the listener's perception and musical understanding of it. He said that there were normally four modes of listening: Listening (*Écouter*), Perceiving (*Ouïr*), Hearing (*Entendre*),[9] and Comprehending (*Comprendre*). These are not intended to be separate or sequential and can occur simultaneously, interacting with one another.

Listening means listening *to* something, trying to identify it, listening while identifying the sound as a sign of the source, e.g., a bark is a sign for a dog.

Perceiving means simply passively receiving a sound: A bark is just background noise which enters our ears without us trying to understand it.

Hearing means intending to listen, focusing on what particularly interests us, so as to be able to describe it. A bark may have unique sonic qualities which distinguish it from other barks.

Comprehending means treating the sound semantically, understanding a linguistic or musical meaning, e.g., "What's that Lassie? A little girl's fallen down the well?" Note that this differs from Listening (*Écouter*) in which a sound is specifically *representative* of its cause.

The term *sound object* (*l'objet sonore*) is an important one in Schaeffer's theory. It is phenomenological in nature and can be considered separately from the environmental and/or musical contexts which produced it: One can consider one's experience of a sound separately from its source or meaning. Schaeffer called this focusing on the aspects of a sound as a phenomenon, *reduced listening* (*l'écoute réduite*).[10]

The approach tended increasingly toward deliberately separating the sounds from their sources, so that the listener would not be distracted by the real-world associations and could focus on its sonic qualities in isolation. In his commentary on Schaeffer's theories, Chion speaks of how repeated listening "exhausts" curiosity and reveals all of a sound's "richness."

Sounds were altered through techniques like filtering (emphasizing or de-emphasising different frequency areas), reverberation, editing and splicing, and looping (see section on classic studio techniques below). The arrival of tape recorders allowed for detailed and micro-level editing and splicing of sounds, and less reliance on the performance skills of the composer.

Gradually the repertoire of techniques expanded, and the initial recognizable sounds of musique concrète were left further and further behind. In his work in the GRM studio, the composer and architect Iannis Xenakis began to develop one such new approach, *microsound*, making up gradually shifting sonic masses from small pieces of sound. Xenakis said he was inspired by real-world phenomena, such as the sounds of the resistance crowds in Athens, and the rain and cicadas he heard when camping in Attica, all examples of sonic composites.[11] His short piece *Concret P.H.*, which was composed in 1958 to be played for the show changeover at the Philips Pavilion at Expo 58 in Brussels (see below), is a good example of this. It consists of short sounds of burning charcoal, layered and played back at different speeds to create textural effects.

Meanwhile, on the banks of the Rhine...

The second major studio we'll discuss, usually referred to as the Cologne Studio, got its start around the same time as Schaeffer's early musique concrète experiments and was also situated within a broadcasting facility.

In 1948, Werner Meyer-Eppler, Director of the Institute of Phonetics at the University of Bonn, had been impressed by a demonstration of a vocoder that had been developed at Bell Laboratories in the US. The vocoder was actually designed

as an attempt to reduce the bandwidth of speech for telecommunications purposes. The basic idea is that a vocal signal is passed through a multiband filter to
obtain a set of simpler amplitude control signals to drive later reconstruction. What
interested Meyer-Eppler, however, was the "dehumanizing" or robotic effect that
resulted.

Meyer-Eppler collaborated with Robert Beyer of the Nordwestdeutscher Rund-
funk (NWDR) in Cologne, who was also interested in the possibilities of electronic
music. The two lectured on this at the Darmstadt Summer Courses for New Music
in 1950. The lectures impressed Beyer's colleague at the NWDR, the musicologist
and composer Herbert Eimert. Together they proposed in 1951 that an experimental
studio be established at the NWDR in Cologne, and the initial work on the facility
was completed in 1952.

The association with the Darmstadt courses proved a productive one: At the time,
Darmstadt was a real hotbed of musical development, and a number of prominent
composers associated with it came to produce work in the new studio, including
Bruno Maderna, Karlheinz Stockhausen, and Gottfried Michael Koenig.

Like Schaeffer, Eimert had an interest in theorizing the new music being created
in his studio, but rather than attempting to create a new framework ad hoc, Eimert's
idea was that serial composition techniques could be adapted for what he called
elektronische Musik.

Serialism grew out of Arnold Schoenberg's twelve-tone method of composition. In
simple terms Schoenberg based each of his serial compositions on a single ordering
of the twelve chromatic pitches. A composition could contain transformations of
that row (transposition up or down, playing it backwards, inverting the intervals,
etc.) as well as the original. Of course, the same principles could be applied to other
"parameters" of music, such as dynamics or timbre, and it seemed straightforward to
use the same procedure to control the various settings of electronic equipment. The
appeal of this for a new medium is clear: its generality makes it infinitely (though
possibly arbitrarily) applicable.[12]

Stockhausen came to have a particular association with the studio. His tape pieces
Studie I and *Studie II* were composed there in 1953 and 1954, using only a sine
wave generator (see textbox below for explanations of classic studio equipment), a
white noise generator, a Melochord (a vacuum tube-based keyboard developed by
Harald Bode, an engineer associated with the studio), and a modified Trautonium.
His *Gesang der Jünglinge*, composed there in 1956, blends electronic sounds with
recordings of a child's voice.

A tale of two cities: The Paris and Cologne studios

Much has been made of the apparent battle between musique concrète and
elektronische Musik. Certainly there was some inflammatory rhetoric, as was quite typical

of the discourse surrounding avant-garde and experimental music at the time.[13] The reality of practice, however, reveals a more fluid situation.

This apparent dichotomy was in fact questioned relatively early on. In an article on the establishment of the radio studio in Milan, the composer Luciano Berio wrote: "Thus far the pursuit of the other Studios has been classified in terms of *musique concrète* and 'electronic music', which have become debatable definitions from today's armchair perspective."[14]

It is often forgotten that Stockhausen visited the Paris studio and composed his *Konkrete Etüde* there. While it is true that in his discussion of *Studie II*, Stockhausen said that he no longer wanted to use acoustic sounds,[15] this is not a position he adheres to, as can be seen by the mixed materials of *Gesang der Jünglinge*, written only two years later (and generally recognized as one of his most significant works). Indeed, despite being the Cologne studio composer par excellence, Stockhausen acknowledged that he learned a lot from his time in Paris, particularly from studies undertaken by the French group on the nature and behavior of sound.[16]

The distinctions made seem fairly aesthetic and grounded in theoretical concerns. Schaeffer felt that serial music techniques, rooted as they were in the intervallic relations of traditional abstract musical thinking, were inappropriate for electronic music.[17] Ironically, the Cologne group preferred electronic sounds for reasons of "purity" and felt that they provided a better medium for serial procedures than instrumental music.[18] In contrast, on a technical level, many techniques were shared between the two studios.

Konrad Boehmer, who would later work at the Institute for Sonology, described the dispute as "a second Cold War," but nevertheless "a very human affair": "It was only in the end of the fifties, that these two opposite genres, the electronic, purely synthetic music of Cologne and the music concrete in Paris, came a little bit closer. It was in some of Stockhausen's and Ferrari's work that you see that. It took quite a lot of time before THIS Cold War was over! I have been educated in both countries in Paris and Cologne. When I was in Paris, it was absolutely unheard of to talk about Cologne and when I came to WDR, it was unheard of to talk about Paris. So, I was a double-spy! (laughs) I've learned quite a lot from both."[19]

And then everybody was doing it . . .

A third important radio studio, the Studio di Fonologia Musicale, was established in 1955 at the Radio Audizioni Italiane (RAI) in Milan by the composers Luciano Berio and Bruno Maderna. Berio had heard a tape music concert at the Museum of Modern Art in New York while in the US in 1952 and was keen to explore the medium. As noted above (see textbox), the practice in Milan was not so tied to the dogma of the Cologne or Paris studios, and focused more on sonic results than the studio or formal techniques used.[20]

A number of significant works were produced there throughout the 1950s by composers including Luigi Nono, John Cage, and Henri Pousseur, as well as by Berio and Maderna themselves.

A number of works for tape and live performers were produced, and even the works for tape alone tended to mix instrumental/vocal and electronic sounds. A particular interest related to voices and speech as an element of electronic music. One great example is Berio's *Thema-Omaggio a Joyce* from 1958, which takes a passage from James Joyce's *Ulysses* as a source.

The BBC started its Radiophonic Workshop in 1958, with a focus more on the development of music and sound effects for its productions than on supporting the work of experimental composers. As such, it was staffed primarily by engineers rather than composers, and many of its innovations were more directly applicable to sound effects or soundtrack production than to avant-garde electronic music.[21]

One of these engineers, Daphne Oram, had a past as a classical musician (she had turned down a place to study at the Royal College of Music in order to work at the BBC), and held ambitions as a composer and experimenter with sound. Her 1950 work *Still Point* was scored for the unusual combination of orchestra, five microphones, and manipulated recordings.[22] Although still unperformed,[23] the 30-minute piece stands out as particularly ambitious for the day. In his obituary for Oram in *The Guardian*, the composer Hugh Davies describes it as "almost certainly the earliest composition to specify the real-time electronic transformation of instrumental sounds."[24] While this is perhaps debatable, it was certainly very forward-looking in this regard.

Having visited Schaeffer and the RTF some time earlier, Oram was inspired along with Desmond Briscoe to advocate for the creation of the Workshop, with both of them serving as studio managers. She stayed only a short period of time, but she stands as a pioneer amongst women in electronic music; we will encounter the Radiophonic Workshop again in Chapter 6, and Oram later in this chapter as well as toward the close of the book.

Numerous other radio studios were established throughout the 1950s and 1960s and beyond, including the Studio di Phonologie de Radio Geneva (1951), the Danmarks Radio Studio in Copenhagen (1953), the Nippon Hoso Kyokai Electronic Music Studio (1954), the Studio Experymentalne in Warsaw (1957), the Elektronmusikstudion (EMS) in Stockholm (1957), the Zvukove Pracovisko in Bratislava (1961), the Norsk Riksringkasting in Oslo (1961), and the expansively named Experimentalistudio für Künstliche Klang and Gerauscherzeugung and its companion facility the Laboratorium für Akustish-Musikalische Grenzprobleme at the East German National Radio (RFZ) in Berlin (1962).[25]

A new peak in "low-downness": Playing *The Sackbut Blues*

Across the water in North America, developments in electronic music were also proceeding rapidly. There, however, things tended to be associated with universities or other public or private research facilities rather than with national broadcasters.

In Canada, the researcher Hugh Le Caine was doing interesting work at the National Research Council (NRC) in Ottawa. During the Second World War he had worked on radar and microwave technology, but in his private life he had always been interested in electronic music. More able to devote time to it after the war, he established a home studio in 1945.[26] In the same year, he produced the first prototype of his most famous invention, the Electronic Sackbut, with a complete version finished in 1948. Le Caine noted: "this choice of name... of a thoroughly obsolete instrument... was thought to afford the designer a certain degree of immunity from criticism."[27]

This keyboard instrument was notable for its fingertip control of expression: Lateral pressure affected pitch, allowing vibrato, portamento, and microtonal variations in tuning. The range was extreme, as much as an octave in either direction. There was also a continuous pitch control, which allowed long glissandi.[28] What Le Caine called "vertical" pressure on the key controlled loudness, allowing crescendi and diminuendi, as well as variations in attack. This foreshadowed later developments in touch-sensitive keyboards. The instrument was monophonic, but this left the left hand free to vary a number of controls that affected the instrument's timbre. It was also one of the first synthesizers to use the technique of voltage control. This involved using varying voltages to control the level of parameters. In the Sackbut these connections were hard-wired, but the idea would be applied in a much more flexible way in later modular analog synthesizers.[29]

Sensitive to the small variation that is a constant feature of instrumental sound, Le Caine was concerned about the "purity" of tone in the instrument. To add irregularity, he introduced devices which added a trumpet-like rasping noise and a flute-like breath sound.[30]

On the strength of demonstrations of the Sackbut and other instruments, the NRC established a lab for Le Caine in 1954 for the purpose of developing new instruments, with the idea that these could be built and sold by Canadian companies. Le Caine's output proved substantial, and all told he would invent some twenty-two new instruments over his lifetime.

One other notable invention was the Special Purpose Tape Recorder (SPTR). Le Caine had spent the years between 1948 and 1951 in England pursuing postgraduate studies in physics at the University of Birmingham.[31] While there, he heard a broadcast of French musique concrète on the BBC. Inspired by Schaeffer's approach,

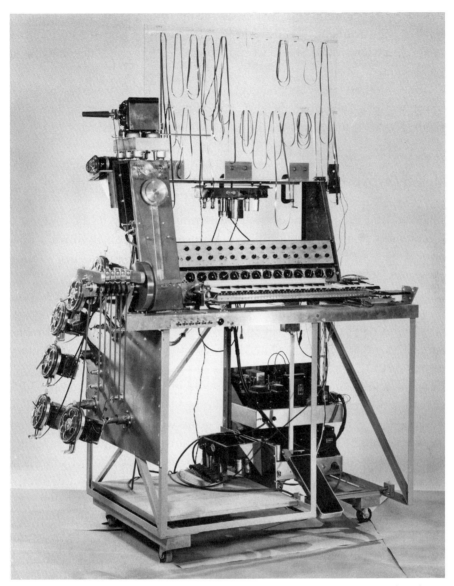

Figure 4.1 Le Caine's Special Purpose Tape Recorder. Image reproduced courtesy of Library and Archives Canada. © Government of Canada. Reproduced with the permission of the Minister of Public Works and Government Services Canada (2012)

he purchased a two-track tape recorder in order to conduct concrète experiments. This eventually led to the SPTR, which was a sort of pre-cursor of the early multi-track machines mentioned in Chapter 2. It allowed six two-track 1/4″ tapes to be played simultaneously, each with separate control of playback speed. He later added a keyboard, with keys varying playback speed and thus pitch, so that the SPTR could be played as an instrument. The instrument ended up as the core of the University of Toronto Electronic Music Studio when it opened in 1959 under the direction of Myron Shaeffer.

Le Caine's designs proved extremely influential and forward-looking. Some aspects of his work only found their way into commercial products in the 1980s. They remain notable for their emphasis on playability and expression.

Analysis: *Dripsody*

Although Le Caine did not consider himself a serious composer, he did compose a number of works, partly as demonstrations of his instruments. Some were whimsical, such as *The Sackbut Blues* of 1948, which Le Caine says achieved a "new peak in low-downness" in his introductory remarks in the recording.[32]

His best-known piece, however, is 1955's *Dripsody*, based upon a single recording of a drop of water. Its economy of material makes it an instructive example of basic musique concrète techniques. We'll use the GRM's Acousmographe software to examine it, which allows layering spectrograms, labels, and other representations.[33]

The primary form of manipulation is the speed of playback of the drop, which Le Caine manipulates to get different pitches using his SPTR. (See also the textbox on classic studio techniques below.) The piece opens with a regular pulse at around 160 beats per minute. (The presence of regular rhythms perhaps shows the influence of Schaeffer's early concrète studies.) After four beats, at just before 2 seconds, a second layer is added, consisting of alternating upwards and downwards sweeps of drops, at a higher pitch than the first layer, but in a slightly slower tempo (see Figure 4.2).

At about 6.5 seconds a three-note repeating figure is added, at roughly a 3/2 tempo ratio to layer 1 and in a lower range.

From this point, the music becomes more dense and irregular, with an effect generally on the border between contrapuntal and textural. At about 13 seconds a prominent low frequency layer appears. At about 38 seconds this becomes a prominent ascending and accelerating line. This repeats, and at about 47.5 seconds Le Caine intensifies things by adding similar but faster layers which go both upwards and downwards, as well as adding echo and reverberation effects (see Figure 4.3).

By about 1:05 this texture has receded, leaving behind a sort of recapitulation based on the opening section, which gradually slows and disintegrates until the end of the piece.[34]

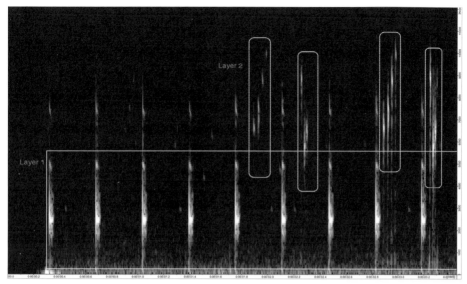

Figure 4.2 Spectrogram of *Dripsody*. Layer 1 is the initial pulse, while Layer 2 is the pattern of upwards and downwards sweeps of drops

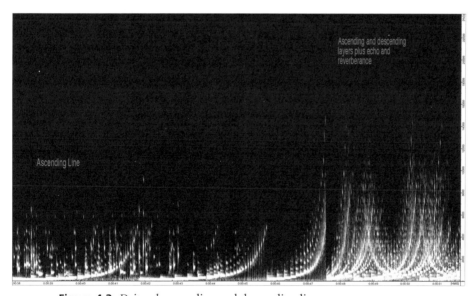

Figure 4.3 *Dripsody* ascending and descending lines

Taped in the US

As noted above, universities played an important role during this period. One notable example in the US was the work of Otto Luening and Vladimir Ussachevsky at Columbia University.

In 1951, an engineer at the university radio station showed Ussachevsky how to produce mechanical reverb and echo effects with a tape recorder by running the tape over two playback heads. Hooked on the potential of magnetic tape for new musical possibilities, Ussachevsky produced five studies of what he called *Tape Music*, exploring octave transposition, reverberation, and other forms of straightforward processing. He presented these in the Composers Forum at Columbia University. Luening was in attendance, and the two began to work together on tape-based compositions. They eventually produced a number of pieces which were presented in the first public concert of tape music in the US, which took place in October 1952 at the Museum of Modern Art in New York. (This is the concert which Berio attended.) In 1955, they were able to establish the first studio at Columbia.[35] The pair eventually established the Columbia-Princeton Electronic Music Center in 1958, with Milton Babbitt from Princeton joining them.[36]

Many of the works the pair produced could in some ways be considered conservative (at least in comparison to what was going on in Europe): They tended to consist of "traditional" musical elements, such as chords, scales, and arpeggios, and they often retained a clear grounding in established instrumental practice, despite their use of changes of speed, echo effects, splicing techniques, etc.

The two went on to explore the possibilities of combining tape with instruments, receiving commissions from the Lousiville Orchestra and the Los Angeles Philharmonic, amongst others.

The classic studios: Some techniques and technologies

Many of the basic techniques and technologies of electronic music originated in this period. Everything described below is in some sense still in use today, albeit perhaps in a different form, e.g., via sound-editing software rather than tape recorders.

Mixing: Simply put, this denotes combining two or more sounds together. In the early days this meant playing them simultaneously and re-recording, with a consequent loss of quality with each generation.

Tape splicing: In the simplest sense, this allows one to re-order sounds in time, literally cutting out one section of tape and inserting it in another place. By making diagonal cuts, one can create crossfades between different sounds (the closer to horizontal the cut, the longer the transition) and construct novel composites, e.g., combining the attack of a clarinet with the sustain of a trumpet.

Tape loops, echos, and delays: These are a family of related techniques. By making a closed loop of tape, one can cause a sound to repeat, as the same bit of tape passes over a playback head repeatedly. Some tape loops were very long – even stretching out of the room or building where the tape recorder was located – while others were quite short. Similar effects on a shorter timescale can be achieved using machines with separate record and playback heads. Tape passes over the record head and an input signal is recorded. A short time later, it passes over the playback head, where the sound is picked up and played. By feeding some of the signal from the playback head (usually at a lower level) back to the record head, a series of decaying echoes results. By running tape between two or more tape recorders, physically separated, it is possible to create longer intervals between recording and playback, to create what are referred to as *delay* effects. Steve Reich's classic pieces *It's Gonna Rain* (1965) and *Come Out* (1966) make use of such techniques to make multiple copies of speech which start in sync, but then gradually shift out of phase. This moves from reverberation, to echo effects, to canons of delays.

Tape speed and direction: By playing a sound back at a different tape speed than the one at which it was recorded (tape speed is usually measured in inches of tape passing a head per second), it was possible to vary both the pitch and duration of a sound. For example, playing back a musical note at half speed would result in the perceived pitch being an octave lower and the duration being twice as long. Tape could also be played in reverse, which would result in a sound being heard backwards.

Reverb: Generally, artificial reverberation aims to simulate the natural resonance of spaces. Almost any environment will have some reverberant properties, but the effect is most prominent in large acoustically reflective spaces such as cathedrals or concert halls. Reverb can provide important information about the size and nature of the space in which a sound is heard. Simulating different sorts of reverb was of interest as it allowed for alternative contexts which a sound could be understood to inhabit. A simple way to create reverb is to play a sound over a loudspeaker in a reverberant space and record the result, but early studios also used artificial reverberators based on spring or plate technology.

Oscillators: Oscillators output a voltage which varies in a pattern that repeats over time. The shape of this pattern is its *waveform*. The rate at which the waveform repeats determines the fundamental frequency of the resulting sound. Although frequency and pitch are not exact analogs (the former being a physical property and the latter a matter of perception), higher repetition rates result in higher perceived pitch. Frequency is usually measured in Hertz (Hz), which is number of cycles per second (cps). The range of variation in voltage determines the amplitude of the sound, roughly speaking how loud it is. The shape of the waveform determines the timbre of the resulting sound and the strength of its harmonics. Harmonics consist of energy at integer multiples of the fundamental frequency. The greater the energy of higher harmonics, the "brighter" sounding the result. The classic waveforms are *Sine* (only the fundamental), *Sawtooth* (the fundamental plus all harmonics, decreasing exponentially in amplitude as you get higher), *Triangle* (the fundamental plus its odd-numbered harmonics, again decreasing in amplitude the higher you go), and *Square* (again the fundamental and all odd-numbered harmonics, but not falling off as fast as with a Triangle wave). Early studios were equipped with standalone oscillators; for example, the Cologne studio had sine and sawtooth oscillators.

Modulators: Modulation is a way of adding frequency content to a sound. One classic example used in many works from this period is *ring modulation*. A basic example can serve to demonstrate the principle. If you ring modulated two sine waves by each other and wave 1 had a lower frequency (f1) than wave 2 (f2), the output would consist of two new frequencies, f1 + f2 and f2 − f1. The effect on more complicated inputs can be understood as composites of this simple case. Numerous pieces produced in the Cologne studio made use of ring modulation, for example, Stockhausen's *Gesang der Jünglinge*.

Noise generators: Early studios were equipped with devices to produce sound with energy at a wide range of frequencies. The classic studios had white noise generators, which (theoretically at least) produced sound with equal energy at all audible frequencies. White noise (and other sounds) could be modified by subtractive techniques using *filters*: These devices altered the spectra of sounds by reducing the energy across some range of frequencies. Common filters are *high pass* (which let through energy above a specified frequency called the *cutoff*, and reduce or remove energy below it), *low pass* (the reverse of high pass, i.e., allow the low-frequency input to pass through and reduce or remove anything above the cutoff), *band pass* (allow content within a range to pass through, and reduce or remove content above or below that range), and *band reject* (the reverse of band pass: reduce or remove within a range and pass everything else). Filters come with a lot of fine variation and are the basis of such things as EQ.

Commercial support and private studios

There was also some commercial support for research (as relatively distinct from product development) in this period. Two notable examples are the Bell Labs facility in New Jersey and the Philips research facilities in Eindhoven in the Netherlands. We'll expand on the latter toward the end of this chapter and on the former in

Chapter 5 (since the most relevant developments there were in the field of computer music).

Although musicians working in the area of electronic music were often dependent on institutions for resources and support, this was also a period during which a number of private studios were first established, for example, Le Caine's 1945 studio mentioned above. Some notable examples were in Britain, perhaps because the BBC was less willing than other broadcasting institutions to allow its facilities to be used for experimental purposes. One early founder was Tristram Cary.

Following his discharge from the Navy in 1946, Cary had established a home studio consisting of a modified disc recorder (he added pickups so that he could create echo effects), a variable speed turntable, and various modified military surplus equipment. By 1952, he had begun to expand the studio with a tape recorder and was experimenting with splicing and editing techniques.[37]

Cary did a lot of work for films and the BBC throughout the 1950s and 1960s. Of particular note was his soundtrack for *The Little Island*, a short film by the Canadian-British animator Richard Williams, which won Best Experimental Film of the Year at the Venice Biennale in 1958. He also did a lot of incidental music for the *Doctor Who* series.[38] Cary went on to establish the first electronic music studio at the Royal College of Music in 1968, before emigrating to Australia in the 1970s.[39]

Daphne Oram left the BBC Radiophonic Workshop in 1959 and established her own studio in Kent. There, in addition to producing a number of compositions, she set to work as an inventor. The most notable output of this work was her Oramics machine, an optically controlled synthesizer which used ten parallel tracks of 35 mm film to control the instrument's various parameters (pitch, amplitude, timbre, etc.). Control signals could be created by hand-drawing on loops of film. In this sense the Oramics machine foreshadows later computer software, in which musicians draw control envelopes to vary parameters over time. More philosophically, it can be understood as an innovative early solution to the problem of notation of electronic music, i.e., how can one visually represent salient aspects of the music in a way that allows them to be understood and edited out of time.[40]

Another early private studio was established in Greenwich Village in New York in 1948 by Bebe and Louis Barron.[41] The two have the distinction of being the creators of the first work for magnetic tape composed in America, their *Heavenly Menagerie* of 1950.[42] Working with both recorded materials and custom-made circuits (Louis had a particular talent for electronics work), they produced a number of film soundtracks, most notably *Forbidden Planet* in 1956 (see Chapter 6).[43]

The Barrons' studio was also used by others, notably by John Cage and David Tudor when they launched the Music for Magnetic Tape Project in 1951, which later included composers Morton Feldman, Christian Wolff, and Earle Brown. By the end of 1952, they had completed Cage's *Williams Mix*, a work whose short duration

Figure 4.4 Daphne Oram at the Oramics machine programmer. Image courtesy of the Daphne Oram Trust, original photograph by Fred Wood

of 4′15″ belies the somewhat epic multiperson effort involved in its construction. Essentially a work of musique concrète (although aesthetically more an exploration of Cage's interests in chance procedures), *Williams Mix* drew upon approximately 600 sounds recorded by the Barrons. These were cataloged and categorized before being spliced together according to a "dress-maker's pattern" generated by Cage using chance procedures. Other pieces produced in the project included Wolff's *For Magnetic Tape* and Brown's *Octet* (for eight loudspeakers).[44]

Varèse and *Poème électronique*: Electronic music comes of age

"Varèse in his music pointed out that music still had room for new thoughts, for new approaches which were thoroughly grounded in the scientific basis, yet made sense musically. I think that's very important because he had, fortunately, a chance to prove that, both in his instrumental compositions and his electronic compositions as well."[45] So wrote Vladimir Ussachevsky about Edgard Varèse, whose interest in René Bertrand's Dynaphone was mentioned in the previous chapter. Varèse's involvement with Bertrand went further than trying to secure funding for Bertrand's instrument. The two had in fact met in 1913 about 14 years before the

Dynaphone had been developed, and their friendship contributed to Varèse's belief that collaboration between composers and technical specialists would be crucial to the future development of music: "What I am looking for are new technical means which can lend themselves to every expression of thought."[46]

Indeed, Varèse's instrumental music could be argued to exhibit many characteristics that would later come to be associated with certain genres of electronic music, such as altering normal patterns of attack and decay (for instance, doubling wind notes with percussion to give them a harsher attack or accumulating a chord from pianissimo entries which together swell to a sudden cutoff), making use of nontempered pitches and glissandi, a broadening of the sonic palette to include "noises," percussion, and nontraditional instruments, and the use of nonstandard orchestrations to create "masses" and "planes" of sound.

Feeling that electronic music would be the ideal medium to express his musical ideas, Varèse had struggled to find facilities and resources throughout the 1920s, 1930s, and 1940s. Although he'd managed to write one work, *Ecuatorial*, involving theremins between 1932 and 1934, it wasn't until 1954 that he completed his first work with a substantial electronic part, *Déserts*, for wind instruments, piano, percussion, and tape. Already in his seventies by this time, Varèse began the work using an anonymously donated tape recorder, modifying recordings of factories and percussion instruments. He was invited by Schaeffer to complete it in Paris in 1954. (Later revisions were done at Columbia-Princeton.)[47]

However, Varèse's most significant contribution to the field would be *Poème électronique*, which was composed for the 1958 World Fair in Brussels. The Dutch electronics company Philips, based in Eindhoven, decided that it wanted to do something special for the event. The architect Le Corbusier worked in collaboration with Iannis Xenakis (who did the bulk of the architectural work) to develop the unique pavilion, which was to host a multimedia event combining light, color, sound, and music. At Corbusier's invitation, Varèse was commissioned to produce the music. In his letter inviting Varèse, he wrote: "There is musical art. There is visual art. There is literary art, etc. Here is *electrical* art."[48]

Poème électronique is an early example of a multimedia installation art piece; it is truly a piece created for a particular specialized space within a unique building, and can be seen as a melding of music, sound, film, lighting, and architecture, all operating at the limits of what was possible at the time.

Working with Philips engineers, Varèse was able to produce a work that was incredibly ambitious for the time and that made use of cutting-edge technology. Indeed, a team of Philips personnel was required on site for the duration of the fair simply to keep it all running. A custom-built spatialization system allowed for sounds on a three-track tape to be moved amongst around 350 loudspeakers arranged along twelve trajectories. The sound material included mechanical noises, bells, organs,

Figure 4.5 Expo 1958 Philips Pavilion. Photograph by Wouter Hagens, July 1958. Reproduced under CC BY-SA 3.0 license

voices, and electronically generated sounds, which were often manipulated. It can thus be understood as incorporating aspects of both the German and the French approach.[49]

Indeed, as the composer Mauricio Kagel, who heard the work numerous times while at the fair himself, said: "Once again Varèse had successfully sidestepped the battles then raging between Paris and Cologne – battles fought with blunt claws and tawdry arguments – and had remained entirely himself . . . Ultimately it was precisely this pragmatism on Varèse's part that set precedents: a vocabulary of rhythmic noises of whatever provenance, commingled with electronic and instrumental timbres, began to spread like wildfire in the 60s."[50]

The music was based partly on material from early works by Varèse, including *Déserts*, and work done for his unfinished piece *Espace*, but also, interestingly a score for an eight-part collective improvisation that Varèse had developed for a series of jam sessions with jazz musicians in New York. Parts of that score seem to have been used directly for the *Poème*, with the jazz instruments replaced by recorded and electronic material. In fact, Varèse's approach to producing the piece seems to have been related to the jazz practice of "head arrangements," i.e., loosely worked-out arrangements performed from memory. The Philips engineers reportedly had some difficulty with the performative aspect of what was expected of them.[51] Visual effects consisting of changing lighting and projections occurred in a synchronized fashion with the music.

Over two million people had visited the pavilion by the time the fair closed, among them many composers and musicians.[52] While it is certainly difficult to assess the full impact of the piece, we will begin Chapter 6 by placing its public impact in context.

Press pause: 1959

Let's pause for a moment at the end of 1959 and consider the general musical landscape, and electronic music's place within it. Dick Clark's *American Bandstand* had been on the air for two years. Early rock and roll had been through its golden age and was reeling from the loss of Buddy Holly, Richie Valens, and the Big Bopper in a tragic plane crash, and with Elvis Presley's departure for military service. The jazz world experienced a standout year, with the release of Charles Mingus' *Mingus Ah Um*, the Dave Brubeck Quartet's *Time Out*, and, amazingly, both Miles Davis' modal jazz manifesto *Kind of Blue* and Ornette Coleman's proto-free jazz debut *The Shape of Jazz to Come*.[53] The American folk music revival was well under way, involving artists like the Kingston Trio and Woody Guthrie, and country music was beginning to be dominated by the "Nashville sound." The classical music world was equally diverse, with many significant avant-garde instrumental works composed that year by some of the composers discussed above, and (at least somewhat) more conventional music by Aaron Copland and Samuel Barber, while the reclusive Italian Giacinto Scelsi produced his provocative *Quattro pezzi per una nota sola* (*Four pieces on a single note*). On Broadway, Rogers and Hammerstein's *The Sound of Music* had just opened, and the winner of the inaugural Grammy award for Album of the Year was Henry Mancini for *The Music from Peter Gunn*.

Against this backdrop, how can we understand early electronic music? One explanation is that it was one of many advanced strands of development active at the time. Each of the areas mentioned above exhibits sophistication in different individual ways, and electronic music was just one more genre. Another way of understanding it is as filling a laboratory role, at least in terms of its impact on other cultural spheres. Doubtless many of the composers mentioned above did not view their *creative* output from this period as consisting of experiments and felt that their electronic pieces should be viewed as complete works of art. That said, already in this period, a process of cross-fertilization was taking place between styles, genres, and cultural contexts. The work of the BBC Radiophonic Workshop, adapting "experimental" techniques to serve the production requirements of popular television and radio productions, provides one great example, and this dissemination of knowledge and technical means only accelerates through the 1960s and beyond. We'll revisit this notion in the following chapters.

Further reading

Chion, Michel (1983). *Guide des objets sonores, Pierre Schaeffer et la recherche musi-cale* (Paris: Ina-GRM/Buchet-Chastel). English translation by John Dack and Christine North, available at www.ears.dmu.ac.uk/spip.php?page=articleEars&id‧article=3597.

Maconie, Robin (2005) *Other Planets: The Music of Karlheinz Stockhausen* (Oxford: Scare-crow Press).

Novati, Maddalena and Dack, John (eds.) (2012) *The Studio di Fonologia – A Musical Journey* (London: Ricordi).

Pritchett, James (1996) *The Music of John Cage* (Cambridge University Press).

Schaeffer, Pierre (1966) *Traité des objets musicaux* (Paris: Le Seuil).

Chapter 5

From analog to digital

This chapter will focus in on technology itself as much as music and will look at the transition in music technology, especially during the second half of the twentieth century, with the gradual introduction and eventual takeover of digital recording and computers. Lest some readers become concerned that this takeover is complete and absolute, let us acknowledge at the outset that the analog remains, from do-it-yourself electronics and circuit bending experiments to the necessity of speakers and microphones.

The story of the move from analog to digital technology is one of accumulating change rather than a single handover point, with a number of salient aspects. First, there was a substantial miniaturization of electronic components in the second half of the twentieth century, following the invention of the transistor (as developed at Bell Labs from 1947, though there are precedents).[1] Second, digital signal processing research earlier in the century gradually made it into practical devices, which came to a head in audio consumer terms around 1982 – the introduction of the CD – but admits pre-cursors much further back. The rise of digital technology also has close links to the rise of the computer following the Second World War, through 1970s video games to a mass market in the 1980s for home computers.

The electronics boom from the mid-twentieth century onward was sparked by intensive war research and fed by post-war economic activity; the availability of war surplus to hobbyists after the Second World War was also a factor in enabling many early electronic music studios and synthesizer experiments to get off the ground. The reduction in component size brought about by replacing older valves with semiconductor-based solid state devices like the transistor was exacerbated by integrated circuits from around 1960, eventually packing millions or billions of components into tiny chips. Moore's Law, coined in 1965, is popularly associated with computer speed, but really talks of the backbone of such machines, the doubling of the number of transistors on an integrated circuit every two years, the exponential increase massively boosting the power of smaller devices.

Early electrical instruments exploited whatever principles of physics could be co-opted to sound generation. Unsurprisingly, musical engineers found ways to utilize the new semiconductor devices where they once might have used valves.

By the 1970s, analog synthesizers were being mass produced and sold in music stores, and during the 1980s, digital devices took over. Although there is early digital music preceding the most well-known analog synths, real-time live digital synths took too long to arrive for the patience of musicians, so that the first music technology boom in the industry was with the likes of Moog, ARP, and EMS, and not with computer music experiments from such figures as Max Mathews or Erkki Kurenniemi.

The companion chapter to this one is Chapter 6, which looks at the rise of electronic music into the mainstream, which was necessarily reliant on the dramatic changes in music technology outlined herein.

Voltage-controlled analog synthesisers

Voltage control is a principle of easy manipulation of the aspects of electronic sound, allowing the simple interconnection of modules. Variation is represented in an electronic circuit by changing voltage against time. For example, although standalone waveform generators were available in 1950s electronic music studios, they could not easily be controlled as music was created, and instead, work was often built up via the intermediary of magnetic tape recording.[2] The pitch control on a 1950s sine oscillator might let you move the fundamental frequency about, perhaps with both coarse and fine tuning, but you could not quickly and stably access a set of discrete pitches with sufficient speed by turning a dial. Voltage control allowed other modules, whether sequencers setting voltages over time or other oscillators, to establish the frequency of a target oscillator, or even for a musician to plug in a keyboard which could set specific pitches on the fly through human action. And what went for frequency could go for any other parameter, like waveform shape or filter cutoff, or allow a signal output to be fed back into its generator. Ease of use and flexibility of patching, with immediate results, was gained through new interconnectivity.

There are many precedents for what became the most popularly known analog synthesizers of the 1970s, from Canadian physicist Hugh Le Caine's experiments – his Electronic Sackbut developed from 1945, for instance – to Harald Bode's work (see also Chapter 3 in particular for many examples of earlier electronic instruments). Often, earlier electronic instruments were cast under the mantle of electric pianos, which are typically electromechanical, and electronic organs. These tended to be restricted to the use of vacuum tubes rather than transistors before 1960. Even if utilizing voltage control principles internally, these devices did not expose flexibility of patching to their users, but only a few tone controls or organ stops. Constant Martin's Clavioline, launched commercially by 1947 and selling in the tens of thousands, was a monophonic synthesizer of some expressive facility with vibrato settings and an awkward volume control.[3] It quickly made it onto a top 10 hit in the UK, *Little Red Monkey* (1953) by Frank Chacksfield's Tunesmiths, and in a custom adapted version, a US No. 1, in Del Shannon's *Runaway* (1961) (further appearing in the work of the Tornados and the Beatles). An even earlier precedent is the Hammond Novachord, presented at the World's Fair in 1939, which was actually polyphonic, but sold poorly and was discontinued from 1942; it did not adapt well to standard keyboardist expectations and had some temperamental quirks.

The most famous name of the analog synthesizer business is that of Robert Moog, a talented audio engineer whose first business enterprise was in selling theremin kits, but who by 1964 had assembled a prototype set of analog synthesizer modules on the principles of voltage control and solid-state circuitry rather than unwieldy vacuum tubes. Orders first came from experimental composers, but gradually grew to the larger market of pop musicians after some promotional breakthroughs, such as a healthy appearance in a booth at the Monterey Pop Festival of 1967.[4] The classical charts smash of Wendy Carlos' *Switched-on Bach* (1968) was entirely created by multitracking monophonic Moog lines, and also featured an unplugged Moog modular system on the cover (along with a bewigged Johann Sebastian). By 1970, the Minimoog was born, a portable and musician-friendly compilation of standard VCO, VCA, and VCF Moog modules, and would eventually find its way into music stores through the efforts of master salesman David van Koevering. Yet, by 1970, rival companies were also seeing the potential of a new mass synthesizer market, such as Alan Robert Pearlman's ARP and the London-based Electronic Music Studios (EMS).

Robert Moog was hardly alone in his work; he sought out the advice of musicians as systems were prototyped, and within his company, talented engineers collaborated on the projects, even pushing ahead the Minimoog on their own initiative against Moog's initial reluctance. Moog also operated in a climate of fellow inventors: Don Buchla has been relegated somewhat to the status of an also-ran in commercial terms, but in truth was far more interested in his experimental goals than mass availability. Moog knew (and had worked for) Raymond Scott, visited Hugh Le Caine, was aware of Paul Ketoff's Synket (1964–5), and was responding to Bode's 1961 article on the potential of transistor-based synthesizers, amongst other pre-cursors of the mass analog waves to come.

Moog's Minimoog sales (around 13,000 over ten years)[5] did not match those of the Clavioline, but were part of the vanguard of a new synthesizer industry. They were accompanied by a critical mass of public exposure that carried over to musical practice in the early 1970s prog rock era. As Rick Wakeman jokes in the *Moog* movie (2004, directed by Hans Fjellestad), a keyboardist could finally scare a lead guitarist.

He also reveals that he bought his first Minimoog from an actor who thought it didn't work because it only played one note at a time!

The original 1960s analog modular systems were notoriously unstable, which could also be part of their creative charm. Oscillators became more trustworthy in later portable models as ARP and Moog developed self-correcting mechanisms, but analog synthesis in general has a somewhat quirky character, and digital memory was only added later in the 1970s to aid in storing effective presets; early synthesists just scribbled down settings in pen on patch diagrams. Handwriting aside, this didn't guarantee perfect recovery. As Pinch and Trocco note, "Analog synthesists tell of producing beautiful pieces of music that vanished when they tried to reassemble the patches the next day – the early synthesizers seldom sounded the same from day-to-day, from patch to patch."[6]

Most of the mass-produced voltage-controlled synthesizers of the late 1960s and early 1970s were from the US, though Japan would come to be the electronic instrument powerhouse by the 1980s. The UK-based EMS were one exception, as they sold 90 percent of their synthesizers to schools! Other countries are sometimes overlooked in histories; whilst lagging behind in terms of date, Russia created many of its own analog synthesizers in the 1980s, at the time of import bans on Western goods.[7] The Estonian prog band Mess built their own modular monophonic synth, developed by Härmo Härm in the mid-1970s for Sven Grünberg to play. The 1970s were an incredibly active time commercially, with Moog beginning the decade in a strong position and, after suffering much company strife, ending it in financial trouble (the same trajectory was true for ARP). It is beyond the scope of this text to list huge numbers of manufacturers and synthesizers of the era, but the flavour is well captured in such books as Mark Vail's *Vintage Synthesizers* in the further reading section for this chapter. That the term "vintage" is used to describe hardware synthesizers from only three or four decades ago at the time of writing shows the huge pace of technological change.

The rise of digital

Digital technology was developing at the same time as the commercial boom in analog synthesizers, and there are experimental digital synths that overlap with the Minimoog. The first commercial digital workstations in the later 1970s were very expensive, but prices soon dropped substantially, and digital synths took over almost entirely in the 1980s, peaking at a new order of sales for professional equipment with the Yamaha DX7 (1983) at around 300,000 units sold. Digital home keyboards from the likes of Casio and Yamaha sold many more than this to hobbyists and schools, however.

The theory of digital audio was outlined by a number of mathematicians earlier in the twentieth century, from Nyquist's theory of sampling (1924) to Claude Shannon's information theory (1948).[8] Telecommunications research was one of the prime beneficiaries and telecommunications companies were unsurprisingly the sites of much R&D; Bell Labs, for instance, where the transistor had been named, played a critical role. Alec Harley Reeves outlined pulse code modulation techniques and practical conversion between analog and digital in a patent of 1937; Bell Labs investigated this in practice for its wartime "Project-X" system for encrypted conversation (1940–3). But practical digitization was also a necessity for early electronic computers, and the rise of digital devices mirrors the rise of computers from 1950s room-filling mainframes through to 1980s home computers.

Early computers had warning hooters, designed to inform a user that a program was under way at a certain stage or complete, but which were co-opted to create sound. A program could be written that literally blasted short toots on the horn at known rates, sufficiently fast to reach definite pitch, and timed to play out a tune as a succession of such horn rolls. The first computer-generated music appeared around 1951 in this way; examples include a recording of a Ferranti Mark I computer made in Manchester, and the Australian CSIR Mk 1.[9]

Computer music can take various forms, though it inevitably involves the number-crunching power of an electronic computer in some sort of musical-arithmetic operation. The two clear early applications (aside from novelty-tune-warning-horn playback) were algorithmic composition and digital synthesis. The most famous early example of the former was research conducted by two chemist-composers, Lejaren Hiller and Leonard Isaacson, into composing a musical score via a computer program; the iconic *Illiac Suite* for string quartet, named after the computer mainframe which did most of the hard calculating work, was first performed on August 9, 1956.[10]

Digital sound synthesis, the later basis for a takeover of commercial digital synths (and eventually a proliferation of virtual synths and mobile applications), was founded by the work of Max Mathews at Bell Labs in 1957. Mathews had access to the computer mainframe for night-time runs, through the enthusiastic support of the research director, John Pierce, who just happened to be the same man who'd coined the term "transistor." After a whole night of rendering digital samples at the incredibly slow rate of 20 minutes per second of output audio, Mathews had to go across town to a specialized data conversion utility housed at another site in order to get an analog magnetic tape for playback. The first composition created in this laborious manner was the 20 second-long *In the Silver Scale*, an exploration of alternative tuning by the psychologist Newman Guttman, which premiered on May 17, 1957.

In order to create the first piece, Mathews had built the world's first audio programming language, Music 1, and a series, summarized as Music N, followed; a descendant, Csound, is still in operation amongst computer music enthusiasts. One of the features introduced in Music 3 was the fundamental idea of unit generators, which turn out to be the same idea as analog modules: fixed packets of synthesis work that can be easily interconnected. At heart, using a computer language to specify the interconnections can lead to complexity and power of an order only hinted at by the tangles of cables draped on the front of analog modular systems.

Bell Labs' mandate to telecommunications research was evident in Mathews' collaborative work on speech synthesis. His most famous work is probably *Bicycle Built for Two* (1961), where a speech synthesizer is turned into a singing voice synthesizer by melodizing the vowels. It turns up in Stanley Kubrick's *2001: A Space Odyssey* (1968) as the swansong for the archetypal computer out of control, HAL. In Mathews' article for the journal *Science* in 1963, "The digital computer as a musical instrument," he notes: "It is very easy to use the computer in this way. The electronic equipment (computer and output equipment) has been constructed once and for all. There are no soldering irons, tape splicings, or even knob-twistings involved, as there are with other electronic equipment for producing music. No manual dexterity is required. Instead, one writes down and gives the computer a sequence of numbers."[11] Whilst he eulogizes the potential of the computer, he is wise to the great challenges of modeling human musical faculty and the complexity of acoustic sound.

With mainframes rare and expensive to access, work on computer music stayed with small groups of researchers and visiting composers until the 1970s, which was even more cliquey than the early studio electronic music of the 1950s. With computer music initially much slower to render than the passing of real time, time had to pass under Moore's Law to reach an adequate rendering rate. Pragmatic transitional arrangement often used computers not to render audio itself, but as live generators of control data for analog synthesizers which themselves provided the real-time sound generation.[12]

A pre-cursor of this capacity was the binary sequencer on the Radio Corporation of America (RCA) Synthesizer, one of electronic music history's eternal sidenotes. A room-filling behemoth in the mold of the mainframe computers of the time, the RCA Synthesizer was a large-scale analog synthesizer, with a punched tape control system for four independent voices and other more fixed sources. Designed by Harry Olson and Herbert Belar (who had first dabbled in automatic composing circuitry in 1949!), and first demonstrated in 1955, the new Columbia-Princeton Electronic Music Center held the Mark I on loan from 1957 and took delivery of a Mark II RCA Synthesizer in 1959. It suited the fastidious work of Milton Babbitt on precision serialism, who created some wonderful pieces – *Philomel* (1964), for example, for soprano and tape. Yet it was hard to maintain and was a clunky tool for composers, few of whom actually bothered with it.[13]

The first full use of a computer to control analog synthesizers seems to be James Gabura and Gustav Ciamaga's 1965–6 experiments at the University of Toronto, using an IBM 1620 to control two Moog oscillators and two custom amplitude regulators.[14] Peter Zinovieff in London experimented at EMS with two PDP-8 computers as sequencers.[15] The most famous experiment was led by Max Mathews, named GROOVE (Generated Real-time Output Operations on Voltage-controlled Equipment, 1970–8); a computer in one room controlled analog electronic synthesis modules in another. Working at night, Laurie Spiegel even adapted this system to control live video processing as well in VAMPIRE (Video And Music Program for Interactive Realtime Exploration/Experimentation, 1974–9).[16] Analog synthesizer manufacturers gradually realized the flexibility of digital control circuits based on the new microprocessors, which became part of designs from around the mid-1970s. It was through microprocessors that E-mu Systems found new ways to manage polyphony in analog keyboards, patenting a digital keyboard scanning system in 1973.[17] Kit computers, such as the Kim-1 introduced in 1975, were readily adopted by some West Coast composers as a component of their own musical electronics.

Fully digital systems for live rendering of sound were simultaneously being investigated. Some amazing anticipations here, especially in sequencers with digital memory, were made by Finnish guru Erkki Kurenniemi.[18] His DIMI-0 (1970–1) system allowed video camera to sound output by hybridizing digital and analog technologies, with a fully digital memory. Unfortunately, he did not achieve international recognition for his work at the time. In Peter Zinovieff's private studio in London, PDP-8 microcomputers were controlling digital oscillators and filters by 1972 in the VOCOM system, while the same year, an all-digital oscillator bank was exhibited in Stockholm. The power of digital systems began to shine through in the number of oscillators: By 1977, Peppino Di Giugno's 4A digital signal processor for IRCAM had 256 real-time digital oscillators.[19] In the same year, the Samson Box was developed at Stanford, which put into dedicated hardware the unit generators from the slower calculating Music V software, for an enormous speed up (it only cost $100,000 too).[20] Though very powerful for the time and used by many composers, it proved ultimately unadaptable as general purpose computers continued to relentlessly speed up.

The early commercial digital synthesizer/samplers (for the two functions were often linked through digital memory) tended to be rather expensive; more expensive than houses, for instance. The US Synclavier (1976) and the Australian Fairlight (1978) are the most famous early digital computer synthesizers. The companies would face off in early 1980s trade shows; the Fairlight's on-monitor light pen usually drew the bigger crowds. These expensive monsters were not alone; for instance,

(a)

(b)

Figure 5.1 a (top) and Figure b (bottom) Electronic and computer music in the "Middle Ages" (mid-1970s): Photos of Laurie Spiegel working with the Bell Labs GROOVE system, in the analog lab at the patchbay connecting some of GROOVE's analog audio modules (top) and at the digital (control) end using the DDP-224 computer console (bottom). Photos by Emmanuel Ghent, circa 1977. Reproduced by permission of Laurie Spiegel

German engineer Wolfgang Palm introduced an all-digital synth in 1978, the 340 System, with a similar combination of keyboard, synthesis hardware boxes, and computer monitor. With computers not yet established in homes, musicians could be intimidated by computer peripherals, and for an accessible price, Palm had used 8-bit digital wavetable synthesis, which tended to produce a harsher sound. Palm turned for some years back to hybrid analog/digital systems (digital oscillators with analog filters) in musician-friendly packages.[21]

As things tend to work in economics, what is introduced as an expensive new system available only to the few becomes a mass-produced product. The cheapness, reliability, and power (in simultaneous voices/mass synthesis) of digital systems compared to analog became evident in the 1980s. The digital sampling capabilities of a Fairlight or a Synclavier were quickly appearing in cheaper equipment; Linn drum machines based on samples first appeared in 1980 with the LM-1 Drum Computer, as did the E-mu Emulator keyboard sampler in 1981. The biggest success outside the home keyboard market for digital sound synthesis was the aforementioned Yamaha DX7 of 1983, costing $2,000. John Chowning had discovered frequency modulation as a digital sound synthesis technique in 1967, and Yamaha licensed the patents from his home institution of Stanford, belatedly gaining him tenure.

The year 1983 also saw the introduction of the Musical Instrument Digital Interface (MIDI) protocol, an interconnectivity standard for digital synthesizers between manufacturers which was enthusiastically adopted by consumers. Home computers could now easily control hardware synthesizers, and a new generation of software sequencers catered to this. They were also being empowered as synthesizer patch librarians, sound editors, and even all-inclusive sampler-sequencers through tracker programs. As a sign of the enthusiasm for the new MIDI standard, the Atari ST (1985) even had built-in MIDI ports. The acceleration into a computer music world reached a new line of behavior by around 1996, as home computers became generally fast enough for real-time digital sound synthesis at high quality in their own right; dedicated hardware modules could gradually be discarded and home studios became almost entirely virtual (but for the necessity of any microphones and loudspeakers connecting to the real acoustic world).

The whole thrust of accessible and increasingly cheap digital music technology led to the demise of many commercial studios, whose main attraction these days is often as more highly controlled acoustic environments rather than for any superiority of music computation over home users. With the availability of huge amounts of powerful computer music freeware programs and music software working through Internet browsers, as well as high-quality mobile music apps that can be obtained for a dollar (like the initial promotion for the Moog company's first virtual iPhone synthesizer), the entry cost to digital music making is just that of a general purpose computation device. We will look in more detail at trends in later computer music in Chapter 12.

Digital versus analog?

There is a tension between the qualities of analog and digital audio systems that often manifests itself, but is in many ways traced more to passion than rational argument. Notions of the supposed superiority of analog over digital are usually attributable to one of two sources:

(1) The quality of digital-to-analog conversion, which was admittedly less effective on some early CD players and digital musical instruments, but is now a well-understood technology.
(2) The nostalgia for certain distortion and noise aspects of the recording medium, for instance, the dynamic compression characteristics and crackle of vinyl, as opposed to the "clinical" and "dry" character of digital recording.

Digital technology does have the largest available dynamic range and the most linear, nondistorting signal of recorders; moreover, it also has that most economically empowered of items in its favor: cheapness.

There are hard limits to the frequency response of digital systems: The maximum reproducible frequency is the Nyquist rate of half the sampling rate. There are some who claim to be able to hear much higher frequency content than normal adults, and some argumentation that human hearing has effective components at higher frequencies than 20 kHz, perhaps through bone conduction. Nonetheless, inasmuch as the cochlea is the clear normal organ of hearing, the physiological evidence tends to support 441.1 kHz as an effective sampling rate as long as the ADC is well engineered. For professional audio, because we now have standard high sampling rate systems (such as 88.2 kHz or even 192 kHz), the weak points in the chain tend to be the analog transducers, microphones, and loudspeakers, and their recording and playback capability.

The debate occasionally re-surfaces, but is in some ways a phantom without teeth, for digital technology has already taken over; the music technology industry has wholeheartedly adopted digital systems and the computer. Trevor Horn discusses the changes over his production career:

> I can't tell the difference between something mixed in *Pro Tools* and something mixed through a board. The only way I can tell the difference is there's more distortion from the board. You can't really tell. These days we all sort of work the same way – "workstation working." You can work on two or three different projects at the same time and it lets you effortlessly move from one session to the other. I think it's very easy to forget that back in the day you used to have to put up a multitrack and throw up the faders. It was much more complicated. That focused you in a certain way but there's no doubt, if you have 20 vocal tracks to go through, it's quicker having them in *Pro Tools* where you can look at them.[22]

Further reading

Cary, Tristram (1992) *Illustrated Compendium of Musical Technology* (London: Faber & Faber).

Collins, Nick (2010) *Introduction to Computer Music* (Chichester: Wiley).

Jenkins, Mark (2007) *Analog Synthesizers: Understanding, Performing, Buying – From the Legacy of Moog to Software Synthesis* (Amsterdam: Focal Press).

Naumann, Joel and Wagoner, James D. (1985) *Analog Electronic Music Techniques: In Tape, Electronic, and Voltage-Controlled Synthesizer Studios* (New York: Schirmer Books).

Pinch, Trevor and Trocco, Frank (2002) *Analog Days: The Invention and Impact of the Moog Synthesizer* (Cambridge, MA: Harvard University Press).

Roads, Curtis (1996) *The Computer Music Tutorial* (Cambridge, MA: MIT Press).

Vail, Mark (2000) *Vintage Synthesizers* (San Francisco, CA: Backbeat Books).

Chapter 6

Into the mainstream

What are the most important landmarks in the popularization of electronic music? Thom Holmes argues that the Philips Pavilion at the World's Fair of 1958 provided the first mass exposure for electronic music,[1] while Andrew Hugill sees this as the apotheosis of Varèse's search through his life for new sound resources.[2] A footfall of two million spectators visited the immersive stomach of the pavilion, hearing Varèse's multimedia work *Poème électronique* and Xenakis' filler piece, *Concret pH*, spread over 350 loudspeakers.[3] Yet, *Forbidden Planet* (1956), with its "electronic tonalities" created by Louis and Bebe Barron, might lay claim to reaching more people; though a relative box office failure, only making $1.5 million,[4] at 50 cents a ticket, this converts to three million attendees. If we credit theremin-laden B-movies earlier in the 1950s as also stirring some consciousness of electronic music (and the Pavilion experience after all was also a film and light show alongside the music), it seems that we should more widely review the various media in which electronic music technology was appearing, rather than conferring all credit on the Pavilion alone.

There are earlier precedents to electronic music reaching public consciousness, through early electrical instruments, as detailed in Chapter 3. Though the Telharmonium had few listeners in its failed pre-radio restaurant music business, the theremin stirred up headlines and audiences, at least in the heyday of the 1920s.[5] At the close of 1927, reporters clamored to get the first interviews with Lev Termen as his ship approached New York from Europe. The healthy success of the Hammond organ from the 1930s, with its innards of tone wheels and valves rather than traditional air, could be seen as a pre-Second World War watershed of adoption. Nonetheless, the Hammond sound is not so hard to accommodate within existing musical practice, and on this basis of an organ replacement, it was sold to many churches in the US.

It is certainly in the 1950s–1970s period that a transition occurred in the public consciousness of electronic music's sound palette, as greater adoption of electronic sound in film, television, and popular music played out. By the 1980s, with cultural phenomena like Jean Michel Jarre's mass laser and fireworks concerts, synth pop and electronic dance music, home computers and video game music, and the standardization of such cheap home digital music production technologies as MIDI, the mainstream had been reached. This chapter will look at some of the work covering this transition time. It also works in parallel with a companion (Chapter 5) on the transition from analog to digital technology, but focuses more on specific musical events.

Electronic music in popular mass media

Whilst we will cover the use of electronic music in popular music in a later section of this chapter and in subsequent chapters, we begin a survey of instances of electronic music's gradual revelation to a mass public by considering the use of electronic techniques in broadcast media. This covers music and sound effects in radio, television, and film, including the commercial music outlet of advertising. The combination of audio with visuals in film and television may be open to a claim that electronic music is not central to the productions. Yet, since the era of sound film, essential roles for diegetic sound (on-screen action correlates) and nondiegetic music (emotional underscoring) have been recognized. It is reported of Ben Burtt, sound designer for *Star Wars* (1977), that he watched a version of the film without his sounds and found that the film played out as an unintended comedy rather than a convincing space opera.[6]

Film music has been a primary avenue of mass publicity for electronic music. We have already seen how sound designers for film were ahead of art music composers in the exploration of recording effects (Chapter 2). A natural fit for the otherworldly sounds of electronic music was other worlds, a statement that already assumes an association so thoroughly made in the twentieth century.[7] These alternative places were often those described in science fiction, though the evocation of putative spirit worlds, or altered psychological state, is also a common theme.

Table 6.1 is a compilation of some noteworthy (mass-released, mainly Hollywood) films from the mid-twentieth century that involve an important aspect of electronic music technique in their sound effects, music, or both. Many more could have been picked out.[8] We have avoided a full discussion of visual music experiments, though many animated films with synchronized music were very successful shorts in cinemas, such as the work of Mary Ellen Bute or the Whitney brothers; although the music set was more often classical music, Pfenninger and Fischinger's drawn sound experiments did achieve some publicity in the 1930s.[9]

How explicit the electronic music elements were to audiences of the time is a tricky question. Herrmann's dueling Theremins in 1951 were only part of his lugubrious scoring. Russell Lack is skeptical, especially for such early examples: "To what extent

Table 6.1 *Electronic music in selected films*

Film	Year	Director	Electronic music relevance
Dr. Jekyll and Mr. Hyde	1931	Rouben Mamoulian	Transformation sound effects created by optical sound-track drawing
Spellbound	1945	Alfred Hitchcock	Miklós Rózsa's Oscar-winning music (occasionally) uses the theremin (played by Samuel J Hoffman)[a] along with full orchestra to evoke disturbed psychological states
The Day the Earth Stood Still	1951	Robert Wise	Bernard Herrmann's score makes double use of the theremin, as well as some studio effects like reverb and tape reversal
Forbidden Planet	1956	Fred M. Wilcox	"Electronic tonalities" by Louis and Bebe Barron in the first fully electronic soundtrack
The Birds	1963	Alfred Hitchcock	Includes Oskar Sala's Mixturtrautonium soundtrack effects
The Andromeda Strain	1971	Robert Wise	Gil Mellé's all-electronic film score with tape effects and synthesis
A Clockwork Orange	1971	Stanley Kubrick	Wendy (née Walter) Carlos' synthesized classical and original music
Solaris	1972	Andrei Tarkovsky	Electronic and orchestral scoring in counterpoint for alien and human presences (composed by Eduard Artemyev)
Apocalypse Now	1979	Francis Ford Coppola	Carmine Coppola score, Walter Murch sound design
Blade Runner	1982	Ridley Scott	Vangelis score, influential on sci-fi noir

[a] Holmes, *Electronic and Experimental Music*, pp. 24–5.

the ominous aspects of electronica have been collectively understood by mass cinema audiences is unclear; certainly there seem to be the same kind of associations for many people with the 'darker' tones of the synthesizer as there were with the traditionally 'frightening' registers on instruments such as the violin or cello."[10] He points out that much electronic music in film blurs the lines of music, sound effects, and even dialogue. Certainly, the importance of sound design work in productions should not be underestimated. *Apocalypse Now* (1979) is often cited for its inventive sound design in these contexts; Lack points to "a painstakingly detailed sound mix by Walter Murch," and in particular the famous urban to jungle sound transformation in the hotel room background.[11]

Nonetheless, the first all-electronic score to a mass-released film is conventionally attributed to *Forbidden Planet* (1956). The textbox below discusses the cybernetic techniques employed by the Barrons in the production of their soundtrack.

The Barrons and the scoring of *Forbidden Planet*

This section draws closely from James Wierzbicki's excellent 2005 book on the score of *Forbidden Planet*,[12] which provides analyses of the soundtrack album and film, as well as the surrounding context.

Louis and Bebe Barron were a husband-and-wife team who received a magnetic tape recorder as a wedding gift in 1948 (they eventually divorced, though continued to make music together until Louis' death in 1989). They were integral to early art music experiments in the "Music for Magnetic Tape" project initiated by John Cage and collaborators in New York in 1951, created the tape work *Heavenly Menagerie* (1951–2), and worked on the all-electronic score for the ten-minute art film *Bells of Atlantis* (1952). Hollywood could provide a better income, and they secured (with some luck) a commission to work on electronic sounds for *Forbidden Planet*. Whilst they were contracted for twenty minutes of effects, they scored the whole movie in three months, and a rough cut with their "electronic tonalities" proved so popular at test screenings that it became the basis of the full release. MGM lawyers' worries over issues from the musicians' union led to the nonstandard terminology of their credit, and some legal issues relating to re-use of materials from the score got the Barrons blacklisted in the Hollywood studio system, so that it remains their one major film score.

The Barrons' compositional techniques were radical for the time, delighting in ambiguity between sound effects supporting action on-screen and ominous electronic textures as background music. They took especial inspiration from the new field of cybernetics and, more like recent hardware hackers than 1950s studio-as-laboratory workers, created short-lived but beautiful feedback circuit hacks that they would record as they burnt out. Captured sounds would then be carefully arranged to the film, with particular circuits' outputs being associated with particular characters as leitmotifs.

In an interview for an oral history project, Bebe Barron recalls that "we used many circuits from Norbert Wiener's book *Cybernetics* . . . we recorded and amplified the electronic activity and endlessly processed it . . . we thought of our circuits as characters in a script . . . once they died, we never could revive them . . . the beauty coming from the circuits . . . we would just sit back and let them take over."[13]

The peak in the early 1970s in electronic sound in film, exemplified by three entries in Table 6.1,[14] fits well with the greater availability of analog synthesizers at the time, following such successes as Wendy Carlos' *Switched-on Bach* (1968) and the mass production of Moogs, ARPs and Synthis. Films in the 1970s also saw starring roles for synthesizers themselves. A Moog modular is a clear prop in the

Mick Jagger gangster/musician vehicle *Performance* (1970), and an ARP 2500 (with ARP engineer Phil Dodds press-ganged into playing a part!) in *Close Encounters of the Third Kind* (1977), with its famous human–alien musical communication duet.[15] In the 1980s, *Ferris Bueller's Day Off* (1986) would provide similar publicity for the Emulator II digital sampling keyboard. By that point, sound synthesis and sampling had became commonplace in popular music, and with the close relation of many commercial films to such trends, the soundtracks often followed suit, whether through film music composers' work or the featuring of popular songs. The often tight relation of "pop theme song" and incidental music is picked out by Russell Lack especially with Harald Faltermeyer's work on *Beverly Hills Cop* (1984) and the *Axel F* theme.[16]

An interest in electronic music soundtracks continues to the present day. Wendy Carlos' original score for *Tron* (1982) was recently treated to a re-make in *Tron: Legacy* (2010) featuring French electronic dance music artists Daft Punk. Pop musicians associated with electronic music have often transitioned to work in film music; Giorgio Moroder and Ryuichi Sakamoto come to mind. Some film directors have shown great interest in creating soundtracks themselves through electronic techniques. For instance, John Carpenter often used synthesizers in composing for his own films, e.g., *Dark Star* (1974), *Halloween* (1978), or *The Fog* (1980),[17] and David Lynch's work takes advantage of hallucinatory sound effects, such as in *Eraserhead* (1977), with its disturbing processed tape soundtrack. If the great majority of films continue to use acoustic instruments for their supporting music,[18] with a general takeover of digital equipment, electronic techniques are ubiquitous in sound design and post-production.

Whilst examples here have been biased toward a Hollywood mainstream, other great cinema traditions have engaged with electronic music. French cinema, for instance, has a close relationship to innovation in musique concrète;[19] in one case, film sound again seems to have trumped Schaefferian sound manipulation. In *Rapt* (1934), Arther Hoérée's storm scene music uses a recording of musicians improvising storm sounds, which are then treated by such concrete effects as reversing, and stripping the attack and decay of notes.[20] Jacques Tati often made humoristic use of unconventional sound effects, sometimes substituting for dialogue, such as in *Les Vacances de M. Hulot* (1953); in Georges Lautner's *Les Tontons Flingueurs* (1963), scenes include a visit to a musique concrète composer's home laboratory, complete with automatic water taps and ping pong ball percussion alongside the tape, and concrète sound effects intruding on gunfights (in one scene, each protagonist has a different gun sound, starting with a conventional gun noise, but becoming more abstract). Not confined to French sound invention, such playful effects work even appears in a 1951 Ealing comedy, *The Man in the White Suit*, where the lab scene stars a contraption voiced by an amusing bubbling tape loop.[21] Electronic treatments find their way into international cinema, whether the subtle processing of instrument sounds in Toru Takemitsu's score for *Woman in the Dunes* (1964)[22] or the East German/Polish film *The Silent Star* (1960) with Andrzej Markowski's rich electronic sounds.[23]

Though we have concentrated strongly on film, electronic music also appeared in radio drama, theatrical productions, and television.[24] As Louis Niebur notes in his book on the BBC Radiophonic Workshop,[25] in the 1950s the Paris and Cologne studios were publicly opposed to the use of electronic music as incidental music and sound effects in television, film, and radio; this is particularly ironic, considering that broadcasting institutions were funding the studios! Yet it is exactly in this sphere that great publicity for nascent electronic techniques were inculcated. In the UK, the BBC's (eventual) adoption of "radiophonic effects" for radio and television, a move pushed by drama more than the traditionalist music department, eventually brought some high-profile exposure of electronic music to the British public, from *Doctor Who* (which began in 1963) to the 1970s children's program *Look and Read*.[26] *The Goon Show* (1951–60) established the use of zany sound effects from multiple "grams operators" (gramophonists); Niebur picks out episode 12 from series 6 (*The Terrible Revenge of Fred Fu-Manchu*, December 6, 1955) as a particular cornucopia of speed manipulation effects. By 1958, after overcoming some wasted years of bureaucracy, the BBC Radiophonic Workshop was finally in operation (it would survive until 1996). The Workshop played a critical role in broadcast "special sound" and was also important for overcoming some gender assumptions about electronic music; the celebrated Daphne Oram, Maddalena Fagandini, and Delia Derbyshire were all involved, though credit to individual composers was not given until 1965,[27] long after Daphne had herself left, and exploitation and inequality of treatment were not entirely absent in relations within the Workshop.

Tropes of film music carry across easily to television and tend again to stick to science fiction or horror genres; comparable to the electronic sounds of *Doctor Who* in the UK, the US is not shy of examples (a later example, the theme from *Knight Rider*, drives into view). Though a conventional brassy theme bookends, the narrative introduction to *The Outer Limits* (1963–5) ("We are controlling transmission") makes use of some isolated electronic sounds and graphics from an oscilloscope.[28] Electronic musicians have also made use of television for promotion. In 1966, Jean-Jacques Perrey and Gershon Kingsley made a charming appearance on the US gameshow *I've Got a Secret*. Perrey used the Ondioline to imitate four orchestral instruments, and Perrey and Kingsley played one track from their recently released *The In Sound From Way Out* (1966). With the launch of MTV in 1981, a lot of coverage went initially to British acts, who as image-conscious New Romantics and Futurists tended to have more videos available, as well as more synthesizers in their line-ups.[29]

One more neglected area of study in electronic music's rise to public consciousness is the use of such techniques in advertising, from commercials to sound signatures for companies. A number of composers at one time or another have worked on such commercial music, and advertising has been quick to grasp the effectiveness of using atypical music and stimulating effects to convey the newness of products. The jazz band leader turned electronic musician and inventor Raymond Scott is often associated with this sort of work, though a surprising number of other musicians have done commercial work, including Daphne Oram and Wendy Carlos; Delia Derbyshire and Brian Hodgson's Unit Delta Plus studio worked on a Philips advert, for instance. Scott's advertising output is nonetheless extensive; a magazine article from 1960 lists recent adverts for "Vicks, Lever Bros., Alcoa, Hamm's Beer"[30] with more on the way, all using his Karloff studio console. Another 1960 interviewer notes of a tour round his facility: "Mr. Scott led us into the beep-swish room to show us his brain-child, and we felt a certain sense of security only because we were wearing rubber-soled shoes. The heart of the unit is a control panel with some hundred or so buttons and dials from which Scott can get an infinite number of rhythms and sound combinations – treble, bass, beeping, swishing, honking – you name it and he'll come up with a reasonable facsimile."[31]

Whilst Scott worked for Nescafé,[32] rival Maxwell House commissioned Eric Siday to create synthesized coffee percolating sounds. Siday also worked on the "CBS presents this program in color" logo used from 1965, making full use of an early Moog modular system.[33] In the 1970s, Suzanne Ciani's work in sound signatures (often using a Buchla modular synthesizer) included "GE dishwasher bleep, the Columbia Pictures logo, the ABC logo, the Merrill Lynch sound, the Energizer battery sound, the Coca Cola logo, and the Pepsi logo";[34] indeed, the honorary appellation of the "Queen of Soft Drinks" covers her work for Sprite and Fanta too! The advertising connection has continued, with advertisers chasing demographics increasingly intersecting with electronic music listening: Aphex Twin's music for the Pirelli advert is a good case in point, or Moby's licensing of every track on *Play* (1999).[35]

Rivaling the passive entertainment of television and film these days is the mass market of video games.[36] Ascendant since the long queues at Pong and Space Invaders machines in the 1970s, through home computers in the 1980s, the gaming market is huge; a recent release, *Call of Duty: Modern Warfare 3* (2011) was touted as the most successful entertainment product on launch in any media to date. Games also make huge use of licensed pop songs, including specifically music-themed games such as *Rock Band* and *Guitar Hero*. We shall return to computer games in Chapter 12.

Oscillate and roll

Simultaneous with appearances as part of other media, electronic technology was making its way into music for a mass market, and we discuss now the transition period of the 1950s to the 1970s. The rise of rock 'n' roll accompanied a post-war baby boom era, catering to a new teen market. We have already covered in Chapter 2 the changes in studio recording technology, germane to this period, such as the post-war appearance of magnetic tape recorders, part of a general electronics boom in studio equipment. Chapter 4 surveyed post-Second World War art music experiments; just as art music composers could create with tape, so too, would the Beatles.

Table 6.2 places some notable tracks in and around mass-marketed music.[37] Some of these were high-profile international No. 1 hits; others had less chart impact, but were influential, or at the very least, prescient, in the longer term.

The first and last records are both purely/predominantly electronic music constructions. The back sleeve of the "electronic popular music" promotional disc by Kid Baltan, *Song of the Second Moon* (1957), backed with a cover re-instrumentation of *Colonel Bogey*, is illuminating of the tensions relating to a transition from art to pop output. It notes that "The views of some composers that electronic music should be without rhythm, melody and harmony is a restriction that should not be applied generally" and either apologetically, or sarcastically, notes that "the composer has used traditional patterns rather than 'advanced' ones" for "'playful' experiments."[38] To pick out one album from the middle of the table's Electrosoniks–Kraftwerk split, Perrey and Kingsley's *The In Sound From Way Out* (1966), the liner notes read:

> Here are a dozen electronic pop tunes. They are the electrifying good-time music of the coming age, the switched-on dance music that will soon be it. This is the lively answer to the question that puzzles – and who knows, even frightens – people who have heard the serious electronic compositions of recent years and wonder, is it the music of the future? As for that avant-garde wing, we say more power to it. But there are other things in the future, such as pleasure.[39]

We otherwise see a transition from records featuring electronic effects or particular electronic instruments against conventional guitar and drums pop to all electronic tracks in the 1970s. The great distraction here perhaps is the electric guitar; even Robert Moog in the mid-1960s was chasing the cheap guitar amplifier business before he eventually found a way to mass-sell synthesizers after the 1967 Monterey Pop Festival. Early uses of electronics in pop can seem like novelty records before the adoption became more commonplace. Note a bit of a pile-up around 1970–2 again, as for the films. Authorial selection bias in choosing items for the tables aside, there is a definite surge in activity, as the availability of analog synths becomes a strong factor with increasingly affordable prices for VCS3s or Minimoogs. Commercial

Table 6.2 *Popular music breakthroughs for electronic music*

Artist	Work	Year	Notes
Electrosoniks	*Song of the Second Moon, Sonik Re-Entry*	1957–8	Tape-loop-built "Electronic Popular Music" (as written on their first single label) experiments from Dutch composers Dick Raaijmakers (a.k.a. Kid Baltan) and Tom Dissevelt
The Tornados	*Telstar*	1962	Joe Meek-produced electronic studio effects evoking a satellite to accompany this instrumental; No. 1 in the US and the UK
The Beach Boys	*Good Vibrations*	1966	Paul Tanner's electro-theremin vibrates very prominently; also a US and UK No. 1
The Beatles	*Tomorrow Never Knows*	1966	From the album *Revolver*, by which point the Beatles were concentrating heavily on studio work. This track is mainly built up from tape loops
Pierre Henry and Michel Colombier	*Messe Pour Le Temps Présent*	1967	Rock tracks with concrète and synthesizer effects, originally for a dance production, selling at least 150,000 copies[a]
Wendy Carlos	*Switched-on Bach*	1968	Bestselling classical album, a painstakingly constructed multitracked Moog showpiece
Silver Apples	*Silver Apples*	1968	Home-made oscillators, voice and drums, influential festival band
Emerson, Lake & Palmer	*Lucky Man*	1970	First-take Moog solo prominent. Heavy US radio airplay at the beginning of the prog rock period
Sly and the Family Stone	*There's a Riot Goin' On*	1971	Organ drum machine guide tracks underlie the whole album
Hot Butter	*Popcorn*	1972	The Gershon Kingsley original from 1969 is less irritating, but its catchiness is undeniable, and an international hit
Roxy Music	*Roxy Music*	1972	Classic VCS3 Brian Eno synth effects processing other instruments; shows the synthesist does not just have to be a Rick Wakeman-like virtuoso of notes
Pink Floyd	*On the Run*	1973	All-synthesizer track from *The Dark Side of the Moon* (which heavily features EMS Synthis)
Kraftwerk	*Autobahn*	1974	A new form of electronic pop is reached as Kraftwerk score a US hit

[a] Taylor, *Strange Sounds*, p. 61.

impact had been proven with Carlos' *Switched-on Bach* (1968), with its iconic cover depicting an unplugged Moog modular system and an actor dressed as J. S. Bach, and its hard-worked analog synth lines, painstakingly played onto multitrack tape. Bach's polyphony fitted well with the needs to record a mono line at a time, to show

Figure 6.1 Cover of an electronic popular music record (1957). Used courtesy of Philips Company Archives (www.philips.com). Scan kindly provided by Marcel Koopman

off the capabilities of synthesis given careful instrumentation; Carlos (with collaborator Rachel Elkind) showed massive determination to realize the recording.[40] It was followed by a legion of lesser imitators cashing in with Moog novelty albums.

Joe Meek's production of *Telstar* (1962) captures once again the enthusiasm for space science at the time.[41] With many exotica records being sold in the 1950s, Meek was neither the first nor the last to tap into post-war economic recovery and technological advances. Indeed, the first color LP cover was for Harry Revel's theremin-featuring album *Music Out of the Moon* (1947).[42] Pierre Henry's "les jerks electroniques" for the *Messe Pour Le Temps Présent* may seem like a gimmicky combination of concrète and rock, but the album proved rather popular, especially for one deriving from a French dance production. *Psyché Rock* in particular has proved influential and is the essential basis for the *Futurama* theme tune!

Though by no means the same impact as the No. 1 smashes from the Tornados and the Beach Boys, Henry's concrète rock crossover is representative of the waves of experimentation on the fringes of popular music (and again indicative of the fact that the term "popular" in popular music means multiple things, not necessarily top chart sellers).[43] Drug and social experimentation in the second half of the 1960s would lead into psychedelia and, in the early 1970s, to a phase of classical-rock crossover in progressive rock; the synthesizer fit naturally with such pursuits. Experimentation was also under way in West Germany, particularly Cologne and Berlin, in a movement eventually dubbed "krautrock" by the British music press, but really just German experimental rock, from whose initial improvisation scenes Kraftwerk and Tangerine Dream formed.

For high-profile appearances, the Beatles are certainly the foremost band of the age. Their retreat to the studio allowed them to avoid the screaming crush of concerts and established important grounds for the foregrounding of studio technologies in music (aided by many Abbey Road engineers and George Martin's production work). The tape manipulation effects are the most overt, whether the drum loop pounding along in *Tomorrow Never Knows* (1966) or the multi-orchestral tune-up tape speed gala of *A Day in the Life* (1967). Synthesizers are a more subtle affectation, though the Beatles had a Moog; it appears for riffs in *Maxwell's Silver Hammer* and *Here Comes the Sun* (both 1969).[44] The huge Moog bass sounds initiating *Save the Life of My Child* (1968), a Simon & Garfunkel track from their *Bookends* album, is more explicit.

By the early 1970s, synths were becoming a common feature of musicians' arsenals, though all-electronic groups would take some time to stabilize; the story from Kraftwerk onward is taken up in Chapter 7. One of the most powerful manifestations of the trend, however, is in adoption in African-American music, always a powerful driver in popular music. After all, the Hammond organ had found its business niche in churches, and electric organs and pianos had made a strong mark on the continuums of jazz, blues, gospel, soul, R&B, and funk. Sun Ra found a Moog an essential adjunct to his inter-stellar message. Sly Stone made continual use of an early organ box drum machine on *There's a Riot Goin' On* (1971) when building up the parts in the studio, often leaving the guide track in the final mix. Timmy Thomas' *Why Can't We Live Together* (1972) has a clear electronic rhythm.[45] Such organist backing rhythms were to transform to literal prominence as sequencers and dedicated drum machines appeared. Stevie Wonder's albums from 1972 to 1974 show a new fascination with the Moog synthesizer, especially for basslines; his synthesis consultants, Malcolm Cecil and Bob Margouleff, were proprietors of the prototype polyphonic system TONTO (The Original Neo-Timbre Orchestra), as used on some tracks for *Talking Book* (1972).[46]

Studio technology of course was ripe for experiment. Here, Jamaican studio experimentalists like Lee Scratch Perry and King Tubby proved resourceful in their pursuit of new dubs from pre-existing studio tracks. Meanwhile, the gathering DJ culture of disco (whether the beat matching of a new wave of skilled DJs or the extended tape remixes of Tom Moulton and his peers) were establishing new avenues for club music. The electronic dance music story is followed further in Chapter 8.

A case study: Björk

Though the main part of this chapter has focused on the transition regions particularly associated with the availability of analog synthesizers, we jump forwards now to a more recent artist, whose work is indicative of reconciliation in popular music with art music, and the complicated relationship of song and technology. Björk Guðmundsdóttir released an album as a child singer and worked in the 1980s with many alternative Icelandic bands; her solo work from *Debut* (1993) is firmly linked into trends in electronic dance music and electronica. Featuring her work is also very important as a counterbalance to the many male names featured through this chapter, providing an example of clear female leadership in electronic music innovation.

An essential source book here is Nicola Dibben's academic study *Björk*,[47] which includes discussion of the social and geographical context of her work, and musical analyses of selected pieces.

The relationship between nature and technology is one of the key themes of Dibben's book. This is encapsulated in part by Iceland itself, with its associated myths of Viking heritage and Northern culture, its dramatic geothermal landscape at the meeting of two continental plates, and the modern highly technologized culture of the island. Björk's 1990s career plays around certain recurring tropes in critical reception such as elfin, Icelander, and exotic, but diversifies increasingly as Björk herself asserts flexibility as an artist beyond any need for stereotypes. As Dibben notes, "Björk's role in the making of her music reflects many of the normative gender roles within contemporary pop; her main compositional tool was her voice, and the beats of her music were often created by or with male musicians. However, she displayed (and claimed) increasing agency within the technological realm."[48]

Whilst much of Björk's solo output utilizes electronic synthesis and recording treatments, source sounds range through many world cultures, and she restlessly explores new mediums of expression and collaboration. In *Medúlla* (2004), the source is purely vocal sounds, sometimes Pro Tooled more overtly, sometimes flowing as relatively complete choral takes. For *Vespertine* (2001), an introverted and tinkling world of micro-beats is fashioned, with high-frequency sounds suitable to laptop or mobile speaker reproduction, often featuring such instruments as harp, celesta, and music box. Her latest project at the time of writing is *Biophilia* (2011), which is heavily integrated with an accompanying iPhone app.

Figure 6.2 Björk in the studio. Photograph by Warren du Preez and Nick Thornton Jones (www.wnstudio.tv). Reproduced by permission

Arrangements are often made around an early vocal take rather than vocals laid at the end of the process on a heavily prepared bed.[49] Rather than 1990s dance trends "in which female vocals were more often fragmented, processed and anonymized," Björk's voice is central to the musical argument, whilst often demonstrating "extreme expressive freedom from the beat."[50] Beats are often heavily processed through distortion and filtering, such as on *Homogenic* (1997) with its combination of strings and electronic percussion: Björk is cited as stating "I wanted the beats to be almost distorted; imagine if there was Icelandic techno. Iceland is one of the youngest countries geographically, it's still in the making. So the sounds would be still in the making."[51] Dibben argues that the natural landscape is brought into an understanding with new technologies, as embodied by Iceland's own journey as a modern country: "this treatment of beats unifies the technological and the natural."[52]

Björk provides her own taxonomy for her work in her *Family Tree* (2002) retrospective, classifying her songs into four categories: roots ("Where we come from"), beats ("our craving for modern times . . . merging my voice with foreign electronic beats"), strings ("our struggle with education and all things academic"), and words ("stories about different emotional states").[53] As Dibben states, "The achievement of Björk's music is its ability to be experimental within the context of Anglophone popular music, and yet be non-elitist. Her music's engagement with beat-based dance music and its call on the body, its inclusive approach to other cultures and genres, and its ability not to take itself too seriously allows it to retain its connection to popular forms."[54] This is why Björk provides such a good example of popularization of electronic music, whilst at the same time exhibiting the sort of flexibility that transcends any category of electronic music alone to enter into twenty-first-century musical practice.

Further reading

Dibben, Nicola (2009) *Björk* (London: Equinox Publishing Ltd.).

Hayward, Phillip (ed.) (2004) *Off the Planet: Music, Sound and Science Fiction Cinema* (Eastleigh: John Libbey Publishing).

Nieber, Louis (2010) *Special Sound: The Creation and Legacy of the BBC Radiophonic Workshop* (New York: Oxford University Press).

Taylor, Timothy D. (2001) *Strange Sounds: Music, Technology, and Culture* (New York: Routledge).

Chapter 7

Synth pop

At the Eurovision Song Contest in 1980, the synthesizer trio Telex performed Belgium's entry. They appeared, swaying, in dapper scarves, in front of a large unplugged modular synthesizer, and sang a deliberately inane tune, appropriately entitled "Euro-vision." Typical of the humor of the band, they were aiming for last place and zero points, but were in turn ironically scuppered by Portugal's award of ten points and were dragged into third from last.

Kraftwerk, the rather more famous German synthesizer band, who pioneered the all-synthesizer ensemble as a force in popular music,[1] also had an underlying sense of humor and humanity. Their albums may seem to be continuing the progressive rock tradition of concept albums, taking on such technological themes as *Autobahn* (1974), *Radio-Activity* (1975), *Trans-Europe Express* (1977), *The Man-Machine* (1978), and *Computer World* (1981), though they are really tightly prepared and marketed packages. Although some longer tracks appear well beyond the duration of a three-minute pop song, the extended improvisation of the German experimental music scene that Kraftwerk grew out of is left far behind in their more well-known work. Their longer tracks promote a mold of extended dance workouts and minimalist tapestries in pop. Exploring a powerful array of analog and later digital equipment, however rigid the sequencing, they emphasized the human being amongst the technology. Their design harks back to earlier eras, such as the clear link to the film *Metropolis* (1927) in *die-Mensch Maschine*,[2] or the doubly meant radio and atomic age of the punning title *Radio-Activity*. On-stage theatrics included much cutting-edge technological exploration, such as the robot mannequins they hoped would supplant them on tour, or the anticipation of mobile instruments in co-option of the pocket calculator. In a German TV performance from 1978, they try to move as little as possible, but on a 1981 world tour, footage exists of the irresistibility of dancing to their music, not just for the audience but the band as well.[3]

Kraftwerk achieved significant success dating from the release of the *Autobahn* single in 1974.[4] They retained a cosmopolitan attitude, often releasing songs with vocals in multiple languages, including French, Russian, and Japanese (the song *Dentaku* is *Pocket Calculator* in Japanese). The scale of their influence is immense,

Figure 7.1 Telex at the 1980 Eurovision Song Contest held in The Hague. Dutch National Archives, The Hague, Fotocollectie Algemeen Nederlands Fotopersbureau (ANEFO), 1945–1989 – negatiefstroken zwart/wit. Finding aid number 2.24.01.05, item number 930–7867. Reproduced under a CC BY-SA 3.0 license

both in popular song and in dance music. They were one of the formative influences on American electronic dance music from electro to techno. The electronic hip hop scene of electro in the early 1980s made the link absolutely clear, with the explicit sampling of *Trans-Europe Express*' melody and *Numbers*' rhythm in Afrika Bambaataa and the Soul Sonic Force's *Planet Rock* (1982).[5]

Many subsequent ensembles have derived their names and manners from the reference point of Kraftwerk, including Komputer, Denmark's Kraftwelt, the all-female Japanese project Kraftwife, and the East (rather than West) German Das Kraftfuttermischwerk.[6] Although *Planet Rock* had sampled Kraftwerk without permission, leading to legal action, Kraftwerk have themselves given their blessing to certain tribute albums, including an album of chiptune remixes, Señor Coconut Y Su Conjunto's electrolatino album *El Baile Alemán* (*The German Dance*, 2000) and re-workings of songs for classical string quartet by the Balanescu Quartet.

Kraftwerk have had an undisputed influence on deploying synths in popular music, though, as Chapter 6 discussed, they are certainly not the only synth-employing chart act of the 1970s. The late 1970s is the primary time of ferment for synth pop, breaking through as a major chart force, and setting the scene for 1980s production trends. Britain had an important role to play, though it took some years before artists really targeted themselves at the charts more than pursuing experimental possibilities. Sheffield's scene, in which Cabaret Voltaire and the earlier incarnations of the Human League were involved, had a vein of bleak sociopolitical outlook and timbral experiment incompatible with mass appeal.[7] These youthful music creators were aware of Eno's sound treatments for Roxy Music and David Bowie, Wendy Carlos' synth-classical soundtrack to Kubrick's *A Clockwork Orange* (1971), and the novels of J. G. Ballard.[8] After 1976, the fortuitous combination of punk's call-to-arms to wannabe musicians, and increasingly affordable synthesizer prices, saw an expansion in synth band activity.

In the UK, it was a solo artist who really brought things to a head in 1979 and gazumped many synth bands-in-waiting. Gary Numan, at first with Tubeway Army and then very quickly following as a solo artist, had massive UK No. 1 hits with *Are Friends Electric?* (June 1979) and *Cars* (September 1979)[9] and rapidly gained the status of a teenage pin-up. Encountering a Minimoog synth in a studio during Tubeway Army recording sessions, Numan tried it out; it happened to be on an impressively raucous sound setting and inspired him to immediately add it to his recordings.[10] A quote from an interview marking his 30-year revival tour reveals the serendipity:

> I went from having never seen a synthesizer before to becoming the "number one expert on synthesizers" in the UK. I had a number one electronic album and people were talking about me being an electronic expert and all that, and I'd only spent about eight hours with a synthesizer because I couldn't afford to buy one.[11]

Numan produced some atmospheric washes from his rented synth and brought prominent lead synth lines to his songs, but did not take the full mechanization steps of Kraftwerk, simply using live keyboardists in a conventional band set-up. Nonetheless, his lyrics of future dystopia, and disquieteningly static and pale stage presence (if lifted from Kraftwerk), struck a chord with British youth, promoted synth pop as a new commercial force, and renewed the efforts of his peers to break out to mass audiences. Within a year or so, Orchestral Manoeuvres in the Dark (OMD) had struck with *Enola Gay*, and Ultravox with *Vienna*. As for the Human League, after a band split (with two founder members going on to success themselves as Heaven 17 and British Electric Foundation), the addition of two teenage nightclubbers, and collaboration with producer Martin Rushent, they became international chart toppers late in 1981.

With hindsight, the clearest inheritors of Kraftwerk's position turned out to be four teenagers from Basildon, Essex. By the time Kraftwerk released *The Mix* in 1991, having already followed a much-reduced release rate in the 1980s for new material, one review stated that "Depeche Mode hang heavier over Kraftwerk than the Germans ever did over them."[12] The backstory to Depeche Mode involves working-class mates achieving unexpected chart success, then spending the 1980s trying to re-invent themselves from teen-marketed pop to something darker and more alternative. But it has an additional fascinating factor; that Daniel Miller, the Mute Records boss who eventually signed them, had created an artificial teen four-piece synth band the preceding year, called the Silicon Teens, releasing the cover album *Music for Parties* to some small success. From the Vince Clarke-led first album to subsequent work with Martin Gore as chief songwriter, Depeche Mode created catchy (if later increasingly somber) songs. Yet their studio textures followed paths suggested by their more radical Mute labelmates such as Fad Gadget and Einstürzende Neubauten (who we'll have more to say about in Chapter 10), including the wholesale adoption of sampling. The combination of dark and intimate lyrical themes and high production quality (through the close early involvement of Daniel Miller and later Alan Wilder in particular) framed atypical slow-burning pop songs that elevated them to stadium status. By 1991, with producer Flood working with both Depeche Mode and U2, a certain convergence in synth-friendly stadium rock had taken place. It is rather ironic that Depeche Mode have survived so long given that their band name means "fast fashion."

Yet whilst Depeche Mode (during their peak years) and Kraftwerk met the mold of the "four men in a band" model, it is not the only template. It is practical with the aid of sequencers and pre-recorded tapes to have only one producer-performer figure and one vocalist, or a single solo artist. Simon Reynolds has picked up on the importance of duos, where the emotional human vocals counterpoint the metronomic machine-programmed backdrops.[13] The duo model is well anticipated in the 1970s by such keyboard and vocalist acts as the Carpenters or Captain & Tennille, and the 1980s brought in particular a wealth of British duos such as Soft Cell, Eurythmics (particularly in their earlier purer synth work), Yazoo, Assembly, and Erasure (all three the product of Vince Clarke's post-Depeche Mode collaborations), or the Pet Shop Boys (with their Fairlight keyboard presets extraordinaire).[14]

Synth pop's relationship to popular music

For a time in the early 1980s, synth pop was mainstream electronic dance music, perhaps with more clearly accessible song form compared to contemporary Italo-disco, electro and the more brutal electronic body music (EBM). Depeche Mode's early success was based as much as anything on their club appeal and the pure danceability of the tracks; pop acts have always had a strong relationship with dance (even when supporting slow dancing with ballads rather than uptempo numbers).

The increasing prominence of underground post-disco music by 1988, and the inexorable rise of hip hop and new strains of electronic R&B, would empower new twists in the role of electronic instrumentation in popular music.

Because of the overlap with the rise of the synthesizer as an affordable band instrument, synth lines and sequenced parts found their way into the work of many bands, such as Duran Duran, which were otherwise more conventional outfits. The Second British Invasion of the US circa 1981–3 was heavily related to the rise of MTV and the greater number of videos available at the time from image-conscious British bands. Nevertheless, it also meant a lot of publicity for the various New Romantic, futurist and synth-pop tribes of the times, and made sure that Thomas Dolby, the Thompson Twins and their ilk introduced certain sounds to market in the US that American producers would respond to in kind.[15] The story of international trends in production is rarely a one-way transference, however, and is more intertwined. The electro and freestyle scenes in New York had themselves been an inspiration to British acts like New Order seeking to embrace new instrumentation, and were the melting pot from which Madonna's long-lived pop career would sprout. Massive-selling international albums, such as Michael Jackson's *Thriller* (1982) and Prince's *Purple Rain* (1984), made timely use of synthesizers.

Ultimately, the sound of synthesizers is welded to much 1980s music production through the widespread availability of the new technology; after all, the 100,000s of Yamaha DX7s sold by Yamaha from 1983 found their way into many studios! 1980s pop production is not just a question of gated snares, but an essential part of the typical sound world is made up of the new digital synths. Quincy Jones' telephone book for session musicians when producing Michael Jackson albums was not short of synth programmers and performers! Even rock acts introduced keyboard players; the posturing rock band Van Halen's most famous international track *Jump* (1984) depends on a synth riff, and in the recording the pre-bridge verses dispense with guitar altogether; ironically, this somewhat unrepresentative track was their only US No. 1, which shows something of the popular appeal of synthesizers at the time even in the supposed stadium rock heartland of the US.

Nonetheless, many bands who broke through riding the wave of synth pop later turned their backs on the style by re-introducing more traditional rock band instrumentation in a more international, generic production mold, including A-ha, the Human League, and Eurythmics. Alphaville's first album *Forever Young* (1984) is seen as a synth-pop classic, though the band themselves gradually diversified into more traditional acoustic and electric instrumentations from them on. But as some synth acts diversified, new waves of synth instrumentation came through; we shall take up the story of electronic dance music proper in the next chapter. Another social current within synth pop is the importance of gay culture. It can be a short step from some Hi-NRG and Italo-disco productions to contemporary synth pop. In the UK, the Hi-NRG gay club sound was re-packaged as a dominant pop market force by the Stock, Aitken and Waterman (SAW) production team, especially in the years 1987–9; you can thank this era for providing the basis of Rickrolling.[16]

As with SAW's production line, we can often follow the flow of synthesizer use by tracking certain producers. Like Kraftwerk, Giorgio Moroder has an essential parallel role in the history of electronic dance, but influenced synth pop as well. Sparks, the quirky American-though-you-would-imagine-Austrian band, worked with Giorgio Moroder on their *No. 1 in Heaven* album (1979). Conny Plank went on from Kraftwerk's earlier albums and other German experimental bands to work with many new wave bands, from Ultravox to D.A.F. (Deutsch Amerikanische Freundschaft). Trevor Horn, who was behind the short-lived Buggles project of 1979–80, was an early adopter of synths in pop production and made them a cornerstone of his career. His obsession with crafting hits is well evidenced by the three months he spent on the mix of Frankie Goes to Hollywood's single *Two Tribes*! His record label ZTT's 1980s peak also included gathering the studio musicians for the influential sampling act the Art of Noise, and he has worked with new technology across his career from a synth-led sound for early 1980s groups Yes and Dollar, through the Pet Shop Boys and Seal, to t.A.T.u. and beyond.[17]

Pop has always been an international market, and synth bands sprang up in many places. One of the most delightful, provocative, and electronically funky ensembles to come through in the late 1970s was Japan's Yellow Magic Orchestra. An aspect of their enduring legacy is the early use of arcade sound tracks; their first eponymous 1978 recorded album includes two "Computer Game Theme" tracks which directly employ arcade sound. Yellow Magic Orchestra did not have to wait for an 8-bit revival in later decades and beat electro's own arcade obsession by four years.

Synth pop has been around for four decades at the time of writing and has gone through many fashions and retro offshoots, in and out of touch with electronic dance music. The relatively short-lived electroclash movement circa 1998–2002 is one case in point, combining synth pop sequenced octave-jumping basslines, electro percussion, and clear dance influence with pop harmony, song structure, and vocals. Instrumentation has waxed and waned between totally and clearly synthetic backing, and such tempering factors as samples of acoustic events and guitars; the human voice always remains somewhere close by, even if vocoded. One welcome factor has been the visibility of female involvement; Alison Moyet (Yazoo) and Annie Lennox (Eurythmics) provide clear precedents, and 1990s acts such as Dubstar, Saint Etienne, and Lamb kept a female vocalist to the fore (even if background production credits still tended to be biased toward men). The 2000s saw a succession of female-fronted acts in the synth pop tradition, including Goldfrapp and La Roux, with greater prominence of collaborative and solo female production work for such artists as Miss Kittin, Ladytron, Little Boots (famously with the Tenori-On), Robots in Disguise, Client, Peaches, and Chicks on Speed. None of these artists would be entirely comfortable with the label of "synth pop," particularly with reference to the 1970s–1980s historical trend, and all tread their own course between outright experimentalism and retaining some accessibility and elements of dance.

Despite all subsequent references to synth pop, the general tactics of electronic instrumentation in song form have been thoroughly absorbed into the pop mainstream, and dance elements have been transformed in many ways throughout electronic dance music. Pop production retains a freedom to lift ideas from many international trends in style, from Jamaican dancehall through the evolving production forms of hip hop. Productions for Britney Spears, Rihanna, Lady Gaga, and Lily Allen are replete with gestures lifted from synth pop and electronic dance music,[18] and share a Scandanavian link in their production credits. The historical link to Norway's A-ha (*Hunting High and Low*, 1985) or the Swedish pop magpies Abba (*The Visitors*, 1981) shouldn't be downplayed, and Sweden in particular has a renowned synth pop scene: Adolphson & Falk and Candide from the 1980s, or more recently Familjen, for example, who show links between electro house and synth pop![19]

The field is rather more widely distributed than a simple Euro–UK–US axis might suggest. Bollywood's ready adoption of synthesizers is only part of Asian pop's connection to the instruments. The highly manufactured pop worlds of South Korea (K-pop) and Japan (J-pop) thrive on synthetic backdrops, going as far as to synthesize the pop singers themselves through virtual pop idols. At a concert in Japan in 2010, virtual idols like Hatsune Miku, Kagamine Rin, and Kagamine Len were projected in 3D on a concert stage, with a live backing band (the idols' parts were pre-rendered on a backing tape).[20]

In treading international pathways, we should also acknowledge that music scenes are not solely about the most prominent acts, but rely on the experimentation of undergrounds. The post-punk milieu of DIY releases and alternative music was a great nourishing ground where trying out synthesizers was a natural part of seeking new avenues. Devo, for example, had turned more to synths by their 1980 album *Freedom of Choice*. Whilst synth pop as a mainstream peaked in the early 1980s, certain more niche underground movements, labeled by some as cold wave, dark wave, and the like, remained active away from the most public eye. Precedents might be found in Suicide's use of distorted electric organ lines and drum patterns in 1977, or Joy Division's and Magazine's use of synth lines in advance of Gary Numan. The Cure readily adopted synths and drum machines in their pursuit of a dark alternative sound, peaking in chilly absorption with *Pornography* (1982).

Obscurer yet rewarding acts to explore might include US synth punks Nervous Gender, New Zealand's Mi-Sex (whose track *Computer Games* from 1979 is nearly as timely as Yellow Magic Orchestra), Australia's Severed Heads, Canada's Rational Youth, Russia's Leningrad Sandwich, the Netherlands' Clan of Xymox, Germany's Trash Groove Girls, and many more.

Techniques and characterization of synth pop

A working definition of synth pop (also called electro pop, techno pop, and the like) might be popular songs with prominent synthesizer instrumentation. It is often difficult to tell whether synth-pop songs are angled primarily at clubs or home listening. Playing to both audiences can be important for breaking singles, and the essence of a lot of pop music is danceability. So there are always overlaps between innovations in pop production and in dance music. The synth bands embraced the use of 12″ dance remixes to cater to the club market in the 1980s, aside from 7″ radio-friendly-length single releases.

Following the Kraftwerk template, many ensembles have featured prominent or total synthesizer and sequencer instrumentation in opposition to the older band model of guitar and drums. Synth pop, particularly in the transitional years from the late 1970s into the 1980s, saw a number of artists committing fully to an electronic music future, and some hedging their bets, perhaps employing a single keyboard player or bringing in electronics under the influence of a particular record producer. If we were to catalog the elements of electronics involved, we might work across a continuum from token low-in-the-mix keyboard parts, through Gary Numan's lead synth lines (against conventional band backing), to the all-sequenced, all-synthesized (all-singing, all-dancing?) ensemble of Kraftwerk and their followers. Individual artists have themselves varied the mixture across their careers; for example, whilst Duran Duran ostensibly have one keyboardist in their line-up, the production of their songs has often involved greater mechanization of the backing (for example, the wild arpeggios of *Rio* (1982) and the full studio artifice of *All She Wants Is* (1988)).

Particularly since sequencers were not as readily available as analog synths in the 1970s, some ensembles aimed for a pure synth sound, but hand-played all the parts, and mixed in some band instruments like bass guitar. OMD's *Bunker Soldiers* (1980), opening their first self-titled album, and especially wonky in the Peel Sessions version, is a good case in point (its post-punk links in vocal mannerism in particular could also be productively pursued). Frustrated that early critics kept writing off their efforts as machine music, Andy McCluskey protested that OMD's work was "all written by real human beings, and all played by hand."[21] Certainly, their early work, even if influenced heavily by Kraftwerk's lead, finds its own alternative path partially through negotiating a more limited technology.

The adoption of synths has often been a surprising process. Joy Division's dark drum and guitar sounds were complimented by icy synths on their late tracks; suffering from insomnia, Bernard Sumner had built a kit synth from an electronics magazine specification![22] After Ian Curtis' suicide, the surviving band members formed New Order, soon involving local musician Gillian Gilbert, and increasingly committed to an electronic sound world; within a few years, the alternative guitar band were closely intersecting with the electro scene, being produced by Arthur Baker, and bankrolling Factory Records' Haçienda nightclub in Manchester. The club would go on to become a pioneering venture in the UK dance music explosion circa 1988, even if it was eventually closed by gang and money problems.[23] New Order's most famous electro-era track, *Blue Monday* (1983), was used by the band as the final track in live sets because they didn't like doing clichéd rock encores; they joked they could just press a button and leave early.[24] *Blue Monday* samples a pad sound from Kraftwerk's *Uranium* (1975), while *Your Silent Face* (1983) has a certain kinship to Kraftwerk's *Franz Schubert* (1977); Ian Curtis had deliberately played Kraftwerk before Joy Division gigs, so these connections seem somewhat fitting in homage.[25]

Whilst the shadow of Kraftwerk falls long over many acts, Kraftwerk themselves cannot be held in isolation as pure pioneers of synth pop. It's not just the wider setting of activity in the 1970s taking in other German electronic bands and electronic disco sound, but also Kraftwerk's own admitted classical heritage. Schubert already appeared in a track title in the last paragraph, amongst Kraftwerk's many harmonic and melodic classical influences. To treat their 1974 breakthrough US hit, a passage from the finale of Robert Schumann's *Viennese Carnival Music* possibly provides the main recurring theme for *Autobahn*, whether consciously lifted or unconsciously part of Ralf Hütter's classical training. Nonetheless, it is important that Kraftwerk stood up for recognizable classical diatonic harmony amongst their other experiments, and this accessibility carried across to many post-punk adventurers. Interviewed in 1976, Ralf Hütter opined: "Most electronic musicians are afraid of tonality. When you see the world of frequencies there is tonality, you cannot deny it. The dictatorship of tonality or the dictatorship of non-tonality is the same."[26]

As an angle on synth pop's ready adoption of popular conventions of song form and general practice harmony, let us consider one model chord sequence in the natural minor Aeolian mode of much pop. The i bVI alternating sequence or its variations, also including bVII (essentially in a home key of natural C minor, Cm, Ab, Bb, Cm), appears as a prototype idea in Kraftwerk's *Radioactivity* title track of their 1975 album, then recurs, amongst other instances,[27] in:

- OMD: *Almost* (1980);
- Eurythmics: *Here Comes the Rain Again* (1984);
- Depeche Mode: *The Things You Said* (1987);
- Pet Shop Boys: *Love Comes Quickly* (1986) and *Domino Dancing* (1988).

Even Matia Bazar's Italian synth-pop standard *Ti sento* (1986) makes extensive use of bVI bVII i! It has a wider history in pop of course, including the Beatles and Abba, but helps demonstrate some of the underlying harmonic connections between synth pop artists and the context of their work. The Pet Shop Boys are especially fond of sequences revolving around a home minor chord, touching on bIII and bVII (*Opportunities*) or i bVI bVII v and bVI bVII i (*Rent*). The Pet Shop Boys' links to pop history are worn on their sleeves, since some of their greatest successes have been electronic cover versions of historic tracks (*Always on My Mind* (1987), *Where the Streets Have No Name (I Can't Take My Eyes Off You)* (1991), *Go West* (1993)) and their ironic knowing-pop-journalist stance is particularly the result of Neil Tennant's own background with the British publication *Smash Hits*.

Another element of synth pop is the riff, sometimes accompanied by layers of countermelodies. Depeche Mode circa *Speak & Spell* (1981) are a great case in point here, since they only owned monophonic analog synths, and their live-honed tracks had to work with combinations of single-note lines. A charming image from the recording sessions is that of Martin Gore eating his takeaway dinner after his daily bank work whilst recording a part with a spare hand. Perhaps he was recording the closing instrumental break part from *Just Can't Get Enough* (1981) shown in counterpoint with the main riff and bassline in Example 7.1. This figure appears in combination with Gahan's chanted "Just can't get enough" line, some vocal "wooah" harmonies, and a fidgety synth tom line, plus the usual danceable drum backing. The instrumentation throughout is synthesized, of course, which establishes a freshness that would only have been undermined by guitar lines and chords. Nonetheless, the album as a whole is anticipated in sound by Daniel Miler's previous solo and collaborative work, and also by other British acts, such as the earlier unsuccessful incarnation of the Human League.

Eurythmics: *Sweet Dreams (Are Made of This)* (1983)

This song, a major international hit (No. 1 in the US on a first single release there for the duo!), is based on a strong riff (Example 7.2) running at 126 bpm. On closer inspection, the integrated riff turns out to be made from two hocketing lines an octave apart. The two-bar pattern is a marvel of economic momentum and the percussion is quite stark to avoid over-tiring the listener, whilst absolutely emphasizing the dance element. It sounds like a flanging effect has been added to the synthesizer line for extra grittiness, and the kick drum marked with an accent on the first beat of each two-bar period is actually boosted by the addition of a heavier further kick sound (this tactic recurs, for instance, in

Example 7.1 Three-part synth line counterpoint from *Just Can't Get Enough* outro (original album version)

Example 7.2 *Sweet Dreams (Are Made of This)* main riff

Example 7.3 *Sweet Dreams (Are Made of This)* synth solo

the Prodigy's *Firestarter* (1996), where it happens on every one of the 4/4 bars). Such a literal two-bar pattern sets a good precedent for techno; hip hop's pursuit of breakbeats had already focused in on critical looping parts for dancers.

The song is driven by repeated instances of the riff in various instrumentations with and without voice, and other separate sections. Cataloging by chordal basis, the building blocks might be listed as:

A: (main riff, verse): Cm (1 bar) Ab G (half bars)
B: (6-bar wordless vocalize interlude) Ab, G, Cm, Fm, Ab, G (later there is a variant B2 based on Fm G Cm Fm Ab G)

C: (chorus "hold your head up") Cm F alternation four times (8 bars)

and the derived form of the standard single version is Ax4 (opening riff), B, Ax8 (verse), B, Ax2 (riff), Ax4 (verse), B, C, Ax4 (with solo), Ax4 (verse), B2, C, Ax4 (with solo), Ax4 (riff), B2, Ax3 (riff), Ax4 (just vocals and kick), A (repeating with vocals, solo, outro).

The literal repeat of the synth solo line over the main riff is an interesting feature; the solo is shown in Example 7.3. In another example of synth pop counterpoint built through recording layers, in the closing stages, the main riff, the chorus vocals, the solo line, and a further synth string part all combine!

As evidence of Reynold's duo model, Annie Lennox's vocals maintain a strong connection to earthier human roots, in a soul tradition of mellismatic elaboration. The contemporary outfit Yazoo were also exploring this at the time through Alison Moyet's bluesy sound against Vince Clarke's electronic backing.

Ultimately, synth pop makes use of mechanisms that are now widespread throughout popular music production. Tracing its heritage depends on inter-relations with musical developments discussed in other chapters in this book, with continuing reference back to a pop mainstream. Synth basslines, effects, drum machines[28] and other sequencing, deadpan, or soulful vocals: Since the days of analog synth lines, sampling has now become a dominant force, but the charm of early synth pop still shines through occasionally in new tracks!

Further reading

Albiez, Sean and Pattie, David (eds.) (2011) *Kraftwerk: Music Non-Stop* (New York: Continuum).

Bussy, Pascal (2005) *Kraftwerk: Man, Machine and Music*, 3rd edn. (London: SAF Publishing Ltd.).

Flür, Wolfgang (2003) *I Was a Robot*, 2nd edn. (London: Sanctuary Publishing Ltd.).

Malins, Steve (2006) *Depeche Mode: Black Celebration*, 3rd edn. (London: Andre Deutsch).

Miller, Jonathan (2003) *Stripped: Depeche Mode* (London: Omnibus Press).

Reynolds, Simon (2005) *Rip It Up and Start Again* (London: Faber & Faber).

Rideout, Ernie, Fortner, Stephen, and Gallant, Michael (eds.) (2008) *Keyboard Presents the Best of the 80s: The Artists, Instruments and Techniques of an Era* (New York: Backbeat Books).

Chapter 8

Electronic dance music

Movement and music are inextricably combined; in pre-historic origins and even surviving in some African languages today, the word for music has overlapped with the word for dance.[1] Dance crazes have been a prominent feature of both ephemeral and longer-lasting movements in popular music, whether the Charleston, Twist or Vogue.[2] Much cultural transfer has occurred through music and dance, especially in popular music, through Latin American styles and the African diaspora. Particular dances can reveal surprisingly distant origins; the acrobatics of break-dancing can be traced back before the twentieth century and moonwalking was not invented by Michael Jackson![3] The human compulsion to dance, whether in couples, groups, or solo, is intimately tied to preferences for clearly regulated, danceable, metronomic music. Electronic perfection of the precision of such metronomic beats, and an ensuing hotbed of dance experiment, seem almost natural in retrospect.

Our working definition is that *electronic dance music* (EDM) features electronic synthesized and sampled instrumentation, with at least some parts of a percussive nature, in tracks designed for dancing. Track lengths can be greatly extended, well beyond the typical three-minute pop song, and the evocation of a beat varies from the absolutely literal "four on the floor" to more complex rhythmic patterning, including deliberately loose and ragged grooves. The sound materials extend from purer synthesized and sequenced instrumental tracks (techno is one possible label here) to raw sample-based collages with prominent rapped vocals (hip hop, rap), also admitting forays into sung vocal hooks or fully fledged songs. Given that much pop music is simultaneously designed to be effective for listening and clubbing, the musical concerns of EDM flow back and forth with general popular music releases.

The evolution of electronic dance music is a convoluted topic, sometimes arousing passionate debate over miniscule musicological differences. A profusion of genre labels is evident in any deeper study of the field.[4] When one considers that artists often invent labels for promotional purposes to differentiate themselves from their many competitors, and that the journalists of the scene have an inbuilt desire to find and promote new offshoots, the profusion is a little more forgivable, if sometimes

Figure 8.1 "The Tell-Tale Beat" cartoon by Randall Munroe from the xkcd online comic, reproduced from http://xkcd.com/740. Reproduced by permission of the artist

rather tiring in pure music theoretical terms.[5] We shall try to steer a middle course herein between acknowledging historic stylistic developments and surveying the panoply of sub-genres.

It is worth making a central caveat about one term in particular. As Brewster and Broughton warn: "if you name a genre of music after a club which was open for ten whole years and which was known for its eclecticism, you're going to run into problems of definition pretty quickly. The word 'garage' is by far the most mangled term in the whole history of music."[6] The club in question is the Paradise Garage in New York (open from 1977 for ten years), with its famously eclectic DJ Larry Levan, though any garage sound of diva vocals over house music was incubated at another club entirely, Zanzibar in New Jersey. But you may be confused by images of 1960s garage bands, Apple's GarageBand software, early 1990s US garage, its pirate-radio-accelerated-playback cousin speed garage, and the later 1990s UK garage scene. The second most multi-use term is probably hardcore, which might evoke US guitar punks circa 1980, a rave scene circa 1990, and more. Now knowing the score, we can proceed with caution.

Origins of EDM

Disco's "party music" brought hedonistic club dancing to a mass market in the 1970s, though the origins of the discothèque and the DJ can be traced back much earlier in the century. A phonograph-based jukebox had appeared as early as 1889 and the first radio DJ broadcast (if more oriented to shipping news than the latest Caruso) was in 1906. The boom in the radio industry, wartime clubs in Paris, glamorous post-war clubs for a new jet-set, and Jamaican sound system clashes (the first in 1952) all had a part to play in the gradual rise of club culture. By 1968/9, DJs such as Francis Grasso were operating in New York, beat-matching records to maintain a continuous flow rather than separately start each track.[7] However, the music was not yet electronically textured.

Although there are popular music prototypes (see Chapter 6), the earliest EDM in its club music form arose in electronic instrumentation experiments in disco. Aside from Kraftwerk's 1970s synth-pop lead, an important popularizing role was played by Giorgio Moroder. His production work with Pete Bellotte for Donna Summer brought a Munich sound of analog synthesizers in disco to international attention. The central track here is *I Feel Love* (1977), which holds an otherworldly allure when compared to more conventional band instrument-based disco tracks of its time. A Moog modular system provided all of the instrumental parts, with a rather famous bassline – think an eighth note spaced C C G Bb on a loop – as the central propulsive thrust; a new sync technique, via a special reference signal on the last track of the 16-track recorder, was used to lay down the various synthesized parts metronomically.[8] Equally amazing is Moroder's anticipation of the general tendencies and sound of electronic dance music, with his 1977 album *From Here to Eternity*. The first five tracks segue directly into one another like an ideal DJ mix, maintaining a model four on the floor; the album takes in vocoders and Abba-esque pop, like Kraftwerk anticipating work to come from synth pop, through electro, to later 1980s dance music.

Although a backlash against disco rocked the US in 1979, the disco movement continued in Europe (in the Italo-disco movement, for example) and in some underground scenes in major cities like Chicago and New York. Whilst synthesizers in pop were highly prominent by the beginning of the 1980s, alternative club music away from the pop mainstream gradually coalesced during the next ten years. As alluded to in Chapter 7, it is worth acknowledging the gay clubbing crowds as particularly driving a demand for post-disco electronic tracks. In the Hi-NRG movement (later subsumed back into popular music), artists like Sylvester or producers like Patrick Cowley and Ian Levine explored higher-tempo, constantly pumping tracks, with an increasing use of electronic instrumentation as the technology became cheaper and more widespread.

Nonetheless, the 1970s were not exclusively about disco; we've already discussed the importance of punk and post-punk in promoting DIY attitudes and indie labels, widening participation in music creation. The use of synthesizers in funk, or recording experiments in Jamaican dub, had their own impact on later developments (see also Chapter 6).

Although now clearly differentiated in record-shop racks, overlaps in origin are also evident in an examination of hip hop and rap music.[9] The functional side to hip hop, with its origins in dance parties, shows a clear parallel to the needs of club music. Whilst new turntable techniques were innovated here, many of the early rap tracks were based around disco-style backing tracks. For example, as an underground movement began to be commercialized by entrepreneurs, Sugarhill Gang's *Rapper's Delight* (1979) became the first mass success for rap; it rested on a session musician re-recording of Chic's *Good Times* of the same year. Hip hop only separated itself gradually over time, with the 1980s being a time of inventive transition.

Hip hop grew up as a local New York development, actually local to the impoverished communities of the Bronx rather than Manhattan's more media-visible downtown. The movement had a long underground time through the 1970s; a true street culture, sound systems used to steal power from street lighting for block parties. As is typical of the cross-currents of life, it was a Jamaican immigrant, Kool Herc, who set the seeds of the new music. Playing two copies of the same record on two turntables in alternation (from around 1973), he extended the b-dancers' favourite sections. Although his turntable skills were quickly surpassed by those he inspired, his powerful sound system, on the Jamaican model, remaining highly prominent and popular. Competitor DJs explored new turntable trickery to make their mark, whether the smooth inter-record flow already practiced by disco DJs or innovative new scratching techniques. Grand Wizard Theodore reputedly invented the scratch when interrupted in his practice by his mother, stopping the current record abruptly! The DJs were joined by MCs to further pump up the crowds, reminiscent of radio presenters and the practice of Jamaican toasting. As surviving recordings show, for some time, hip hop was a live performance medium; an early document like *The Adventures of Grandmaster Flash on the Wheels of Steel* (1981) is a testament to one-take turntable skills.

Once rap came to public prominence, recording became a more visible focus than the parties. Drum machines and synths were prominent by 1982's electro, with sample-based production becoming big by the late 1980s. Many 1990s EDM artists (such as the Chemical Brothers or, more obliquely, Autechre) acknowledged the importance of hip hop in their musical upbringing. This influence is most readily seen perhaps in the sample-based UK house productions circa 1987 and the short-lived trend for "hip-house" in the late 1980s. And whilst much rap, when tending to slower tempi and lyrical content, diversified away from club dance, the inter-flow of production trends has continued to this day. One cross-connecting example is Missy Elliott's *Lose Control* (2005), which heavily lifts from Cybotron's *Clear* (1983).

House and techno: Chicago and Detroit

"Such global forms as house and techno are really nothing more than disco continued by other means."[10]

Frankie Knuckles was the main DJ at Chicago's Warehouse club from 1977 to 1983 and then worked at the Power Plant club while Ron Hardy took over at the re-named Warehouse (the Music Box). Through the activities of a small number of DJs, including the proselytizing of a popular local radio station, WBMX-FM, Chicago was one of the crucibles of a new dance music sound. It is likely that the Warehouse club's name provides the best originating explanation of the term *house*, as the records played there were sought out in record stores. Although the main tracks at the club were originally sourced from international artists, a home-grown music scene gradually arose in the early 1980s; the well spring of disco had begun to dry after 1979's collapse of the disco bubble. Knuckles had been preparing his own mix-tapes grafting Philly soul to harder drum machine rhythms and looping popular sections of tracks, and local pioneers began to create records that fitted the needs of the scene. The pioneering spirit quickly took off in 1984, particularly after Jesse Saunders' effort *On and On* sold so quickly.[11] As Farley Keith Williams (also known by the pseudonym Farley "Jackmaster" Funk) later noted:

> all you need is a feel for music. There are people who've been to college to study music and they can't make a simple rhythm track, let alone a hit record. It's weird. And it seems like a waste of time to learn that, because now a little kid can pick up a computer, get lucky with it, and write a hit.[12]

Whilst people may turn to computers first these days when producing dance music, for the house pioneers, the favored equipment was drawn from Japanese corporation Roland's x0x line. The TR-808 drum machine (TR = Transistor Rhythm) was released in 1980, followed in 1981 by its TB-303 bass synthesizer (TB = Transistorized Bass).[13] Both machines incorporated pattern sequencers, which, if fiddly to program, could set up the sorts of metronomic repetition critical to the electronically abetted dancefloor. Crucially, both machines were commercial failures when first released, so could be picked up relatively cheaply.

A whole musical sub-genre, acid house, eventually flowered from the TB-303 in particular;[14] the analog bass synthesizer had such a resonant filter that extreme settings could create weirdly energized warblings. Almost the entire basis of one of dance music's most tightly looping yet effective works, Phuture's *Acid Tracks* (created in 1985, reaching mass European distribution by 1987), burbles away manically through a series of highly resonant overdriven filter settings, against subtly changing percussion.

Chicago house's success, the energetic production of highly dancefloor-oriented tracks, was also its failure, when, after imports hit European markets, European producers quickly realized their own takes on the formula. Whilst international exposure and chart hits came to some of the Chicago producers – Farley "Jackmaster" Funk's *Love Can't Turn Around* was a top ten UK hit in September 1986 and Steve "Silk" Hurley's *Jack Your Body* reached No. 1 in January 1987[15] – most of the artists had short-lived careers. By 1988, Chicago police were clamping down on the club scene, the influential WBMX radio station was off air, and Frankie Knuckles had moved back to New York.[16] At the same time, however, the *techno* artists of nearby Detroit were managing to establish their own momentum as a musical force.

The links between Chicago and Detroit were close, since they are separated by only a five-hour drive, and the Detroit artists used to visit the Chicago clubs and sell their records in the larger market there (Detroit artists were discovered by UK A&R agents via Chicago record stores). Derrick May even sold his 909 to Frankie Knuckles to pay rent, giving away one of the differentiators of the Detroit DJ sound, much to Juan Atkins' chagrin. Eddie "Flashin'" Fowlkes recalls:

> For me my first record was more of a house record even though it was hard. But back then you didn't think too much about how to call it. When Neil Rushton put this compilation together Derrick wanted to call it "The Best of Detroit House." But then Juan said: "You can all call your music house but what I do is techno music."[17]

The etymology of the word techno is actually in the techniques of the arts;[18] it was only in the nineteenth century that "technology" began to take on its modern connotation of engineering. Alvin Toffler features the "techno-society" prominently in his influential tract *Future Shock* (1970), and the follow-up *The Third Wave* (1980) uses the term "techno rebels" in a way that was picked up by Juan Atkins. Although Atkins' Cybotron electro project (1981–5) had a track called *Techno City* (1985), Yellow Magic Orchestra released *Technopolis* in 1979, and the Buggles created a track entitled *Techno Pop* in 1979 (Kraftwerk's *Electric Café* album of 1986 also has a prominent *Techno Pop* track, and was later re-named to make this link even more explicit).[19] Techno on its own as a genre label is commonly attributed to the need for a marketable compilation title for what became *Techno! The New Dance Sound of Detroit* (1988).[20] The growth of the term techno was such that many writers used it as a synonym for all electronic dance music, especially in the 1990s, though we would usually distinctly identify *Detroit techno* as the seed movement.

The first wave of Detroit production grew out of a Eurocentric party scene. Creation myths have tended to focus on the Belleville Three (Juan Atkins, Derrick

May, Kevin Saunderson), though there certainly were other active producers in the first stages, like Eddie Fowlkes quoted above, and other locations for the parties than the Belleville suburb.[21] Of the famous trio, Atkins, a little older, with his earlier record releases, was initially the leading figure, and his serious and futurist attitude set a mood for a darker instrumental sound. Whilst overlaps are clear, a possible characterization of the differences between Chicago and Detroit might focus on Chicago as a sort of more ecstatic drum machine-based disco sound and Detroit as a cooler sequenced future funk. As Derrick May famously declared in the liner notes to the *Techno!* compilation of 1988, "It's like George Clinton and Kraftwerk are stuck in an elevator with only a sequencer to keep them company."[22] However, he also claimed, with exaggerated caricature, "House still has its heart in 70s disco; we don't have any of that respect for the past, its strictly future music. We have a much greater aptitude for experiment."[23]

Controversy has continued as to the extent of Detroit techno's originality and centrality of contribution, though it is clear that Europe alone could not have produced the twists on the synth-dance formula incubated by African-American producers in the US. With the tendency that all mass-communicated music tends to become international property, anxieties about ownership of local creative ventures are always stirred as scenes break into wider exposure. Detroit techno became a local industry of sorts, with new waves of producers following the success of the first, including the hard industrial techno of Jeff Mills and Mike Banks, the jazzier links of Carl Craig, and, through Detroit's proximity across the river to Windsor in Ontario, Canadian artists like Richie Hawtin.

International dance music

Tracing the international growth of all styles of electronic dance music is an impossible task. By 2000, dance music had become an international hit phenomenon, the basis of the backing of most new pop tracks, heard throughout the holiday islands of the world, mutating in character as new production styles encountered the world musics of local communities. Superstar DJs jet-setted, often attracting a much greater level of fame and demand than the musicians who supplied their tracks. If they lugged large boxes of records with them in the 1990s, after the millennium a tendency was evident toward lighter-weight luggage allowed by fully digital track management in hard-drive disc jockeying. EDM also grew along with the Internet, with a wealth of resources to support would-be producers. Home production could be followed up (in the ideal) by distribution without intermediaries, and popular forum sites discussed the merits of new releases and the minutiae of stylistic difference. Although some of the popularity of clubbing itself as an activity may have waned by the millennium, the wide stylistic family tree of EDM has kept many branches active to the present day.

Europe, which had contributed so strongly to the development of electronic pop and dance in the 1970s, had a very important economic part to play for EDM releases and became a center of production work above and beyond the smaller US communities of the 1980s. Although the UK's music industry had an unquestionable role in the adoption of EDM, it remains important to acknowledge the many wider scenes of European producers, from the traditions of Italo-disco and Euro-pop to the new waves of European chart techno and more alternative styles. After all, many of the pioneer UK DJs who established new clubs around 1987 had actually encountered inspirational elements of the scene in the (Spanish) Balearic Islands in the mid-1980s, and wanted to translate these back to their home nation.

After the UK became the main export market for US house and techno releases, by 1988 dance music underwrote a full social explosion, in acid house's "Second Summer of Love." The love in question was popularly linked to the copious distribution of the drug ecstasy alongside crowd euphoria; the UK press, initially enthusiastic, turned quickly to horror stories particularly emphasizing the drug angle. The UK's enthusiasm made it a hotbed of production in the new styles; from sample-based UK house circa 1987–8 to the South Yorkshire bleep scene of 1989, the UK would head off on a multicultural trajectory of its own leading through rave hardcore, jungle, UK garage, and beyond, sometimes called the "UK hardcore continuum."[24] Such was the sudden ubiquity of the lifestyle and sounds by 1988 that crossover fertilization from dance to rock genres was quickly pursued, as in the Madchester scene of the Happy Mondays and the Stone Roses. In retrospect, a political backlash was inevitable: Given a manic scene where existing clubs could not cater for the sheer demand, unlicensed raves took the custom. Limiting such unauthorized gatherings of youth was the primary target of the 1994 Criminal Justice and Public Order Act, though police intervention had been happening for years before this. EDM, which had spread to fields, was formally forced to retreat to inner-city clubs or to escape back to those holiday islands, like Ibiza, which had first prompted the scene. Pirate radio continued to keep many an underground active.

Simultaneously, US dance music was affecting people across the European continent. The Belgian and Dutch mania for EBM in the early 1980s translated straight through to an embrace of the new US styles, and their transformation in new currents. The UK's 1992 jungle innovations can point to a background in hardcore rave, itself detoured via these European producers. In the 1990s, stratospheric increases in basic event rates in the music pushed tempi ever faster in the pursuit of some ultimate gabba-rate.

Germany remains a center for EDM to the present day and had developed a
mass youth culture for techno by the mid-1990s.[25] Given Kraftwerk's original work,
Germany was well positioned as a focal arena of electronic music development,
and unification with East Germany from 1989 substantially extended youth enthusiasm for club musics, and beyond that into Eastern Europe in general. As Mark
Reeder notes: "The techno scene symbolized the revolutionary excitement of those
times . . . It was pure energy and it seemed to express everything for the kids of that
moment."[26] After initial waves of hard "tekkkno," German producers explored different poles: They created dub and minimal techno avoiding almost all non-essential
elements in tracks, but also played a key role in the creation of an international
trance-techno music from the early 1990s. It would be unfair not to mention France
in the 1990s as its own hotbed of chic through such artists as Daft Punk, but, in any
case, by such points, EDM was becoming a fully global phenomenon, and Brazilian
or South African producers might equally lay claim to fame.

The international appeal of electronic dance music can be traced not just to the
effectiveness of the basic dance functionality (readily adaptable to local preferences
in the fine detail placed over the top) and ease of use of the production technology,
but also to the reaching of large markets. Where English-language pop required a
certain basic mastery of the language, EDM production could thrive on a count-in
in Italian or Spanish, some off-the-shelf diva samples, or the avoidance of vocals
altogether, making it easy for anyone to create records with international appeal.
Dance music often took on exotic associations, reflecting partying on holiday islands
from Ibiza to Goa. Beyond the sometimes crude incorporation of ethnic samples
in psy trance or ambient dance acts like Enigma, vibrant new dance musics have
formed; South Africa's kwaito, for example, took early inspiration from original US
house and techno artists, bypassing in part later European rave developments.[27]
The inter-relations are complex, following certain trade routes for the flow of
records; for example, Brazil's funk carioca took inspiration from late 1980s US
Miami bass and New York freestyle. International encounters have led to many
addictive sounds; Buraka Som Sistema are a Portuguese-Angolan collaboration,
founded in the Angolan kuduro dance sound.

Figure 8.2 attempts to chart some rough stylistic shifts across the decades from
the 1970s to 2010, with a bias toward European and North American genres.[28]
In constructing such a chart, we must accept that styles do not spring cleanly
into existence, but have blurred origins and cross-pollinate in their evolution. By
no means are the dates and genre breakdown definitive, but they are an honest
attempt to give some guidelines to the reader before encountering the mass profusion of stylistic variants within EDM. The more experimental listening-oriented
styles are left to Chapter 10. Whilst the Jamaican contribution is clearly marked,
and African-American contributions central to US popular music, many cultural

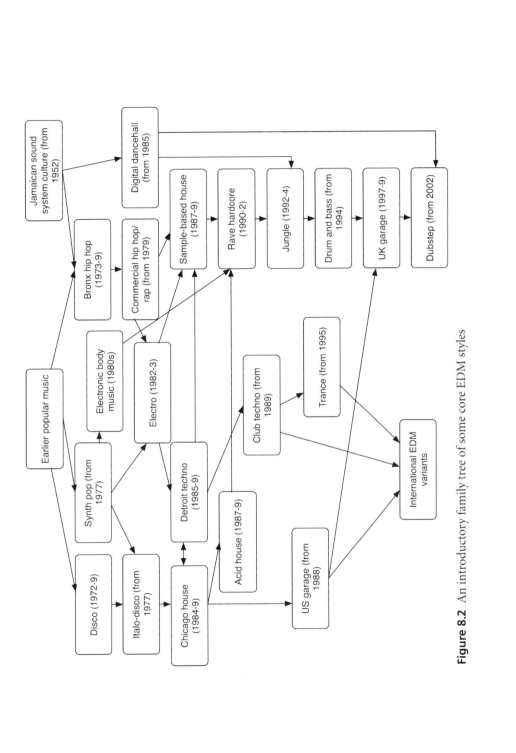

Figure 8.2 An introductory family tree of some core EDM styles

groups have had an input. For example, synth pop could not exist without 1960s pop music in general, whether Motown or the Beatles. International dance music really has brought into play a worldwide network of producers, whose innovations often feed back to multicultural centers like New York or London, but may also be promoted far more directly via the Internet.

Musical analysis of EDM

A universal description of electronic dance music is a dangerous proposition, given the breadth of styles. If we include the whole of hip hop and rap along with faster club musics, few consistent features may remain aside from the influence of certain core technologies, like sequencers and samplers, and a certain draw to loop-based cyclical repetition as a strong constructive principle for dance function. Different sub-genres emphasize different musical attributes, so that while we might investigate harmonic rhythm in international trance-techno, it may be irrelevant to minimal techno.

Simon Reynolds provides a thirteen-point breakdown of key elements of electronic dance music which is worth paraphrasing here.[29] It illuminates social factors in the main rave/club scenes as much as directly musical attributes:

(1) Technology obsessive machine music.
(2) Texture and rhythm promoted above melody and harmony.
(3) Physical responses to the music important (e.g., bass at high volume rattling bodies).
(4) Mass communion for dancing crowds.
(5) Pleasures clearly on the surface of the music, showy if shallow.
(6) Drugs.
(7) Primacy of sound over visuals, and crowd over any specific artist.
(8) Facelessness, anti-personality cult.
(9) Democratic, collective, generic.
(10) Full of cultural taxonomists impatient for new scenes and trends.
(11) Valuing underground tracks over sell-out mainstream hits.
(12) Site-specific (e.g., music created for the sound systems of particular clubs).
(13) Mixed crowds and mashed-up tracks.

Reynolds' list is by no means definitive, in that counter-examples can be found for many of the assertions, and the attributes often overlap or could do with further fleshing out. Point (2), on the musical priorities, varies substantially within the many styles of EDM; international trance-techno tracks often make use of thick harmonies, and even hardcore rave's "hoover" riffs are melodies, if featuring the multi-octave and portamento sound of the Roland Alpha Juno 2 keyboard's "WhatThe?" preset. The cult of DJ personality for a time seemed to overtake the cult of any individual musicians, but some artists established a strong market presence out of the rave scenes (Liam Howlett's the Prodigy, for example), and some musicians took on DJ gigs!

In analyzing musical components, researchers have worked further at dissecting tracks, both by a more traditional music analysis approach and also by analysis-by-synthesis in devising computer algorithms to emulate the character of particular styles. The latter forces the analysts to be absolutely explicit about the musical rules; it also has an interesting intersection with EDM practice, in that some artists have begun to themselves devise EDM-generating algorithms as part of their work. Admittedly, at present, this is usually on the experimental fringes discussed in more detail in Chapters 10 and 12, though some mass-marketed devices like the MadPlayer MP3 player (released in 2002) have offered this kind of functionality, inspiring use in hip-hop tournaments, for example.

From the direct analysis side, Mark Butler has published a much-cited volume, *Unlocking the Groove* (2006), included in this chapter's recommended further reading section, that especially treats the case of techno music construction and DJ performance. Butler particularly investigates the rhythmic properties of the music, emphasizing timbre and texture over pitch materials, and concentrating most strongly on the genre of techno rather than a wider set of styles.

We can trace the core properties of EDM back to the typical sequencer-based construction of the music; basic patterns are auditioned and prepared, in looping cyclical time. Pieces are built up from combinations of layers, where looped layers are sometimes of different lengths. The layers tend to correspond to the inherent multitrack layout of digital audio workstation packages and earlier sequencers. Butler's essential identified features are this "textural layering" where multiple seed loop patterns are juxtaposed in parallel streams, and the phenomena of "metrical dissonance" where "non-congruent" patterns operate in counterpoint to each other. The latter is reminiscent of aspects of isorhythm, cross-rhythm, and rhythmic polyphony, typically with larger-scale return points rather than continual non-alignment. The different lengths and rhythmic components of loops lead to metrical dissonance where they imply different local pulsation rates, though they will typically repeat on a larger hyper-measure scale; imagine, for instance, a four on the floor kick juxtaposed with an eighth note repeating hi-hat, and a further element based on dotted eighth notes; the latter will match to a beat every 3 beats and will repeat exactly with respect to a 4/4 bar every 12 beats/3 measures (12 is the lowest common multiple of 3 and 4). A common divisor of the rhythmic durations in each layer is usually found; thus, a sixteenth note grid fits comfortably within both the 4-beat and the 3-beat pattern.

The form of the music is also investigated by Butler. Built up from layers, a common strategy in the music's unraveling is to introduce, or drop out, layers one or more parts at a time. At certain sections, the bulk of the material is removed in favor of a breakdown (a moment particularly prevalent in trance or some drum and bass) only to allow the increasing tension of building up once more. Live performance with sequencers by some dance acts, for instance, work by Adamski or Orbital, reveals this dropping in or out of layers over time as a fundamental of the dynamic. DJ work also extends over long sets; compelled to maintain a ceaseless flow in beat-matching, the DJ-friendly records are those which have clear and explicit beats on extended intros and outros.

To speak more generally outside of Butler's core techno waves, we find a continuing inventiveness and skill of the producers. Encounters with music technology often lead to new musical directions, as creators take advantage of technological tricks to overcome problems of traditional musical skill. Gradually preparing sequenced parts allows the slowest of keyboard players to create the fastest and most elaborate lines, only given a little patience. A good example of an innovation is the sampling of whole chords, which are then assigned to individual keys; frantic chord punching lines are then sequenced, a hardcore rave and chart music stalwart circa 1990–2.

To summarize some musical attributes of core EDM styles, we might then note the following points:

- The presence of multiple complementary layers, some co-dependent in creating aggregate effects, most capable of being independently dropped in and out.
- Prominent bass, careful EQing of highs, mids, and lows.
- Percussion parts, from synthesized instruments to sampled loops such as breakbeats.
- Groove, from tight sixteenth note grids to looser swing patterns (the latter naturally working better at mid to slow tempi).
- A variable role for melody and harmony, from no deliberate harmonic or melodic associations (material as texture) to explicit chord sequences and riffs.
- The status of vocals, from instrumental tracks, through vocal cut-ups and vocoded manipulations, to diva vocals and MCing.
- Dance-orientation, leading to extended workouts, establishing substantial and addictive repetition sufficient to continually energize dancefloors and assist DJ set construction.

The reader might like to consider their own favorite EDM style and consider how well these properties hold there; what else might be essential to that style that differentiates it from others?

Certain recurring archetypes appear in EDM, from the four on the floor kick to more syncopated alternative rhythmic patterns. Example 8.1 shows three basic

Example 8.1 Some basic rhythmic figures from EDM

drum patterns of some import to EDM styles. The first is actually used very literally in Jamaican dancehall productions, particularly from the late 1980s into the 1990s, but is also a basic syncopated figure which appears in many world musics. Aside from digital dancehall, in EDM it appears for instance as a basic cut-up pattern in jungle, where a drum loop is re-triggered in groups of 3, 3, and 2 eighth notes (3+3+3+3+2+2 also appears frequently, in eighths or sixteenths, from skittering R&B productions to indie guitar tracks!). The central pattern is a disco template, and the starting point for house, where live drums become absolutely metronomic drum machine beats. Techno, US garage, gabba, and many more appropriate that four on the floor kick, whilst varying the hi-hat patterns and prominence of the snare (an archetypal dubstep drum pattern, for example, might keep the four on the floor but place a single snare on the third beat; drums tend to feel like they move at half rate in that style). A popular four on the floor variant is to just have a strong open hat sound on the offbeat eighth notes and no closed hat, and even to join this with an offbeat bass as well! Finally, the third pattern is a studio drum and bass beat, circa the mid-1990s. The secondary snare figure (and, in extensions, an intricately programmed ghost snare part) lends extra drive to the aggregate, but the fundamental here is the "2 step" kick-and-snare combination, which avoids the four on the floor with inter-linked streams. Intriguingly, a UK garage beat is very similar, just slower (perhaps 140bpm to a drum and bass 160bpm) and with swing on the sixteenths.

Analysis: Lil Louis, *French Kiss* (1989)

The analysis presented here follows a similar design to Mark Butler's analyses in his book. We list the basic patterns of different loop lengths – what Butler denotes the sound palette. We don't supply the full form of the work showing where all parts drop in and out, though we do examine layerings in the first three minutes, and discuss the most salient features of the piece.

Lil Louis is the pseudonym of Chicago house producer Marvin Louis Burns. *French Kiss* was an international success, reaching No. 1 in the US dance charts and the Netherlands main chart, and No. 2 in the UK and German charts, on the back of which Burns signed to major labels. The sexually explicit female vocal part (or should that be pant?) is reminiscent of Donna Summer's own breakthrough *Love to Love You Baby* (1975), with all vestiges of singing removed and only the orgasms remaining.

A definitive version of the piece is hard to source; discogs.com lists 25 versions of the single![30] However, the core patterns of the 1989 versions at least are stable in the most well-known mixes. The version dissected here is the London-printed FFRR 1989 maxi-CD, listed as having a 10:02 duration on the sleeve (as Lil Louis' Diamond Records self-published original), but actually running under 9:56 when ripped and in an audio editor.

An interesting curiosity of the track is the extreme tempo slow down to a standstill, and speed back up again, in the second half of the piece. *French Kiss* slows from 5:19, with a breakdown without drums from 6:10–6:23, then speeds up back to normal tempo (124 bpm); there is a further mini-break at 7:12 on the way, and a full return by 7:32, held for the remainder of the track. This no doubt had a novelty effect on the dancefloor, but also shows the possibilities of breaking out of functional dance loops to a more abstract section, to leverage the excitement of returning once more. Tempo is also an interesting aspect if encountering the piece on vinyl, as it would have originally been DJed; the ability of a DJ turntable to vary playback rate has an effect on the base rate (and home pitch) of the track, and could even be manipulated through the piece, perhaps to close the speed up much faster than the original rate. The inbuilt slow down and speed up in the recording was effected via a sequencer, however, for the pitch materials keep a constant reference pitch.

Example 8.2 presents the fundamental patterns utilized in the piece. Pitch is notated in F rather than F# to minimize accidentals; the real reference pitch on the CD master is midway between the two (a quartertone between F and F#). At a couple of points in the piece, following a Kraftwerkian transposition idea, the music drops by a tone for a few measures before the home pitch is restored. Although presented on a single stave, the repeat marks denote particular loops, and in the work these appear as different layers in counterpoint. Some variations are shown; the more complicated hi-hat pattern 1 which starts the work is replaced by 2 when the shaker pattern also starts up (1 later returns before 2 again). There is also no real bassline: *French Kiss* is one of those records, like Rhythim is Rhythim's *Strings of Life* (1987), where the kick drum is so important that it removes any real need for a bassline to compete at the low frequencies.

Table 8.1 lists the use of the patterns in the first three minutes of the piece, from measures 1 to 90. Preceding any of the bars is a teasing keyboard glissando figure, first running down then running up. The entire piece has a high held F in the background. From the table, note the large proportion of measures with four on the floor kick drum, but also the nonsquare constructions for changes in the layered patterns, not always following 4 or 8 measure changes (though always on measure boundaries, and with a

Table 8.1 *Formal structure of layering in the first three minutes of* French Kiss

Measures	Kick	Synth riff 1	Hi-hat 1	Snare fill	Snare 1	Shaker	Snare 2	Hi-hat 2	Synth riff 2	Synth riff 3a
1–27	X	X	X							
28	X	X	X	X						
29–36	X	X	X		X	X				
37–44	X	X			X	X		X		
45–56	X	X			X	X		X	X	
57–60	X	X	X		X	X			X	
61–70	X	X	X		X	X	X		X	
71–76	X	X			X	X	X	X		
77–80		X			X	X	X	X	X	
81		X	X		X	X	X		X	X (fade in)
82		X	X	X	X	X	X		X	X
83–4	X	X	X	X	X	X	X		X	X
85–90	x	X	X		X	X	X		X	X

Example 8.2 Basic patterns in Lil Louis' *French Kiss* (1989). Repeat marks denote particular looped patterns of lengths of 1, 2, 4 and 16 beats. The numbering of patterns denotes the order of appearance in the version of the track discussed here. Synth riffs 3a and 3b are related, are performed via the same instrument with delay, and are further modified in places in the work

4-bar temporary drop out of the kick). There are some subtle changes between the two hi-hat patterns, possibly just improvised or accidental at the sequencer. The whole work has a glorious combination of looser human playing/panting and decision making, and exciting rigid sequenced elements.

EDM is not universally admired, and aside from the many differences fans and producers have on the subject of its sub-genres, and the annoyances of everyday overhearing of headphone techno, some critics have tried to dismiss the music in general. Pioneering electroacoustic composer Pierre Henry has argued that the music is "far too dependent on the loudness, which allows the bass to be powerful. It's a music far too much connected to physiological reactions and not enough to mental reactions."[31] Yet, this critique seems to deny the central function of dancing intimately tied to the music's reception. Brewster and Broughton stage a defense through an Albert Goldman quote: "the time scale and the momentum of any physical activity is vastly different from the attention span of listening."[32] We might go further and state that some of the most appealing EDM can cater both to listening and dancing simultaneously; after all, as was mentioned at the outset of this chapter, there are strong evolutionary and cognitive links between these activities! Underground and chart dance music is not necessarily musicologically simple and should be approached with some respect. As Mark Butler notes on the importance of ambiguities of interpretation in EDM's multilayered rhythmic schemes: "dancers and listeners challenge the oft-expressed contention that rhythm in dance music (in general, not just in EDM) must be simple and obvious – a view that hinges upon a conception of the dancers as passive recipients of the rhythms they are given."[33]

Given EDM's massive family tree, this book can only begin to point you toward the rich web of work available. EDM's evolution is ongoing, from musics of London pirate radio to the international variations and dialogue in progress. EDM provides a wonderful opportunity to encounter stylistic change in the wild. "Ishkur's guide to electronic music" website (http://techno.org/electronic-music-guide), whilst providing some idiosyncratic biases in its creator's opinions and categorizations, is a good resource to start a journey through EDM styles. It is remarkable to hear tracks from different years and supposedly different genres alongside one another, and to realize how much overlap is really going on, and how much subtle differences are the foundation of ostensibly great separations of "style" diverging over time.

As a fitting cyclical close to a music of cycles, mention can be given to a later invasion of Chicago innovation circa 2010: juke house and Chicago footwork! The dance steps concentrate on fast footwork, like breakdancing with less arm movement, and the music mixes up some electro and house-tinged beats, with very literal and hypnotic repeating short vocal loops. Yet again, from a small US community scene, the music is inspiring other producers around the world to adopt, respond, and transform in "an ongoing transatlantic electronic dance music conversation."[34]

Further reading

Brewster, Bill and Broughton, Frank (2006) *Last Night a DJ Saved My Life* (London: Headline Book Publishing).

Butler, Mark J. (2006) *Unlocking the Groove* (Bloomington, IN: Indiana University Press).

Haslam, Dave (2001) *Adventures on the Wheels of Steel: The Rise of the Superstar DJs* (London: Fourth Estate).

Redhead, Steve (ed.) (1997) *The Clubcultures Reader* (Oxford: Blackwell).

Reynolds, Simon (2008) *Energy Flash: A Journey Through Rave Music and Dance Culture*, 2nd edn. (London: Picador).

Reynolds, Simon (1999) *Generation Ecstasy: Into the World of Techno and Rave Culture* (New York: Routledge).

Shapiro, Peter (ed.) (2000) *Modulations. A History of Electronic Music: Throbbing Words on Sound* (New York: Distributed Art Publishers Inc.).

Shapiro, Peter (2005) *Turn the Beat Around: The Secret History of Disco* (London: Faber & Faber).

Sicko, Dan (2010) *Techno Rebels: The Renegades of Electronic Funk*, 2nd edn. (Detroit, MI: Wayne State University Press).

Snowman, Rick (2004) *The Dance Music Manual: Tools, Toys and Techniques* (Oxford: Focal Press).

Thornton, Sarah (1995) *Club Cultures: Music, Media and Subcultural Capital* (Cambridge: Polity Press).

Toop, David (2000) *Rap Attack 3: African Rap to Global Hip Hop* (London: Serpent's Tail).

Chapter 9

Continuing the classical?

While recent chapters have dealt with aspects of popular culture and electronic music technology, in this one we'll return to some continuing lines of development from the golden age of experimentation in the 1950s described in Chapter 4. But before we dig in, let's pause to spend a moment on the ever-thorny problem of definitions.

Who says we have no class?

What do we mean by the word "classical" in relation to electronic music? It's certainly not a term in common use and seems as if it might allude to the sort of early experimental work we looked at in Chapter 4. However, as the title of the chapter suggests, we'll use the term "classical" here to refer in loose terms to some lines of musical development that can be traced back (perhaps along a somewhat bumpy path) to the traditions of Western art music. As we've seen, much electronic music development has and continues to take place in universities and conservatories associated with classical music, and many important electronic music composers and musicians were trained in such institutions.

That said, as a distinction the term "classical" is not unproblematic. Under its overarching umbrella, a huge variety of styles and approaches can be found; there is also considerable overlap between what we'll discuss here and material in other chapters. Aspects such as multimedia, sound art, digital sampling, etc., all find their place within the conservatoire electronic music world, itself just one area within a ubiquity of electronic music in the world today. As such, we should keep in mind that we'll be making only a few stops within a rough and heterogeneous geographical area, with rather indistinct borders that blur into other domains in surprising ways.

As we go through, we'll pause from time to time to look at (and query) some of the terms used for more common genres, styles, or practices. Note that these are not really distinct categories, or an exhaustive listing, but "centers of gravity." In many cases there is some confusion in terms of usage, with words that have technical meanings also being used colloquially to refer to styles, cultures, and ways of working.[1]

We'll also briefly discuss a few artists and their works. Given the space available and the range of things we could choose from, our selection cannot help but be little more than a sample, but will nevertheless hopefully give the reader a taste of what's happened since the 1960s.

Institutionalized music

As noted above, institutions and organizations have continued to play an important role in the development of electronic music.[2] That said, the heavy dependency on institutions for resources that we saw in the 1950s is now set against the widespread availability of relatively cheap commodity hardware and software for electronic music production. Indeed much, or even most, of the work that goes on in many institutions involved in electronic music is done using such resources. While commercial products (such as much Digital Audio Workstation software)[3] may not be perfectly suited to things like experimental music production, broader marketability allows for a high degree of refinement in terms of interface, features, and usability at a relatively low cost. The availability of such resources has also allowed for a great broadening of access, and the situation of the second half of the twentieth century – in which university studios were sometimes in use twenty-four hours a day – has been replaced with the cliché of every teenager composing music on a laptop in his or her bedroom.

Nevertheless, institutions still play an important role in terms of supporting custom development and research, particularly in areas that do not necessarily have widespread potential for commercial development. One important aspect of this has been their support for open source software projects such as the music programming language SuperCollider.[4] While the open source movement is not limited to academic involvement, this is a recent example of a long tradition of the public sharing of knowledge and the role of institutions as a public good.

Since the 1950s, a number of important electronic music institutions (some associated with universities, some not) have been established. One notable example is the Institut de Recherche et Coordination Acoustique/Musique (IRCAM), which was opened in Paris in 1977 with Pierre Boulez as Director. IRCAM's work has involved both scientific research and creative output, with a particular interest in works for instruments and electronics. Initially, at least, the pattern of development for the latter took the form of the Varèsian dream of composers collaborating with engineers, scientists, and programmers.[5]

To sample some other important institutions, we might mention the Institute for Music and Acoustics at the Center for Art and Media (ZKM)[6] in Karlsruhe,

Germany, the Studio for Electro-Instrumental Music (STEIM)[7] in Amsterdam, the Center for New Music and Audio Technologies (CNMAT)[8] at the University of California, Berkeley, the Center for Computer Research in Music and Acoustics (CCRMA)[9] at Stanford University, and (more recently) the Centro Mexicano para la Música y Artes Sonoras (CNMAS)[10] in Morelia (Michoacán), Mexico, the Centre for Interdisciplinary Research in Music, Media and Technology (CIRMMT)[11] at McGill University, and the Sonic Arts Research Centre (SARC)[12] at Queen's University in Belfast. (As you can see, the enthusiasm of electronic musicians for acronyms remains undiminished.)

It's also worth noting of course that despite a significant range of activity still going on in European and North American centers, "classically inclined" electronic music has evolved into a truly international culture, with significant studios throughout the Americas (for example, the Laboratorio de Investigación y Producción Musical in Buenos Aires), in Asia (for example, the China Electronic Music Center in Beijing),[13] and elsewhere in the world.

Elektronische Muzik

While the equipment of the Cologne studio is now in the process of being transferred to a museum, during its decades of operation, it provided a model for numerous other studios established around the world, many of them by composers who had worked there, such as Herbert Brün and Gottfried Michael Koenig.

Koenig's story also involved the fate of the Philips studio. In 1960, Philips decided that its research facilities could no longer house an electronic music studio, and its equipment passed to the University of Utrecht, where the Studio for Electronic Music (STEM) was founded. Koenig became Director there in 1964, and, with the acquisition of a PDP-15 computer in 1971, moved its research in the direction of algorithmic composition and digital sound synthesis. In 1986 – by then much larger and re-dubbed the Institute for Sonology – the institution was incorporated into the Royal Conservatory in The Hague, where it remains to this day. One of the first places where one could pursue degrees specializing in electronic music, numerous significant composers and computer musicians have trained there over the years, including Paul Berg, Kees Tazelaar, and Barry Truax.[14]

Reinforced concrète[15]

France's GRM[16] has remained a major center for production and presentation, commissioning works from numerous international composers. Further afield, musique acousmatique has proven to be an influential trend, with a number of communities of practice springing up around various institutions in different places in the world.

In 1970, the composers Françoise Barrière and Christian Clozier established the Institut International de Musique Électroacoustique de Bourges, whose studios hosted a plethora of international artists over its four decades of operation. They also supported a major international competition and festival: *Synthèse*.[17] Unfortunately, funding for the Institute was cut starting in 2008, and it closed in 2011.[18]

Another important locale for musique acousmatique is Montréal, where a vibrant local scene developed following the arrival of the French composer Francis Dhomont as a guest researcher at the Université de Montréal in 1979.[19] He ended up lecturing there from 1980 until 1996, and taught a number of prominent electroacoustic composers, including Robert Normandeau. Across town, Concordia University would also prove to be forward-looking in terms of electronic music, establishing a major in Electroacoustic Studies.[20] The Montréal style sometimes involves "cinematic," or quasi-narrative approaches, and there has been a particular interest in acousmatic music with video (contradiction in terms though that might seem to be).

In Belgium, the composer Annette Vande Gorne – a student of Schaeffer – established the L'Espace du son festival of acousmatic music in Brussels in 1984.[21] She taught electroacoustic composition at the conservatories in Liège, Brussels, and Mons, establishing another electroacoustics program at the latter.

While the prominence of Schaeffer's legacy is perhaps not unsurprising within the French-speaking world, the active acousmatic scene that has developed within the UK might have been harder to predict. One might speculate that this is in part a result of the fact that the BBC did not support a home-grown electronic music tradition in the way that other national broadcasters did, but in any case the UK has become something of a hotbed of acousmatic activity.

The New Zealand-born composer Denis Smalley, who taught for many years at the University of East Anglia and City University in London, received training at the GRM before moving to Britain in 1971. Largely responsible for bringing the French school's ideas to Britain (prior to which there had been greater interest in Stockhausen and the Cologne traditions), Smalley has been extremely active both as a teacher and as a post-Schaefferian theorist of electroacoustic music.[22] His work *Pentes* (1974), which evokes ideas of landscape and contains sounds of the Northumbrian pipes, remains a classic of British acousmatics.

The composer Jonty Harrison joined the faculty at the University of Birmingham in 1980, where he both built up the existing facilities and established BEAST (Birmingham ElectroAcoustic Sound Theatre), a loudspeaker orchestra for the presentation of electroacoustic music (see below). His 1982 work *Klang* is considered another classic. He has been particularly active in recent years in the area of multichannel composition, notably in the collection of four works, *ReCycle*, which was completed in 2006.[23] Like Smalley, Harrison has been extremely active as a teacher, and his former students have established numerous studios around the world on the Birmingham model.

There are pockets of acousmatic activity elsewhere in the world as well. One very active area is Latin America, which has produced many interesting composers, such as Alejandro Viñao, Javier Alvarez, and Julio d'Escriván. All of these artists trained at City University in London. While on the one hand, this provides an example of techniques and practice influencing people from other parts of the world, on the other hand, it is important to realize that this works in both directions. Alvarez and Normandeau, for example, are both very influential composers, whose individual takes on acousmatic music are highly respected in Europe.[24]

Presentation systems

The question of how to present electronic music, particularly in terms of aspects of space, has seen considerable development since the early idiosyncratic experiments of works like *Poème électronique* and *Kontakte*. Much of this work has been in the area of multi-loudspeaker systems. One interesting distinction that can be made is between systems and approaches intended to be used *interpretively*, and those that aspire to *neutrality*.

In 1974, the GRM established the Acousmonium as its concert system.[25] François Bayle says that he was partly inspired by the symphony orchestra, with its arrangements of specialized sound makers of different types:[26] "It seemed to me that the complexity of our mixes could only comfortably define itself across an analogue terracing of diffusers of differing calibre, whose positioning all over the stage would assure when in public a large scale legibility, comparable to, and adjustable like, that which was so carefully regulated in the composition studio."[27] Bayle's original layouts were largely frontal, with most of the loudspeakers on stage and in groups of different types. Other "acousmonia," such as BEAST, distribute loudspeakers more widely around the space (including at different distances) and may be somewhat more uniform in terms of loudspeaker types.[28]

Presenting a piece on such a system usually involves the practice of *sound diffusion*. In the classic case, this would involve using a fader board to route the two channels of a stereo piece to one or more pairs of speakers.[29] The diffuser may have any of a number of goals in mind, including localizing the sound in different parts of the performance space, making the sound *less* localized (i.e., more immersive or diffuse), providing a consistent stereo image across a wider area of the audience, enhancing the musical content already inherent in the piece (including any spatial aspects which may be implicit in the material), or interpreting the piece by playing it on loudspeakers with different (and hopefully appropriate) characters. Some systems (for example, the Gmebaphone, developed by the Bourges group) allow for processing the sound to aid in realizing these goals.[30]

Diffusion is a pragmatic approach to both the performance and spatialization of electronic music, in the sense that it makes it possible to adapt a piece to a particular performance context, perhaps exploiting unique idiosyncrasies of the space or set-up. It also grounds its practice in the musical material, with the general goal being the enhancement of the music, rather than that of replicating a precise spatial scene.

Other approaches aspire to the latter and tend to require systems consisting of (more or less) equally spaced and equally distant matched loudspeakers. The two most notable approaches are *Ambisonics*[31] and *Vector Base Amplitude Panning* (VBAP).[32] Both of these are concerned with simulating direction and are flexible (within certain limitations) in terms of speaker layouts. Some composers use such techniques to create multichannel fixed media pieces that target particular set-ups. (A ring of eight equally spaced speakers is one particularly common layout, as are 5.1 systems like those found in home cinema set-ups.) Conversely, they also form the technical basis of several emerging "object-based" spatialization schemes, which usually pair soundfiles with time-varying information about direction, etc. One example of a system that makes use of such an approach is the ZKM Klangdom.[33]

Hybridization is of course possible and in recent years the BEAST system, for example, has evolved to accommodate stereo and multichannel diffusion, fixed layout pieces, and various approaches to "massively multichannel" composition, all using a custom software system.[34]

Definition check: Acousmatic or "fixed media" music

Strictly speaking, acousmatic music is no more a style than electronic music is. In a loose sense, it might simply mean music played over loudspeakers, in which the sound source is neither present nor apparent. In this sense, it can be said to encompass all *fixed media* (in old parlance "tape") music, without live performers or other media, regardless of whether it is based on recorded or synthetic sounds. (In many cases, the source is impossible to distinguish anyway!) In a broad sense, one can see that there is an international community of people doing such fixed media work, which long ago transcended the old disputes about material, whatever the locally favored dialects and techniques.

Figure 9.1 BEAST in rehearsal at the Sound Around Festival in Copenhagen. Photo by Scott Wilson

In contrast to this general usage, the term "acousmatic music" is also sometimes used colloquially to refer to music that derives in some way from the practice of the Paris studio – doubtless because the term originated there – and various post-Schaefferian commentators (Bayle, Smalley) have questioned or attempted to refine the definition of the term "acousmatic" over the years.[35] In an article describing some of the debates that took place about this, Dhomont spoke of the need for a new term, calling acousmatic music a "genre" and speaking of the need to distinguish acousmatic practice from other sorts of electronic music.[36]

With such caveats in mind, we can attempt to paint some broad strokes in terms of what people mean when they say "acousmatic music":

- Acousmatic pieces take the form of fixed media (these days, digital sound files) and are meant to be played over loudspeakers, including multi-loudspeaker set-ups.
- Acousmatic music does not limit itself to (but does not exclude) sonic material having the scale or properties of instrumental music (e.g., using traditional systems of pitch).

- Despite the focus in Schaefferian theory on sonic properties and reduced listening, much acousmatic music deliberately plays with the recognizability of recorded sound material.
- Harrison says acousmatic music "evolves from characteristics inherent in the specific material, [and is] not conceptualised before the sonic event."[37] This point renders acousmatic compositional practice distinct from "conceptual" approaches such as Eimert's preferred serial techniques, and outlines a strategy for the development of material and form. (This is probably a more specifically "French" definition.)
- Some acousmatic music is cinematic or narrative-driven, deliberately evoking particular soundscapes or telling a story (e.g., the works of Normandeau for the former and those of Katharine Norman for the latter).
- Acousmatic music uses timbre as an element in its musical discourse. This is also true of percussion music, for example. (This is not such a difficult concept to grasp. If we view contrast as a basic principle of musical form, timbre becomes simply another element to contrast.) In a more rigorously Schaefferian sense, some would say that acousmatic composers should have an "acousmatic intent" with regard to their material,[38] but it should be noted that again this describes a compositional attitude rather than a sonic result.

Caged music

The lines of development established by John Cage in his works and writings on music (electronic and otherwise) have also proved very influential, and electronics have proved particularly fertile ground for the development of "experimental" music.

Cage's collaborator David Tudor was recognized initially as a virtuoso pianist (he provided definitive interpretations of works by Cage, Stockhausen, and Boulez), but gradually abandoned performing and became a composer of electronic music. Tudor's pieces often crossed the line between music and installation art, and made use of both custom and off-the-shelf electronics (the latter often subverted from their original purpose). His best-known works are the four *Rainforest* pieces. Often realized collaboratively, *Rainforest IV* (1973) consists of a number of (usually resonant) physical objects, which are attached to acoustic transducers. (Imagine a loudspeaker where the speaker cone has been replaced with an object such as a sheet of metal or a jar.) The transducers are fed with electronic signals carefully designed to activate the object's resonance. The sounds produced can be picked up and (if need be) amplified, or in more elaborate versions fed into other objects to create an ecosystem of resonance (the rainforest!). *Rainforest IV* is a good example of a system-as-composition. As Nicolas Collins wrote, in Tudor's pieces "the circuit – whether built from scratch, a customized commercial device, or store-bought and scrutinized to death – became the score."[39] Because of its inclusiveness, *Rainforest IV* has remained a popular workshop piece. Indeed, the collective Composers Inside Electronics (which ultimately included Tudor, Paul DeMarinis, John Driscoll, Phil Edelstein, Linda Fisher, Russell Frehling, Ralph Jones, Martin Kalve, and Bill Viola) grew out of its first realization.

Alvin Lucier's music has been described as having a kind of "distilled simplicity,"[40] and it is certainly true that his most significant pieces often seem to consist less of traditional musical discourse than of (often surprisingly beautiful) demonstrations of acoustic phenomena. His *In Memoriam Jon Higgins* (1984) for clarinet and sine wave oscillator demonstrates this reductive quality well. Over the course of about twenty minutes, the frequency of the oscillator rises "from the marrow of the bones to the very centre of the eyes," as one reviewer put it,[41] while the clarinet sustains tones at close to the oscillator's pitch. The result is a series of acoustic beating effects, which are further enhanced when the oscillator crosses through the resonant frequencies of the room, creating illusions in terms of location. The overall effect is surprisingly beautiful and difficult to follow in time, probably because it so rigorously eschews traditional musical discourse. When once asked why he chose to have a single, constant, twenty-minute unidirectional sweep, rather than a more elaborate form involving changes of direction and speed, Lucier replied, "Because then you would have language. I just want you to hear the beats!"[42]

Lucier's best-known work, 1969's *"I am sitting in a room,"* also highlights room resonance.[43] A realization of the piece consists of the performer reading a text within a given room while recording it. This recording is then played back and is in turn recorded. This cycle repeats until the original text has been completely dissolved by the resonances of the individual room, with the words replaced by patterns of pitch that reflect the rhythm of the original. The result will vary considerably depending on the speaker, the text, and (especially) the room. In this sense, the piece is as much a set of instructions for a process as it is a composition. For the most part, performances of *"I am sitting in a room"* are prepared in advance (possibly played back in a different room), but real-time versions are possible, as are variants with multiple rooms, moving the microphone, etc.[44]

Lucier was part of a generation of experimental composers working with electronics and exchanging ideas and techniques. Among the many worth mentioning are David Behrman, Gordon Mumma, and Robert Ashley, who together with Lucier made up the Sonic Arts Union.[45] He taught for many years at Wesleyan University in Middletown, CT, and like Tudor he has served as a mentor and inspiration for many young composers and sound artists.

Definition check: Experimental music™ (electronic department)

Experimental music is another one of those terms that seems to resist a uniform definition.[46] In a general sense, it might mean any music whose outcome was unknown at the time of its development, or which experimented with musical language, techniques, or resources in some way. Certainly, up until the mid-twentieth century, it was used very broadly (including by Schaeffer).

Another of the great musical arguments of the twentieth century took place between "European avant-garde" composers such as Stockhausen and Boulez, and the followers of more "American" developments; most specifically the ideas of Cage. In much usage, "experimental music" has come to distinguish the latter as distinct from the former,[47] and for the purposes of this discussion we'll consider work in the post-Cageian tradition.[48]

Some possible examples of typically post-Cageian experimental music (not only of the electronic variety) are as follows:

- Works in which the realization is in some way not pre-determined ("indeterminancy" in Cage's parlance). Many experimental electronic works have no pre-determined form and may blur the lines between music and sound art (see Chapter 11).
- Works which make use of random elements to vary the result (chance). Note that this is not the same as indeterminacy. Works can be indeterminate because of the use of real-time chance operations, for instance, but also for other reasons, and works can be generated using chance procedures without being indeterminate at the time of realization. Cage's piece *Williams Mix* (1953) is an example of the latter, in that a given realization is fixed and repeatable.
- Works which explore the notion of "system-as-piece." Works by post-Lucier/Tudor artists such as Nicolas Collins and Ron Kuivila often explore the properties (acoustic and otherwise) of spaces and/or electronic systems. Collins' *Pea Soup* (1974) uses a feedback system to explore the resonant properties of the space in which it presented.[49] Rather than a pre-determined sequence of events (which might form a sort of "narrative" structure), a performance of such a piece might consist of a reasonably exhaustive exploration of the system's possibilities or the playing out of a process.

Soundmarks not sound objects, Schafer not Schaeffer

In 1971, the Canadian composer R. Murray Schafer established the World Sound-scape Project (WSP) at Simon Fraser University in Vancouver. Joined by numerous composers and researchers – including Barry Truax (also known for his pioneering work in granular synthesis and granulation of sampled sound) and Hildegard Westerkamp – Schafer set out to establish an ecological approach to the study of sound in the environment.[50] This ultimately led to the establishment of *acoustic ecology* as a discipline, which Truax defines as "the study of the effects of the acoustic environment, or soundscape, on the physical responses or behavioural characteristics of those living within it. Its particular aim is to draw attention to imbalances which may have unhealthy or inimical effects."[51] For this reason, acoustic ecology can be seen as the sonic wing of the environmental movement.[52]

The group produced a number of books, including Schafer's *The Tuning of the World* and Truax's *Handbook for Acoustic Ecology*, as well as a number of recordings documenting natural and artificial soundscapes (which in some cases were under threat). These recordings formed a tape archive potentially analogous to a cultural history museum or a sampling seedbank, and were the basis of a number of record releases.

In the process of producing these, a compositional practice gradually emerged. At first, this was for practical reasons – i.e., artificially constructing soundscapes out of separate recordings which could not be captured through straightforward documentation – or to compress timescales so that changes related to the passage of time or moving location could be more easily appreciated. One classic example was a recording made to capture the experience of entering the Vancouver harbor by boat. The recording was assembled artificially so as to prevent motor noise from dominating, and what would have been a thirty-minute journey was condensed into seven minutes, in order to highlight the significant aspects of the soundscape in a more accessible format.

Eventually, composers such as Westerkamp and Truax began producing *soundscape compositions* which were intended to stand alone as works of art, separate from the activities of the WSP. Perhaps inevitably, this led to an increased artificiality, but the works tended to retain their focus on environmental and ecological concerns. In contrast to early Schaefferian ideas, which (according to acousmatic listening practice) emphasized sonic properties over source signification, soundscape compositions tend to use recorded sounds *precisely for* their semantic implications. In response to the notion of the *l'objet sonore*, acoustic ecology posits the *soundmark*, the acoustic equivalent of a landmark, a sound that has particular social or cultural significance for a given community.

Westerkamp's *Beneath the Forest Floor* (1992) remains a seminal work in the genre, creating a sort of hyper-real composed soundscape from recordings made in old-growth forests in British Columbia. A variety of natural sounds and (perhaps inevitably) unnatural ones, such as the sounds of logging, pass by the listener at different distances, sometimes alone, sometimes in carefully framed environmental vignettes.

The ideas of the WSP eventually fed into the World Forum for Acoustic Ecology, an international collective of composers and researchers interested in the social, cultural, and ecological aspects of sonic environments.[53] Meanwhile, a variety of similar practices have grown up in other contexts, some influenced by the WSP, some not. As elsewhere in this chapter, these are incredibly varied, including such work as the detailed and revealing field recordings of Chris Watson[54] and the "sound sculptures" and installations of Bill Fontana (see also Chapter 11).[55]

Definition check: Soundscape composition

As noted above, soundscape composition of the sort deriving from the practice of the WSP tends to have "green" concerns at heart. That said, not all of the similar practices which have developed around the world involving the use of clearly recognizable real-world sound are as "politically minded" as the Vancouver tradition. While bearing in mind that there is a fair amount of variety in practice, characteristics that are common in this genre include the following:

- Environmental concerns, and an ecological approach to sound.
- The use of recorded sound *for* its semantic effect, i.e., sounds are symbols of their sources, their environments, and/or related aspects of the real world, rather than elements of an abstract musical discourse.
- The use of the microphone as microscope, or focusing device, providing emphasis where it would not occur in the natural soundscape or allowing us to hear what we can't or wouldn't hear normally.
- A tendency to frame or edit soundscapes for dramatic or narrative effect.

Instrumentally conceived electronic music and electronically conceived instrumental music

As we've seen throughout this book, one common line of development is replacing instrumental resources with electronic ones, for reasons of convenience, cost, access to new sounds, etc. Classically trained electronic musicians do this as well, some-times using electronic sounds which behave like instruments, sometimes combining acoustic instruments with electroacoustic textures. What is certain from this is that instrumental and electroacoustic compositional practice have informed each other considerably over the last half-century.

The Argentinian-born American composer Mario Davidovsky is well known for his *Synchronisms* series of pieces, written for various instruments and tape. At the time of this writing, there are twelve such works, written between 1963 and 2006.[56] The pieces are interesting in that they generally take the sonic properties of the instruments as starting points for the tape material, but diverge, sometimes creating interesting sonic composites. In many cases, the tape parts "behave" instrumen-tally, that is, use tempered pitch structures, instrumentally informed gestures, and "sound" on a human scale. One could almost imagine them being arranged for a live ensemble, were it not for the sounds produced. A contrary example can be found in *Synchronisms No. 5* for percussion ensemble and tape. The composer Eric Chaslow has described the percussionists as behaving like an "electronic ensemble" in their own right.[57]

Electronic keyboards and amplification were stock features of early minimalist music, and post-minimal composers have continued and expanded upon the elec-tronic element. The composers Julia Wolfe, Michael Gordon, and David Lang – collectively responsible for the multifaceted *Bang on a Can* organization in New York[58] – create music which combines the pulse and repetitive patterns of minimal-ism with the language and sounds of jazz, world music, and especially rock, with all the electrification that implies. Gordon's *Industry* from 1992 severely processes a solo cello using guitar effects such as distortion, thereby creating a sort of "heavy metal" string sound. His fifty-two-minute *Trance* from 1995 is scored for a large ensemble which includes winds, percussion, strings, three keyboards, accordion, electric guitar, bass guitar, and tape, all heavily amplified.

The Hungarian composer György Ligeti's works provide an interesting example of electronic music informing instrumental composition practice. Following some exploration into electronic composition at the Cologne studio, Ligeti returned to instrumental work, but his later compositions (particularly those of the 1960s such as *Atmosphères* (1961) and *Lux Aeterna* (1966)) exhibit a sensitivity to timbre and the design of complex textures that would seem to have been informed by electroacoustic techniques.[59]

The composers whose practice falls under the label of *spectralism* represent another example of the influence of electronic music on instrumental practice. In a strange echo of history, both French and German schools of spectralism developed – each influenced by the classic studio practice in their countries and each practicing its own kind of "instrumental synthesis," both with and without electronic components.

The French group *L'Itinéraire*, which included composers such as Gérard Grisey and Tristan Murail, made use of spectrographic analysis to derive time-varying pitch material. They would take the partials of an analyzed acoustic sound (for example, a gong), possibly altered via modulation procedures, and orchestrate this for instrumental ensembles. The opening of Grisey's *Partiels* (1975) is a classic example, in which a trombone spectrum is repeatedly "synthesized" by an ensemble, in gradually modified form. While not really sounding like a trombone (it's not really intended to), the result rests on the border between harmony and timbre. The German "Feedback" group consisted largely of former students and assistants of Stockhausen (not necessarily Germans), and included Johannes Fritsch, Clarence Barlow, Peter Eotvos, and the Québécois composer Claude Vivier. Vivier's best-known work is 1980's *Lonely Child* for soprano and orchestra. It consists of a kind of gradually more elaborated monody, in which a single line becomes timbrally richer through the addition of homophonic lines calculated using ring modulation techniques.[60]

Definition check: Mixed music

Categories with names like "mixed music" are common these days in calls for competitions or festivals. Usually this refers to some mixing of electroacoustic sounds with acoustic, or at least partially acoustic (think electric guitar!) instrumental performance.

The classic model for this is the "instrument and tape" piece, but in practice a mixed music piece might include any of the following aspects:

(1) Live processing of the instrumental sound – this in itself is a huge area, with a range of possibilities including anything from simple amplification to rendering the source unrecognizable.

(2) Meta-instruments – this could include new or modified versions of traditional instruments (for example, the *Hyperbow*, developed at MIT)[61] and range from almost unnoticeable additions to invasive changes which require the performer to learn new techniques. Wiring the performer with sensors would also fall under this category.

(3) What we might call "Tape Plus," i.e., the use of software to provide more flexible playback of pre-recorded material – this often takes the form of a series of cues, allowing performers more scope in phrasing and interpretation than a single fixed-media part (which might require a stop watch or click track in headphones for synchronization).

(4) Live performance of the electroacoustic element – this could be anything from triggering a simple series of cues to a virtuoso performance on a custom-built instrument.

(5) Some form of machine listening or interactivity – again, a huge area, which runs the gamut from using instrumental input in order to trigger electronic events to fully fledged computer improvisers such as George Lewis' *Voyager* software.[62]

(6) Computer-assisted instrumental composition using software such as *Open Music* – strictly speaking, this is not *mixed* music, falling under the related category of *computer-assisted composition*, but can appear in electronic music festivals because of the machine element in composition.

Conclusions

Let's end the chapter as we began, by questioning our definitions and assumptions, and trying to fill in some of the ground between the few stops we've made on our whirlwind tour. How meaningful are the distinctions we've made between genres and practices? Certainly, we can find many examples of crossover. One example is the composer Luc Ferrari, who was closely associated for many years with the GRM and was its director from 1962 to 1963. Ferrari is perhaps best known for his series of *Presque rien* (*Almost nothing*) pieces. These began in 1970 with his *Presque rien No. 1 "Le Lever du jour au bord de la mer,"* which in essence consists of a day-long field recording of a beach edited down to twenty-one minutes. In this we can see a composer operating in the heart of *musique acousmatique* who is nevertheless most noted for his quasi-minimalist proto-soundscape compositions.[63] Moreover, we would not have to look very hard to find examples of pieces from any of the loose categories above that exhibit characteristics of the others, and while making strict distinctions about a type of music may serve to emphasize what makes it unique or interesting (or to advance one's career!), it is often the case that rhetoric and practice are not in agreement.

On closer examination, the boundaries between the "classical" and other areas of electronic music also prove surprisingly porous. Many popular artists received their training in programs in "classical music" institutions. Some members of the Montréal band Arcade Fire are graduates of Concordia's electroacoustic composition program, for instance.[64] Conversely, many "classical" composers are influenced by popular electronic music. One example is Gabriel Prokofiev (the grandson of Sergei and trained at the University of Birmingham and the University of York) whose *Concerto for Turntables and Orchestra* was performed at the BBC Proms in 2011.[65] DJ Spooky (otherwise known as Paul D. Miller)[66] has worked with a number of classical music composers such as Iannis Xenakis and Pierre Boulez, including remixing the latter's *Pli Selon Pli* (1957–62, rev. 1989). New generations of electroa-coustic composers may be found inside and outside of educational institutions and new music institutes; they may consider work in art music traditions the core of their output or only part of a wide-ranging portfolio. We could mention Manuella Blackburn, Sheongah Sheh, Daniel Blinkhorn, and Natasha Barrett, amongst many others, but the most important thing to understand is that these developments are continuing worldwide, with all the freedom of exchange afforded by the Internet era.

In a broader sense, all of this is indicative of a broader electronic music culture in which (any knee-jerk assertions about ivory towerism aside), the "classical" contin-ues to play an important part, both informing and being informed by other sorts of electronic music and techniques.

Further reading

Collins, Nicolas (2004) "Composers inside electronics: Music after David Tudor," *Leonardo Music Journal*, 14(1): 1–3.

Emmerson, Simon (ed.) (1986) *The Language of Electroacoustic Music* (London: Macmillan).

Landy, Leigh (2007) *Understanding the Art of Sound Organisation* (Cambridge, MA: MIT Press).

Schrader, Barry (1982) *Introduction to Electro-Acoustic Music* (Englewood Cliffs, NJ: Pren-tice Hall).

Truax, Barry (2001) *Handbook for Acoustic Ecology* [CD-ROM] (Vancouver: Cambridge Street Publishing).

Wishart, Trevor (1996) *On Sonic Art* (Amsterdam: Harwood Academic Publishers).

Chapter 10

Experimental electronica

Not all experimental electronic music artists are associated with a formalized art world or academia. This chapter explores rich musics that have grown through the enthusiasm and graft of practitioners on the fringes of popular music, or just simply exploring their own path in alternative and underground culture. It would hardly be accurate to call these exponents of experimental electronica popular musicians, since their audiences are certainly not the mass audiences of the pop charts, even though there are sometimes sufficient followers to support distinct niches of activity and a few chief exponents in full-time creation. Further, this chapter will bring together diverse sonic bedfellows that may sit rather uncomfortably alongside one another in their aesthetics, noise music being chief amongst the dissenters. Nonetheless, the historical overlap of the development of these forms often looks back to 1970s counterculture.

The term "electronica" itself was adopted in the US as a marketing umbrella in the late 1990s, particularly to cover electronic dance music acts, and the influence of this on popular music in general (such as Madonna's collaboration with William Orbit on *Ray of Light* (1998)). In Europe, the term has more generally alluded to electronic music in general (perhaps particularly some of the musics touched on in this chapter, post-1970) and in Latin-derived languages simply means electronic music.[1] We title the chapter "Experimental electronica" to make it clear that the majority of artists considered herein are not exactly mainstream pop musicians, but new experimenters in electronic music. For example, rather than the Cabaret Voltaire of the 1980s, who became more commercially focused, we might prefer to consider the model of Cabaret Voltaire in 1970s Sheffield, primarily concerned with experiment in new sounds.

From ambient music to electronic listening music

We begin gently. Music's listening modes are varied, and electronic music is certainly not restricted to explicit, percussion-heavy music for dancing, though we shall investigate an interesting link to club culture later in this section. We treat here some of the sparser, sometimes colder, certainly more abstract and chilled-out music, often intended for reflective listening and occasionally exactly designed for non-intrusion. Although such listening roles are not new in world music, a cursory listen to compression-heavy rock and pop radio might conceal the presence of less overtly stated music.

Ambient music did not start with Brian Eno, though he is often credited with it, and certainly had a hand in the popularization and naming of the genre in the 1970s.[2] It is a peculiar genre, inasmuch as to be consistent with its own spirit, it might not want to call total attention to itself. Satie's *Furniture Music* (1920) espoused the art of blending into the background,[3] and notions of functional background music abound, for example, for centuries of receptions, restaurants, and dinner parties. A related notion is music intended to influence mood without becoming the full focus of attention, from film music to Muzak's elevator productivity (the company was established in 1934).

Inasmuch as ambient music might tend to be characterized by certain restrained sonic gestures, like nature recordings, isolated synthesized strings, slow or unintrusive sequenced patterns, and stripped-down textures, we can identify many precursors before Eno's *Ambient 1: Music for Airports* (1978). Raymond Scott, the prodigious inventor-musician, had explored the potential of sleepy electronic music for the very young with his trio of volumes of *Soothing Sounds for Baby* (1964). Beaver and Krause's *In a Wild Sanctuary* (1970) juxtaposes environmental with synthesized sound, though is mostly more raucous than ambient in feeling. Wendy Carlos' *Sonic Seasonings* (1972) is a combination of nature recordings and soft analog synthesis that achieves a more peaceful symbiosis. Particularly implicated in the chain of influence on Eno are the German experimental group Cluster (who released their first eponymous album in 1971, but had been active under the guise of Kluster preceding this) and their later manifestation as Harmonia, who Eno joined in 1976 for the Harmonia album *Tracks and Traces* (1976) and continued in collaboration with for a few years. The hypnotism of sequenced synthesizer patterns is found explicitly in such progressive synth acts as Tangerine Dream, and the aesthetic of chilly atmosphere turns up in post-punk releases like *Eskimo* (1979) by the Residents.[4] As Eno's focus on an aesthetic of non-intrusion, explicitly separate from elevator music, is itself not original in the longer context of experimental music, so the sonic material is also not isolated.

If ambient music was relatively dormant in the 1980s, its purer principles were often confused with the vapidity of new age music. Eno's work had been critically noted, but was not massively successful commercially. Ironically, within a decade or so, the very musics which seemed most in opposition, such as the massive amplified beats of club electronic dance music, led to an opportunity for ambient to re-invent itself, if shorn of Eno's aesthetic argument, as chill-out and after-club music. Clubbers needed places of refuge from the storm of bass and percussion, music which operated down-tempo of the main rooms. Chill-out rooms begin to be specifically established from around 1989 in UK clubs, such as with the Orb's residency at Heaven (though precedents could be found in Ibiza bars, dub reggae, or original 1960s psychedelia, for example). The Orb's *A Huge Ever Growing Pulsating Brain That Rules from the Centre of the Ultraworld* (1989) or the KLF's *Chill Out* (1990) (born after the Orb's Alex Paterson fell out with his original collaborator, the KLF's Jimmy Cauty) are audio documents from this period revealing a textural sensibility tending toward the reverberant, as well as a use of samples commensurate with the times, often lifted from exotic shores. From such seeds, new breeds of electronic listening music were formed, as new listeners to electronic music, perhaps tempted in by club culture, found new music to listen to away from the club setting.

The fringes of electronic dance music provide much ground for experiment. Whilst Warp Records began as a Sheffield bleep and bass outfit, it actively pursued the possibilities of electronic listening music, sometimes for alternative clubbing experiences, but mainly for home consumption. The cover of *Artificial Intelligence* (1992) models a robot relaxing in its living room. The press notes Warp felt compelled to release in 1994 on the subject are very interesting for their insights. On the relation of electronic listening music to ambient music, Warp was fully aware of the aesthetic distinction of the background and pushed its releases to the foreground: "music which has a mellow feel or has no beats is often mistakenly called Ambient. Pure ambient music, as the name suggests, is music which sets an ambient feel to the room you are in. The music on this Album is structured and melodic and requires attentive listening. It is not an ambient album."[5] On the other hand, Richard James, involved in the *Artificial Intelligence* project as Polygon Window, simultaneously released *Selected Ambient Works 85–92* (1992) as Aphex Twin. His 1994 follow-up on Warp, all stark synthesis with huge reverb, was hailed as the true heir of Eno's 1970s work.

Controversy has lingered over Warp's *Artificial Intelligence* project since mailing lists adopted terms such as intelligent dance music, intelligent techno, and brain-dance. The label certainly did not intend that all other EDM-influenced music be judged "unintelligent." As Warp's press team noted: "Artificial Intelligence is not a term that was intended to be bastardised into the word Intelligent-Techno. The phrase was never intended to be aimed at 'intelligent' people (whatever *they* are), it was simply computer terminology which seemed appropriate to the style of music and was supposed to be a bit of a tongue-in-cheek dig at the people who said it was music made by computers that had no soul. We were trying to say that the computer was merely a tool to make music and that there was as much emotion in this music as in any other genre."[6] Whatever these terminological anxieties, Warp artists associated with the first *Artificial Intelligence* compilation, such as Autechre and Plaid, have gone on to establish careers in electronic music which flirt around the intersection of EDM and listening experience. Most aspects of their work are far removed from any gentle notion of chill-out music, though the beauties of washing sound and moments away from simple percussive beats are often pursued.

Though one of the most famous, Warp was not the only record label to make a name for itself in an intensive era of new electronic listening music accompanying the EDM boom. British artists might cluster to Warp, although relations extended to, for example, peers on Rephlex (from 1991) or Planet Mu (from 1995). Other famous labels include Germany's Mille-Plateaux (from 1993) and Austria's Mego (from 1994), whose artists took their own paths through this field, often in territory closer to the upcoming sections of this chapter. Individual relationships with the weight of electronic music history are negotiated, for example, in Autechre's acknowledgement of Bernard Parmegiani and Paul Lansky. Paul Lansky also provided an element of a Radiohead track as that supposed guitar band took a sidestep into electronica with *Kid A* (2000); arguably, no extra publicity was needed here for electronic listening music, which had proved its commercial viability and remains an active field of endeavor for home studio artists.

Noise musics

" . . . an offensive accumulation of whacks of a scalpel in your ears at the highest level of the potentiometer"[7] is how Pierre Schaeffer described Iannis Xenakis' work *Bohor* (1962), despite its dedication to him, premiered at immense playback volume. Heavily injured whilst in a resistance group in Greece in the Second World War, Xenakis' hearing was compromised and caused him to push electronic amplification harder than others found reasonable.[8] His exploration of harsh and uncompromising sound has made him a revered spiritual father figure in some noise scenes.

If the ambient music of the previous section provided too peaceful a moment of repose, the subversive response might be to blast out a very loud and scary sound. However, we should avoid the idea that all noise music is continuous extremes of loudness, much as the limits of amplification are tempting to so many of its artists. Noise music's texture varies greatly and explores many points across a wide range of dynamics: Subversion in the context of a very noisy concert may be a quiet work. If noise music's developmental path is traced back to the 1970s, we find that subversive statements are its foundation and that the pioneers were performance artists.

Throbbing Gristle (TG) grew as a rock performance outlet for artists who had previously performed in art galleries as COUM Transmissions (1969–76). Some of their early art gallery performances were just as shocking, if not more so, given their sexually explicit bodily nature, as the later controversial imagery and sounds of

TG's live shows. Just as Roxy Music had formed with a core of art school graduates, other experimental bands saw this as a viable route to bring art concepts to a wider audience. In doing so, TG spawned the term "industrial" (used for their record label name), which later took on harder set ramifications as a music of metallic percussion and machine recordings.

Here again, precedents can be traced to the Futurist art movement of the 1910s and especially Luigi Russolo's Intonarumori, noise makers built to expand the palette of instrumental sound toward the industrial age soundscape of factories and motorized vehicles. Russolo wrote in his 1913 tract *The Art of Noise* that "Futurist musicians must continually enlarge and enrich the field of sounds . . . We therefore invite young musicians of talent to conduct a sustained observation of all noises . . . the motors and machines of our industrial cities will one day be consciously attuned, so that every factory will be transformed into an intoxicating orchestra of noises."[9] Sirens, military technology, and industrial engines fashionably occurred in the work of composers of the 1920s such as Edgard Varèse, George Antheil, and Arseny Avraamov. The manifesto name was later adopted, appropriately enough, by a sample-band of the 1980s.

TG's music is itself rather variable in stylistic pre-occupation, from improvised freak-outs and punk looseness to hypnotic beats and electronic chaos, all against distorted utterances and frantic cut-ups. It does not firmly establish the highly sustained blast of noise, or the industrial percussion and sound sampling, of later acts, but does make clear the possibilities of a highly liberated attitude to sound, anarchist political edges to presentation and content, and a backbone of custom-built electronics (through such means as Chris Carter's Gristlizer effect[10] and tape delays). Genesis P-Orridge's vocal screams and roars on a track like *Discipline* (1981) are quite close to the later thrash metal vocalists.

The artists who quickly followed these paths operated in the freedoms of the post-punk period, when synthesizers were but one easily accessible route to noise making. Gritty distorted tape loops (often through push-button editing of cassettes) were a common resource, as in Boyd Rice/Non's piece *Knife Ladder* (1979) or the work of Whitehouse (as with TG, flirtation with extremes of imagery and ideology often accompanied extreme pushing of sound resources). Whilst some artists might have thought they operated free of history, others admitted rich precedents in experimental music, as noted by Nurse with Wounds' list of influences in the liner notes of *Chance Meeting on a Dissecting Table of a Sewing Machine and an Umbrella* (1979). Any sounding object could be organized, recorded, and amplified; Einstürzende Neubauten (Collapsing New Buildings), when they weren't trying to apply a pneumatic drill to the central pillar from the newly opened Haçienda nightclub[11] or running a *Concerto for Voice and Machinery* at the ICA (in 1984),[12] might pursue "noise of blood captured with a foetal heartbeat detector."[13] They weren't the only metal-bashing band, given the metal percussion often underpinning 1980s industrial music acts like Test Dept or Die Krupps, who also interfaced with the more rhythmic EBM.[14] The attraction of sheer power enabled by synths is revealed in this quote from Robert Görl of D.A.F., who empowered the transition from synth pop into EBM: "Most bands get a synthesizer and their first idea is to tune it! . . . They want a clean normal sound. They don't work with the POWER you get from a synthesizer . . . We want to bring together this high technique with body power so you have the past time mixed with the future."[15] The push to extremes is a natural part of exploring the space of sonic possibility.

Lou Reed's *Metal Machine Music* (1975) had already made the attraction of sheer noise clear, through a double album of guitar feedback designed to snub a nose at a recording contract. He was beaten to the punch in turn by the 1960s work of American experimental composers like Robert Ashley and Gordon Mumma exploring squeals of feedback. The sound (if not the action) of parts of Ashley's *The Wolfman* (1964) is not so far from the much later improvised feedback microphone belting of Masonna or Kylie Minoise, and demonstrates the continuing importance of amplification in these musics. The take-up of noise music has been particularly active in Japan. Masami Akita (Merzbow) has gradually established a huge body of work, from early cassettes (Lowest Music & Arts mail-order cassettes from 1979) to later (1990s) laptop-created digital noise, confronting taboos, fetishes, and noise levels that have contributed to hearing loss through Akita's career.

The descendants of noise music extend from those who embraced industrial music, through speedy movements in thrash metal, to interconnections even with electronic listening music; the breakcore movement (circa 2000) interfaces the extremes of speedcore, gabba, and drill and bass via the prism of noise music. Characterizing noise, the artists are typically men wanting to drive musical equipment faster and faster, and who create attention deficit syndrome music with a lot to say about aggression, drug use, rebellion, and impatience, as almost a polar opposite to ambient music.

Yet noise music is one of those wide nets whose skirts can hold many interfaces to other areas. Motivations for making noise music might include the following:

- Raw physical sensation: Extreme loudness has a physical effect on the body, while sensory dissonance is an interesting timbral area for exploration.
- Cultural dissonance: Noise as the "other," disturbing the status quo, not necessarily through extreme sound, but in a context-dependent fashion.
- Representations of an overload of information, of undiluted complexity, as a catharsis for rage at the human condition.

A recurrent danger for practitioners who blithely follow extremes of action and rebellion is that their actions quickly become formulaic, just another orthodoxy, their audience inured, in Simon Reynolds' marvelous description, by "screeching to the converted."[16] The ultimate noise is an unattainable asymptote beyond diminishing musical returns; despite the title *Unhearable*, Chinese musician Wang Changcun's 2002 piece can still be appreciated!

Glitch

One of life's aural pleasures is a fashion boutique music player choking on the latest chart releases and stuttering until a beleaguered shop assistant can swap to another source. This sounds curiously similar to many deliberate experimental tracks that you might have preferred to be on that player in the first place. Glitch is a form of electronic listening music for which such hiccups are a natural part of communication.[17] Artists have recorded their crashing computers, deliberately skewed sample values at high zoom in audio editors, connected outputs to inputs, loaded the audio editor program binary into an audio editor as if it were a raw audio file, and sought innumerable ways to subvert by interesting failure the normal behavior of the technologies essential to electronic music. Especially treating new digital systems in the 1990s rather than analog technologies, glitch music as a genre embraces accidents and human subversion of machines.

Nevertheless, the pursuit of error as a creative tactic has a long heritage, for much that is creative is driven by serendipity, and trial and error necessitates learning from errors; new aesthetic directions are driven by promoting a particular "error" – an error according to old systems – to the center of new innovation. More generally, art needs something to stand against, can center-ground what seemed impermissible, and can undermine the sureties of prior art. Milan Knizak, for example, a fluxus artist, had a *Destroyed Music* series in the 1960s, scratching, splicing, and otherwise altering records;[18] the deliberate CD damage which Yasunao Tone instigated in 1984 is just a later manifestation of this sort of productive-destructive tendency. As Holger Czukay and Irmin Schmidt (active particularly in early 1970s German experimental rock groups who often used electronics) noted in an interview: "the most inventive way to use a synthesiser is to misuse it."[19]

An influential German trio (as they were from 1991–5) for a developing digital glitch scene were Oval. With albums like *Wohnton* (1993), *Systemisch* (1994), and *94 Diskont* (1995), they established that forced CD skips and other equipment failures could be the basis of new textures. They loop scratched shards of sound and juxtapose multiple layers of processed source material. Drifting across from sample stutter-backed songs and ambient soundscapes to more propulsive abstracted techno, their listening music has a rich textural bent. Their production techniques, whilst not always isolated examples even at the time, given the mass production exploration of samplers, contributed significantly to the shift of emphasis in glitch to the beauty of what might otherwise have been overlooked, unwanted, and undesired artifacts. But whilst textural preferences of source and processing may be perturbed, the eventual outcomes in new electronic listening music overlap with territories already introduced in this chapter.

Kim Cascone sets out various foundational techniques of digital experimental glitch music, as they arose in the 1990s, in his supposedly "post-digital" article.[20] To paraphrase:

- test tone drones and stark landscapes;
- buffer skipping;
- time stretching and bit reduction;
- microsound – manipulating tiny grains of sound, re-drawing waveforms sample by sample;
- data transformation – from image files to audio, from Word document to sound.

The computer is the primary device, the electron microscope allowing the viewing and disturbing of individual atoms of sound. A trial-and-error approach is productive – as Cascone writes:

> Because the tools used in this style of music embody advanced concepts of digital signal processing, their usage by glitch artists tends to be based on experimentation rather than empirical investigation. In this fashion, unintended usage has become the second permission granted. It has been said that one does not need advanced training to use digital signal processing programs – just "mess around" until you obtain the desired result.[21]

Although computer glitches have appeared to be central to this scene, a related arena of hardware hacking (also termed circuit bending) has grown over the same time period.[22] This is particularly apposite, given that the origins of digital glitch are in the hacking of CD players, carried out through physical manipulations rather than software warping! In hardware hacking, wires, fingers, or worms[23] touch integrated circuits directly, forming momentary connections. The circuits are those found in 1970s and 1980s gear, especially when components in the circuits are easily accessed and not overly miniaturized. As well as musical hardware, any sounding gadgets will do, especially toys. Finding productive short circuits, these glitching routes can be hard-wired in to create a hacked device. A classic target for hacking is the Texas Instruments Speak & Spell toy (released in 1978) and numerous hacks are publicized online for 1980s Casio and Yamaha home keyboards. This hobbyist hacking has risen greatly in popularity in recent decades: Magazines such as *Make*, and a plethora of online blogs and information sites such as www.instructables.com, disgorge the secrets of building hardware.

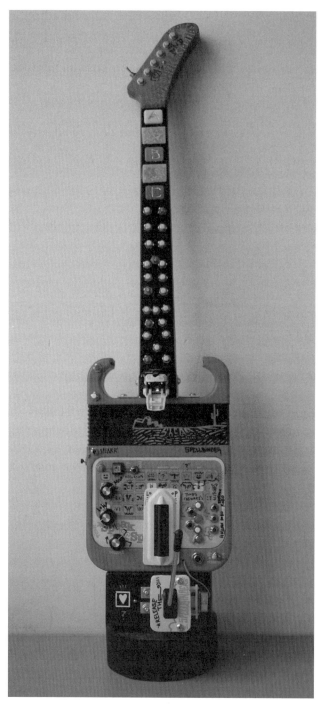

Figure 10.1 Aj Pyatak's Speak & Spellbinder hack, a Frankensteinian Speak & Spell/Guitar Hero controller combination (www.mygannon.com). Reproduced by permission

Whether digital or analog, mistakes continue to be highly productive territory for artists, and a slip of the pen at this point seems inerrortable.

Analysis of experimental electronica

Though we have split the exposition of experimental electronica into three sections, it should be clear to the reader that the boundaries are fluid between these sections and across the chapters of this book. A glitchscape could be played at ear-splitting volume, taking on some attribute of noise music, or be intended for quiet contemplative listening. The fringes of electronic dance music are full of strange composites, and tight repetitive loops are found in many of TG's pieces. A physical response to energetic noise music can drive a listener into wild dancing even if the "beat" is not cast-iron.

John Latartara has argued that the primary attributes of "laptop composition" circa 2000 are repetition and noise,[24] though the argument might extend more generally to much experimental electronica pre-dating any laptop culture. Repetition covers the use of loops (including explicit rhythmic beats as well as more abstract repeating textures) or of stable unyielding drones, whilst noise here in pure audio terms is a reference to nonperiodic sound, of blasting broadband spectral content rather than the linear harmonics necessitated in pitched sound. Perhaps Latartara's case is too broad; repetition and nonrepetition are after all an all-encompassing set at the most general level of detail, but the evocation of loops and noisy signals is a useful starting point. A lot of electronica seems to be setting up a situation, a particular delimited sound world, and letting it run for a while.

To some observers, especially those in the world of art music, repetition is always suspicious, with political overtones of military drill and imposed routine. Stockhausen criticized four fringe electronic dance music producers for their conceptions of electronic music, which clashed with his own stance against repetitive rhythm (the four artists in question had a chance to defend themselves).[25] Autechre's statement against the 1994 Criminal Justice Bill in the UK (which restricted the right for groups to gather and sought to outlaw rave culture), the *Anti EP* (1994), makes a claim that the track "Flutter has been programmed in such a way that no bars contain identical beats and can therefore be played under the proposed new law. However, we advise DJs to have a lawyer and a musicologist present at all times to confirm the non-repetitive nature of the music in the event of police harassment."[26] Actually, the track fails the "repetitive beats" condition, since a uniform sense of metrical structure is present, even if the individual rhythmic details are varying; perceptually beats are different from events! Nonetheless, *Flutter* does evidence an interesting generativity within the piece. More widely, uneven (nonsquare) loops, co-prime co-repetitions of layers, and the like are all employed in experiemental electronica as it diverges from regularized EDM.

Latartara in his article provides spectrographic analyses of works by Oval, Merzbow, and Kid606, a trio of artists perhaps representing the glitch, noise, and warped EDM constituencies. We shall illustrate the analysis of the type of music encountered in this chapter by applying a spectrographic approach to the analysis of three alternative pieces, one by the arch-Japanoise artist Merzbow (Masami Akita), one by the collectible producer Muslimgauze (Bryn Jones, who sadly died in 1999), and one by the laptop duo Blectum from Blechdom.[27] The first two acts can be highly charged: The context of work of Merzbow is related to interests including animal rights and bondage photography, and Muslimgauze, to the political situation of the Middle East, especially Palestine. Through the aggression of noise or sampling of the sonic textures of Islamic culture, such a backstory makes its way into the foreground of the sound world. Compared to this extreme, Blectum from Blechdom are often more lighthearted and varied in their approach, though they are highly trained musicians who are serious in their creation of work.

The Muslimgauze track is *Hafizz Maidan* from *Wish of the Flayed* (Muslimtape 01, 2008, originally recorded June 1996, available as a free download at http://arabbox. free.fr/muslimtape01.html). Figure 10.2 provides an overview. The track makes substantial use of a resonant chirp percussion against two kicks, strong bass tones with a higher modulated component, and a background wash of ominous lower-frequency ambience, which is pushed louder in the mix at points. The common loop is over four beats at 136bpm, but avoids typical Western club patterns even though constructed on sixteenths. The basic form is:

Resonant chirp 1:   x0xx 00xx xxxx x000
Resonant chirp 2:   x000 00x0 0000 0x00
Kick 1:   0000 x000 0000 0000
Kick 2:   0000 0000 0000 00x0

the kicks on the second and in the fourth beat, signifying a partial avoidance of Western rhythmic convention.

A (sample of a) traditional instrument (a Turkish Ney or Arabic Kawala end-blown cane flute) floats in four times; at the fourth presentation, the noise backdrop is suddenly removed (this is clear in the spectral view by the drop out of the band of noise between 0 to 3kHz). The points of silence for the resonant percussion are also clear in the spectrogram, between around 0:41–0:45, 1:40–1:45, and 2:00–2:10. The production quality keeps the elements clear to the ear, whilst the repetition is hypnotic; you can hear why Mulsimgauze pieces, shorn of their political imagery, have been used for Ashtanga yoga classes!

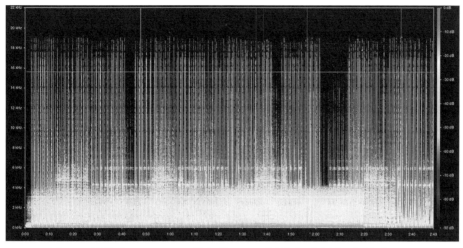

Figure 10.2 Spectrogram of Muslimgauze's *Hafizz Maidan* (1996)

Merzbow's eschews any rhythmic frame and in his nearly fourteen-minute piece *Space Metalizer Pt. 1* (from the LP *Space Metalizer* (1997), Alien8 Recordings) transports us directly to an angst-ridden world of distorted sound, directly conjured far away from any popular music trope. The overall texture is highly distorted, original sources warped to unrecognizability by overdrive effects pedals. The performative nature of the rendition seems clear: The piece may well be one live improvised take, spontaneity captured on recording and then mixed further (perhaps not much at all!) in post-production. Masami Akita is credited in the liner notes as the performer using "Noise Electronics, Metals, Novation Synthe Rack." The overall sound world is uncomfortable, particularly for a first-time listener unused to the noise music genre; a more experienced listener begins to find instances of great beauty within the onslaught. The CD is mastered extremely hot, with highly compressed and full frequency range distortion prevalent.

It is clear from the spectrogram of this Merzbow track in Figure 10.3 that there is variation of texture throughout the track, sometimes subtly shifting (one imagines a control on a piece of equipment slowly moved) and at other points jumping with a sudden jerk of controls, or a phase shift in the chaotic response of the processing chain. The swoops in the spectrogram between 2–4kHz in the 2:50–3:45 area of the track relate to sweeps of the center frequency of a highly peaked resonant filter. Drops from wide-band noise to low-frequency distortions can be seem in the spectrogram as transitions from blocks of high energy across the vertical to more restricted low-frequency bands (5:29–5:45, for example). Four horizontal harmonics are visible for around a minute from 9:30, from a fundamental squealing just above 4kHz. The spectrogram gives some clue to the fury of the noisescape, since music more

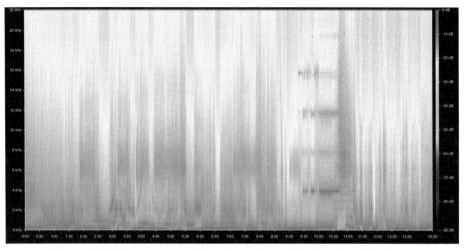

Figure 10.3 Spectrogram of Merzbow's *Space Metalizer Pt. 1* (1997)

typically has a spectral roll off where higher frequencies are attenuated; it's a wonder that Masami Akita has any hearing left at all.

In Kevin Blechdom's own words, "Blectum From Blechdom is a computer, sampler, and synthesizer duo that formed while Kristin Erickson and Bevin Kelley were studying at Mills College in 1998. Electronic music that embraces malfunction and malformation, including rhythms synchronized by ear, absurdist mythologies, a penchant for bad taste, and a costume built for two"[28] (Kevin Blechdom and Blevin Blectum are the respective performing personas of Erickson and Kelley). *The Messy Jesse Fiesta* (Deluxe Records, 2000) was awarded the second prize at the 2001 Ars Electronica in Digital Music.[29] The album as a whole ranges widely and sometimes psychotically, from children's music and musicals to harder electronic dance music, glitch, and digital noise.

The track represented here, with a spectrogram overview in Figure 10.4, is *Shedspace*, a more instrumental track and less overtly comic in effect than some of the others on the album. The soundscape is more varied than either the Muslimgauze or Merzbow examples, using variable-rate sample playback (lower speeds to gritty effect), synthesized tones, granulation, sample stuttering, and distortion. A frequency-modulation synthesis texture recurs twice in the outer areas of the track (0:00–0:57.5 and 1:45 to the end), and the central part has a number of abrupt jumps, interrupting the listening flow, to create an ABA form where A is more static than the disruptive B section. This breakdown can be seen clearly in the spectrogram, with similar textures at the start and the end, and broad-band effects in the central section. The piece ends abruptly, transitioning quickly to the next track on

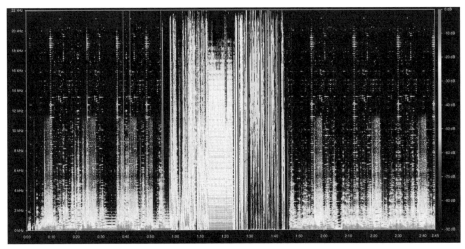

Figure 10.4 Spectrogram of Blectum from Blechdom's *Shedspace* (2000)

the album, from an abstract texture to a quirky rhythmic groove (which in turn transforms to other places; the whole fiesta is full of such shifts).

The Messy Jesse Fiesta is appropriately named; experimental artists have no incentive to be neat and tidy. Merzbow or Muslimgauze make a mockery of exhaustive collecting, with always another release (even posthumously!), and too many formats to follow . . . their recording careers parallel the huge amount of material released every week, which makes it impossible for a single musicologist to keep up with. Identities are confused; Richard James appears under many aliases and has gained such notoriety that rumors fly around messageboards at lightning speed; it is likely, but not absolutely certain, that the Tuss is also Aphex Twin.[30] Artists are often irreverent, at least with respect to academic conventions and art music seriousness. Humor, sometimes puerile, sometimes very funny, abounds in song titles; alongside the good humors of Blectum from Blechdom, the digital band Stock, Hausen and Walkman provide ribald brilliance lost somewhere to the side of their namesakes Stockhausen and late 1980s pop producers Stock, Aitken and Waterman.

The arrival of new technologies is often a cue for new groups of people to get involved. They may reproduce many past ideas, but may also forge some paths ahead, if tempered by the affordances of the devices they hold. As "laptop music" became a buzzterm around the millennium, "mobile music" holds sway at the close of the first decade of the twenty-first century. New waves of artists arise constantly, inspired by a technological generation only one year, one week, one idea older, always pushing onwards, if not toward any well-determined end goal, but determined to push all the same. Finding their own experimental music, they are sometimes ignorant of historical precedent, at other times attracted by previous experiments, but always involved. They may only release one album, one track, perform once, but all contribute to the ongoing adventures of experimental electronica.

Further reading

Bailey, Thomas Bey William (2009) *Microbionic: Radical Electronic Music and Sound Art in the 21st Century* (London: Creation Books).

Demers, Joanna (2010) *Listening Through the Noise: The Aesthetics of Experimental Electronic Music* (New York: Oxford University Press).

Hegarty, Paul (2007) *Noise/Music: A History* (New York: Continuum).

Kelly, Caleb (2009) *Cracked Media: The Sound of Malfunction* (Cambridge, MA: MIT Press).

Prendergast, Mark (2003) *The Ambient Century: From Mahler to Moby – The Evolution of Sound in the Electronic Age* (London: Bloomsbury).

Chapter 11

Sound art

Although there have been entire books, numerous journal issues, and countless articles written about *sound art*, it remains difficult to agree on a single definition. It is worth initially evoking the idea of a publicly visited artwork; it may help to consider the art gallery setting as one common option, where an artist presents an installation work with a significant sound-based element, awaiting visitors to experience it. Yet we shall see a diversity of practices herein beyond this starting point. For the purposes of this chapter, pieces "performed" from beginning to end with an expectation that the audience remain in the space will be generally exempt from the term, as evoking too strongly the art or rock music concert setting.[1]

Issues of definition arise because of the gradual way sound art has come to prominence. Sound art is as much linked to experimental music in the twentieth century, whether Russolo or Cage, as it is to the exploration of alternative media in the fine arts. Not coincidentally, Russolo's involvement with the futurist movement (he was himself a painter) and Cage's New York drinking sessions with abstract expressionists in the early 1950s point to the inter-relations of music and visual arts.[2] The famous conceptual art pioneer Marcel Duchamp had explored change music in *Erratum Musical* (1913), while Yves Klein anticipated extreme minimalism in his monotone symphony of 1949. But since the middle of the twentieth century, fine artists, more traditionally associated with painting or sculpture, have taken on work in the medium of sound as a possibility for their work; musicians, too, have found themselves working on installations for gallery settings as they have sought to escape the concert hall. The color music of the experimental film makers or the sound synaesthesic pre-occupations of Kandinsky in his abstract art indicate further early connections.

Francisco López, one of the major figures of the sound art and experimental music scene, blindfolds his audience so that they can experience what Christoph Cox calls sound-in-itself.[3] Sound-in-itself can be found in a concert hall, in a gallery, or a site-specific installation (and Lopez is very familiar with the acousmatic traditions discussed in Chapter 9). La Monte Young, Tony Conrad, and Alvin Lucier all created pieces which could be considered sound art, but they are recognized mainly as musicians and identify themselves as such. John Cage thought that all sound could be music; he had no need for an additional category of sound art. Noted sound art historian Alan Licht has called musicians who identify themselves as sound artists "playing the art card,"[4] the habit among musicians of claiming cultural capital through association with galleries and exhibitions instead of concert halls and performances. (Of course, artists can also be accused of playing the music card; we are all just trying to maximize our audiences!) Other practitioners insist that sound art simply cannot qualify as, or does not seek to place itself in the realm of, music, but is rather a form of art incorporating sound, acoustics or sonic phenomena, space or architecture, spoken word, or even art which simply references sonic culture.[5]

Sound art can be heard in a museum or gallery, in a dedicated architectural or public space, it can be heard best standing still, sitting or lying down, walking, or even driving in a car. To listen to Israel Martinez's 2007 work *Piece in three movements to share with strangers or friends on a ride around the metropolis*, you must drive a pre-established route through Mexico City while listening to a pre-recorded cassette. Amazingly, there are even pieces for audiences submerged in water; in the early 1970s, Max Neuhaus' *Water Whistle* series required the public to float in pools with their heads underwater in order to hear his work.

Sound art can be passive or require audience participation in order to activate the sound. In David Byrne's 2008 sound work *Playing the Building*, people waited in line for over two hours to play an organ which had been wired to parts of the building structure, vibrating metal beams, striking structural columns, and blowing air through the electrical conduits in response to the audience pushing down keys and pedals. Sound art can be heard over headphones, over home stereo systems, can require hundreds of speakers, or, as in the case of *Playing the Building*, can be purely acoustic.

Sound art can exist for only a second, as in Tom Marioni's *One Second Sculpture* (1969), or can play for years – La Monte Young's sound and light environment *Dream House* has been permanently outputting some high overtones on the harmonic series since 1993 (plus or minus power outages). Sound art can be pure sound or include other media; the *Dream House* features lighting by Marian Zazeela. Sound art can be referential: Martinez's *Piece in three movements* has the final movement end with the car in the central Plaza de la Constitución with sounds of protest playing over the sound system. Sound art can also be conceptual, as in Annea Lockwood's *Piano Transplants*, one of which took twenty years to be performed.

Piano Transplants

The scores for Annea Lockwood's *Piano Transplants* are simply text, and it should be noted that the pianos used should already be beyond repair. Pianos are placed in certain situations, including the gradual engulfment of the famous *Piano Burning* (1968) and the gradually vegetative state of *Piano Garden* (1969–70). The score for *Southern Exposure* (1982, realized 2005) reads:

"Chain a ship's anchor to the back leg of a grand piano.
Set the piano at the high tide mark, lid raised.
Leave it there until it vanishes."[6]

Sound art doesn't even have to make audible sound – sounds can be too low in volume or outside our hearing range – more shockingly, sound art doesn't have to make any sound at all. In Christian Marclay's collaboration with Graphicstudio, *Cyanotypes*, a range of images are created on photosensitive paper in the aspect ratio of cassette tapes.[7] The titles of these works reference the tapes which he found in thrift stores in Florida, including the Dixie Chicks, LeVert, and Nat King Cole. From careful grids of the tapes themselves to abstract snarls of unspooled magnetic tape, these large-scale photograms do not make sound and in fact capture the destruction of recorded media, yet they could still be at home in an exhibit of sound art. Marclay's most famous work might be *Record Without a Cover* (1985), a record sold with no cover and no jacket, so that it deteriorates every time it is played or even moved. This might be the ultimate expression of sound-in-itself short of an unattributed and meta-data-less MP3, for there are no graphics to create extra-sonic associations.[8]

Joanna Demers has identified three sub-genres of sound art:[9]

(1) An installed sound environment that is defined by the space rather than presentation in time and can be exhibited in a similar way to a visual artwork.
(2) A visual artwork that also has a sound-producing function such as a sound sculpture.
(3) Sound by visual artists that serves as an extension of the artist's particular aesthetic, where they normally express themselves in other media.

Sound art is not simply a combination of music and art – it intersects electronic music, concrete poetry, and video arts. George Lewis believes "if you're not prepared to accept the problems that come with being mobile, with having a sort of nonfixed way, in which you're receiving multiple influences and acting in multiple ways, you're going to have a hard time."[10] Although such complexity may hinder investigation, William Furlong believes that sound art has benefited from its inability to create a distinct category, because these sorts of labels become limiting and the work circumscribed and marginalized.[11] One of the so-called fathers of sound art, Max Neuhaus, didn't even like the term, writing that "much of what has been called 'Sound Art' has not much to do with either sound or art."[12] He much preferred the term "Sound Sculpture." Although presenting his work in traditional music venues,

Trevor Wishart associated himself with the term "Sonic Arts" in order to describe a wider range of musical sounds. Demers thinks this leads to a "schizophrenic condition in which electroacoustic music is simultaneously music and something other than music, such as sound art."[13] The sound artist Bill Fontana understands this schizophrenia, describing himself as a "composer and artist whose work exists with one foot in and out of contemporary music, one foot in and out of contemporary art, on the edge of some science, on the edge of philosophy."[14]

With these caveats in mind, the artists mentioned in this chapter are commonly identified with the term "sound art," though many reject the label. Although museums still struggle with exhibiting shows of sound art, the contemporary art world is beginning to recognize this new hybrid form. There has been an explosion of publications on the subject in recent years, and in 2010 Susan Philipsz became the first sound artist to win the British Turner Prize. Her work *Lowlands* consisted of the artist recording herself singing three different versions of an ancient Scottish lament and then editing them together. The piece was originally installed using invisible speakers under the Caledonian, George V, and Glasgow Bridges in Glasgow, and after the site-specific installation was completed, the piece was moved to three empty rooms in the Tate Britain Museum. Some critics wrote that the piece was music, not art;[15] this is a debate which will continue and expand as chimeric forms of expression incorporating sound flourish in the twenty-first century.

Site-specific work

One of the primary ways sound art can be distinguished is site-specificity, either placing the piece in a site, transmitting sound from one site to another, or specifically referencing a site. One artist who works with all three methods is Bill Fontana. In 1976, while experimenting with multitracking, he made an eight-channel recording of Kirribilli Wharf in Australia, which he played back over eight channels. Inspired by the spatial complexity of the percussive sounds answering each other from eight points in space, he called it a "sounding sculpture." He revisited the piece twelve years later, placing microphones in the same location, but rather than recording the waves, he transmitted the live sound to an art gallery in Sydney. His work often uses microphones installed in one location which transmit their resulting sound continuums to another location, transforming the visible (retinal) by the invisible (sound). For his 1992 *Earth Tones*, he buried six low-frequency exciters in Sonoma County. Visitors to the Oliver Ranch heard low tones from five parts of the world emanating from, and occasionally shaking, the ground. Oliver Ranch is also the site of Ann Hamilton's *The Tower*, a "unique, acoustic environment and a new type of entertainment space defined by two staircases built in a double helix form."[16] One entrance and staircase is for the audience and the other is for the performers, creating a unique site for performances. While the pieces in the tower are "performed" from beginning to end with an expectation that the audience remain in the space, the tower itself is a kind of sound art piece, a structure created to have a specific acoustic experience (though the reader might be forgiven for reflecting on the uniqueness of any given concert hall).

Another sound artist who worked with site-specific sound, and a powerful case study for this chapter, is Max Neuhaus, who began his musical career as a percussion-ist specializing in John Cage's works. He then began performing with live electronics and became so intrigued by the possibilities of electronic sounds that he gave up performing entirely in 1968 after issuing his seminal recording *Electronics and Per-cussion: Five Realizations by Max Neuhaus.* He built all the circuitry and speakers for his pieces himself, and was insistent that the pieces exist simply as sound; he hid all the speakers and wiring, and would not let the works be labeled. He felt that seeing a speaker would make it part of the sound sculpture; he wanted his pieces to be made only of sound and hoped that at least fifty percent of people wouldn't even notice his work!

His most well-known piece is installed in a New York City traffic island in Times Square. He did not normally title his works, but this one has become known simply as *Times Square*. His audio combines and augments the sounds of the subway system; many people aren't even aware there is a sonic sculpture at work. Rumor has it that he surreptitiously installed the initial piece, running it illegally off the New York City power grid from 1977 to 1992, and then turned it off when he moved to Europe. In 2002, Dia Beacon convinced him to reinstate the work; they are now listed as the owners and have promised to oversee the upkeep permanently.

Neuhaus worked intuitively with his sites, changing the content of the sound and the placement of the speakers until he had created a sculpture which satisfied him. Initially, he did not leave any documentation of his pieces, but in 1989 he began creating what he titled "Circumscription Drawings" to find a way to publish something without destroying the integrity of the work.

He realized he was functioning in the world of contemporary art, which is a world of exhibitions, and he needed a way to capture the piece after it was completed:

> After finishing a sound work, if time allows, I wait several months before listening to it again. This is the first time I can stand outside the work and see what it is that I have made. It is only at this point after experiencing the work with distance that I make its circumscription drawing. This drawing, two panels, a visual image and a handwritten text, integrates two traditional forms of communication to circumscribe something both invisible and indescribable. The image is not the drawing nor is the text: the drawing is what they synthesize together. When read

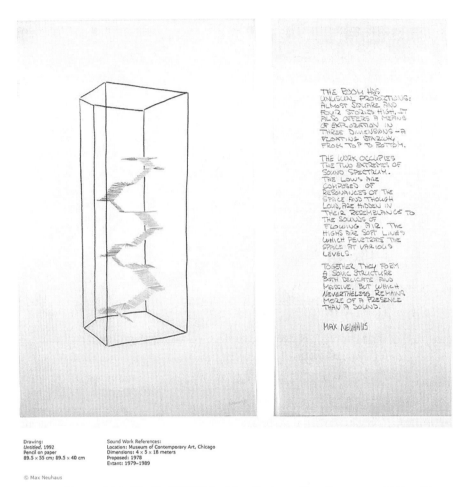

Drawing:
Untitled, 1992
Pencil on paper
89.5 × 55 cm; 89.5 × 40 cm

Sound Work References:
Location: Museum of Contemporary Art, Chicago
Dimensions: 4 × 5 × 18 meters
Proposed: 1978
Extant: 1979–1989

© Max Neuhaus

Figure 11.1 *Untitled* (1992) by Max Neuhaus. Pencil on paper 89.5 × 55 cm; 89.5 × 40 cm. Reproduced by permission

in parallel, they evoke a central idea of the sound work, a point of departure and a reference, for reflection.[17]

He was a perfectionist about his pieces and invalidated his *Untitled* (1979) Chicago Museum of Contemporary Art installation. Although the piece ran until the museum closed in 1996, Neuhaus did not recognize the work after 1989, the year in which he visited the installation unannounced and found that the winners of an electronic music contest were being played over his speakers. He compared this to letting art students have a graffiti contest on a Richard Serra sculpture. The original agreement with the museum indicated that the work would never be turned off and no other artwork would be shown in its space. The museum had already violated this agreement multiple times, receiving complaints from Neuhaus each time. In

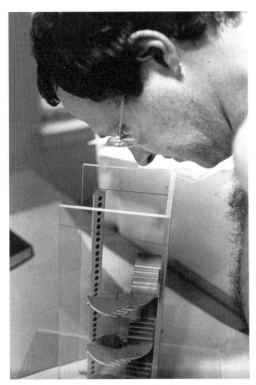

Figure 11.2 Photo of Max Neuhaus working with a scale model of the Chicago Museum Stairwell. Reproduced by permission

1996, the building and Neuhaus' custom-designed equipment were destroyed. The curators "never got it: they even asked me if I would make a new work for them out of the pieces."[18] His electronics represented months if not years of work and were created for each unique space. This disregard for his artistic process must have been extremely hurtful to the man who declared that "The important idea about this kind of work of mine is that it's not music . . . it doesn't exist in time. I've taken sound out of time and made it into an entity."[19]

Max Neuhaus' patent for sound

Max Neuhaus was the first person to be awarded an American patent for sound. In 1978, he decided to try to design a better set of sound signals for emergency vehicles because it was clear the sirens themselves had never actually been designed and were instead the product of whatever could be found to make a loud noise. He believed the main problem was that it is almost impossible to pinpoint the location and path of sirens through sound alone. He tried to raise funding from both the city of New York and his artistic patrons, but:

> Being an artist didn't help. The scientific community was not interested; they felt threatened by someone who refused to acknowledge that quantification was the only truth. My own community, art sponsors, were always out to lunch; they didn't feel it was within their purview. So much for the rhetoric of the grand union of art and science.[20]
>
> In 1989, he finally got the funding to test his ideas. He chose a site in the California desert and began his intuitive process of designing sound, this time mounted on moving cars. He chose this stretch of highway because the nearest housing was forty miles away and the highway ran through a steep-walled canyon with a double "S" curve with acoustics surprisingly similar to the canyons of Manhattan. On April 30, 1991, the US Patent Office issued Patent Number 5,012,221, embodying forty-six ideas on how to use sound to move an emergency vehicle through traffic.

From galleries to soundwalks

Both Neuhaus and Fontana have shown work in galleries and museums, as well as building site-specific installations. Showing multiple sonic works in a gallery is difficult, because the sound is not contained and can cross-contaminate with sonic bleed-through from one piece to another. For Sonic Boom (2000), the first major exhibition about sound art in the UK, curator David Toop presented 23 sounding works. He did not try to keep the sounds separate because:

> the character of music in the present time is that it all overlaps... We are saturated by sound now. We walk around and we move through constantly changing soundscapes, different types of music, different genres of music overlap all the time... And you are almost walking through an environment where one sound overlaps and then you walk away from that sound and it fades and you walk into a new sound. So the gallery is the total, immersed experience and hopefully that transforms the gallery from what we think of as being a rather sterile space for showing art to something which is much more alive and human.[21]

Most museums and galleries are oriented toward visual work – they know how to hang art on a wall and how to light it. As Marclay notes, "nobody knows anything about sound – how you hang a speaker, how you EQ it to the room... more and more museums have a lounge-type listening room, but there are still a lot of changes that need to happen before the art world is ready to present sound as art."[22] No matter how well the gallery presents a sonic work, it is sometimes impossible to hear because of other visitors talking, and popular works which are meant to be heard over headphones or require audience interaction might entail a long waiting time. Some curators resort to only showing one piece of sonic art at a time, but even that

Figure 11.3 Zimoun: 361 prepared DC-motors, filler wire 1.0 mm, 2010.
Reproduced by permission

can cause problems with visual artists who feel that their work is compromised by
the sonic art work. Curators often resort to using headphones, but not all sound art
is amenable to being presented in this way.

The sound artist Zimoun creates work that cannot possibly be heard over headphones. He doesn't use microphones or speakers, but instead creates mechanical
sound works from rigorous iterative displays of commonplace industrial objects
such as plastic bags, cardboard boxes, and tubing activated by motors. His sculptures create sonic and visual chaos out of a seemingly ordered system. Inspired by
the sciences of generative systems, robotics, and swarm behaviors, he creates very
simple synthetic structures, which unfold into complex, almost biological systems.
Licht differentiates Zimoun's particular type of minimalism from the work of musicians like La Monte Young and Steve Reich, describing "hive-like structures which
remove the factor of duration by physically stacking the repetitions on top of each
other."[23] The sound is the essence of his artistic practice; the form of the sculpture
develops from the function of its sound production. What you hear is what you see,
an electromechanical sound-making organism.

One way to avoid the problems of presenting sound art in a gallery is to have
the sound outside the gallery. In the Sonic Boom exhibition, Christina Kubisch's
because tomorrow comes #2 allowed visitors to wander into an outdoor sculpture
garden receiving the soundscape via special headphones which used electromagnetic
induction.[24] The sounds were generated from the "mutual interaction of magnetic
fields, which arise on the one hand from electrical wires traversing the room, in

which sounds circulate, and on the other from headphones with magnetic coils, which [she] developed [her]self."[25] Kubisch has developed an entire series of works called *Electrical Walks* where listeners are given these special headphones along with maps which indicate particularly interesting sonic locations. In this mode, Kubisch's work is an electronically mediated form of soundwalk, related to some practice in soundscape composition (see Chapter 9); R. Murray Schafer defines a soundwalk as an "exploration of the soundscape of a given area using a score as a guide . . . the score consists of a map, drawing the listener's attention to unusual sounds and ambiences to be heard along the way."[26] In 1967, Neuhaus had also begun taking audiences on listening walks, stamping their hands with the word "listen" and instructing them to silently take note of their sonic environment.

The sound artist Janet Cardiff is well known for her soundwalks, in which the audience listens to binaural narrative recordings through headphones while navigating through museum or city spaces (binaural recordings give an incredible sense of three-dimensional space to the listener). With her partner George Bures Miller, she also creates theatrical sets with video and sound viewed from the perspective of an audience or actor. Her audio installations present an array of speakers, matching or varied, to create a spatially sonic atmosphere that the audience can walk through. Her most famous work is probably the *Forty Part Motet*, which is a re-working of *Spem in alium nunquam habui*, composed in 1573 by Thomas Tallis. Cardiff recorded the forty members of the Salisbury Cathedral Choir with identical individual microphones, including their warm-up and discussion afterward. The piece is presented as forty matching loudspeakers mounted at head height inscribing an oval. The *Forty Part Motet* has been exhibited in lavish period rooms, ecclesiastical settings, and sparse gallery spaces.

This work stands in contrast to her soundwalk pieces, which require an incredible amount of site specificity. Cardiff records naturally occurring sounds from the site and then adds other layers, almost always including breathing and footsteps combined with internal and external dialogue defined by the quality and immediacy of the voice:

> The idea for the walk came to me by accident. I was in a graveyard . . . recording what I saw in front of me on my small voice recorder like the names on the gravesites, the plants and what I smelt. I inadvertently pushed the wrong button and rewound the machine. When I played back the tape to find where I had left off, I heard the sound of my body while walking, my voice describing what was in front of me and also my breathing. I began to walk with my virtual body. It was one of those "aha" experiences. I knew I had to use the format because it was so peculiar. I produced the first walk, *Forest Walk*, about two weeks later.[27]

Figure 11.4 Janet Cardiff's *Forest Walk* (1991). Courtesy of the artist, Luhring Augustine, New York, and Galerie Barbara Weiss, Berlin

In her soundwalk pieces, Cardiff is attracted to the closeness of the sound and the audio bridge between the visual, physical world and her body. These walks do not adhere to the common classifications of the multimedia installation, performance art, the site-specific artwork, or the audioguide, yet they draw upon all of these genres or categories.

Another work which blends multimedia installation, site-specific artwork, and informative guide is George Lewis' *Information Station No.1* (2000). Most of his installations "chronicle the social and cultural implications of popular music, particularly its affirmation of identity."[28] This installation examines the social, cultural, and sonic implications of the Point Loma sewage treatment plant. The viewer is encouraged to sit in front of three video monitors surrounded by four speakers. Webcams capture the viewer's gestures and produce an overwhelming flood of information about the plant, including interviews with workers, scanned newspaper articles about the plant, and pictures of the sewage equipment. Movements are also sonified, with the noises of the plant's sludge pipes, digesters, and machinery brought to life as the viewer interacts with the system.

The viscerality and sensory presence of sound itself has been used to create art objects. Alvin Lucier's work was discussed in Chapter 9 and often reflects fundamental acoustic and psychoacoustic properties. Bill Viola's *Hallway Nodes* (1973) sets

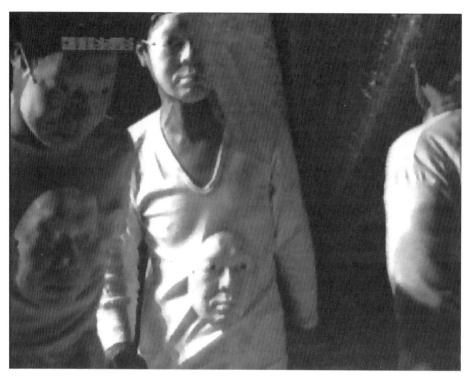

Figure 11.5 George Lewis, *Information Station No. 1* (2000). Multiscreen
videosonic interactive installation for the Point Loma Wastewater Treatment
Plant, San Diego, California. Commisioned by the San Diego Commission for
Arts and Culture, with support from the National Endowment for the Arts.
Software: Harry Castle. Videography: Hans Fjellestad. Reproduced by permission

up physically palpable low-frequency standing waves.[29] Viola placed two speakers
at opposite ends of a long corridor so that the resultant sound waves intersected at
a particular point, where their interference could be felt as a sort of sound pressure
on the body rather than heard. Ryoji Ikeda also creates "sound pieces whose quality
is determined by one's listening point in relation to the loudspeakers. Furthermore,
the listener can experience a particular difference between speaker playback and
headphone listening."[30] By using extremely precise techniques utilized by audiolo-
gists and sound engineers to test for psychoacoustics, Ikeda makes solo audio work
highlighting the specific qualities of headphone listening.[31] His album +/– (1997)
is in part an example of glitch music (see Chapter 10), but with the twist of considering listening environments. Composed using sine tones and short bursts of
sound, the sound image transforms as the listener moves around the room. Even
small shifts of the head can result in large changes in timbre, frequency, rhythm, and
volume.

Sound art is just one example of the crossovers that are occurring at an ever-increasing pace as technology enables a network of connections between various types of artists, practices, and concerns. In the next chapter, we will discuss more of these hybrid art forms, but given its increased prominence in recent decades, sound art has deserved its own chapter. Other pieces and composers discussed in this book might also fall near the examples presented of sound art works. Whilst in 2008 Gascia Ouzounian wrote that an "in-depth examination of sound installation has been neglected by musicologists and art historians alike,"[32] this is being rectified by a plethora of new scholarship in this field "beyond music, between categories."[33]

Further reading

Carlyle, Angus (ed.) (2008) *Autumn Leaves: Sound and the Environment in Artistic Practice* (London: University of the Arts London).

Kahn, Douglas (1999) *Noise, Water, Meat: A History of Sound in the Arts* (Cambridge, MA: MIT Press).

Kelley, Caleb (ed.) (2011) *Sound* (Cambridge, MA: MIT Press/London: Whitechapel Gallery).

Kim-Cohen, Seth (2009) *In the Blink of an Ear: Toward a Non-cochlear Sonic Art* (New York: Continuum).

LaBelle, Brandon (2007) *Background Noise: Perspectives on Sound Art* (New York: Continuum).

Licht, Alan (2007) *Sound Art: Beyond Music, Between Categories* (New York: Rizzoli).

Voegelin, Salomé (2010) *Listening to Noise and Silence: Towards a Philosophy of Sound Art* (New York: Continuum).

Wilson, Stephen (2002) *Information Arts: Intersections of Science, Art and Technology* (Cambridge, MA: MIT Press).

Chapter 12

Further connections

Electronic music is a particularly adaptable medium and fluently blends with other art forms; in the previous chapter, we discussed one such hybrid, sound art. In this chapter, we will explore other areas of intersection, from opera to video games, including the intensive new developments in computer music brought about through the Internet. The section headings evoke the varied artistic aspects and paradigms.

In 1849, Richard Wagner used the term "Gesamtkunstwerk" in two essays to describe a "total artwork," or the combination of many art forms into one.[1] In the 1990s, the term "multimedia" became popularized as any combination of text, graphic art, sound, animation, and video.[2] Technology companies used the term multimedia extensively, and some art historians prefer to use the term "intermedia" to suggest a connection between art forms. Dick Higgins is often credited with the invention of the term "intermedia" in the 1960s,[3] though he himself traced his inspiration back to Samuel Taylor Coleridge.[4] Intermedia does not have to include a computational component, but many contemporary artists work with digital tools which make it especially easy to combine art forms. Not all works can be considered Gesamtkunstwerk, or even intermedia; rather, they "exist between, among, and above the genres, rigid categories, and tools solidified by the institutions of culture."[5]

In the 1990s, electronic music became more accessible not only because the tools dropped in cost but also because they decreased in size and increased in power. For example, in June 2012, BeagleBoard released its latest machine, the BeagleBone, a 700MHz computer with 256MB of RAM, a USB port, and an Ethernet port for around ninety US dollars.[6] The board is only 3.4 × 2.1 inches, improving the portability, autonomy, extensibility, and longevity of designed systems.[7] Designers can now build the computer directly into their installation, instrument, or robotic system. In the 2000s, portable touchscreen devices proliferated, supporting new kinds of interaction with sound from audience participation to gaming. During these two decades, the Internet became fast enough to transmit uncompressed audio in real time to people's homes, and has become a central medium of social and musical interaction for electronic music.

Opera

Wagner is best known for his operas, and opera is the archetypal intermedia form, regularly including a set, staged theatrics, dance, and lighting. Contemporary opera often uses amplification, electronic sounds, and video projection. Even the relatively conservative composer John Adams used pre-recorded sounds and video projections in his opera about the first nuclear bomb test, *Doctor Atomic* (2005). Experimental composers have gone even further to fuse together art forms. The Austrian composer Olga Neuwirth wrote an opera based on David Lynch's cult film classic *Lost Highway*. Scored for five singers, six actors, six instrumental soloists, and a small orchestra of winds and percussion with samplers, live electronics, and tape, *Lost Highway* "challenges our perceptions of opera" by merging video, dialogue, and music.[8] Ms. Neuwirth, who studied both music and art at the San Francisco Conservatory and contemplated becoming a film maker, has a particularly broad compositional palette. On her website, she breaks her creative output into works, radio plays, theater music, film music, and installations.[9] Sometimes two categories intersect, such as her *... miramondo multiplo...*, which exists both as a trumpet concerto and is also for sale as an installation consisting of a video of her handwritten score and sonic excerpts of the concerto played by trumpet soloist Håkan Hardenberger and the Vienna Philharmonic under Pierre Boulez.[10]

Electroacoustic composers have written operas, notably Barry Truax with *Powers of Two* and Alice Shield's *Mass for the Dead* and *Apocalypse*, while Robert Ashley is often associated with incorporating electronics into his theatrical works. The pioneers of musique concrète, Pierre Schaeffer and Pierre Henry, tackled the Orpheus myth with their *Orphée 53*, which premiered (with some controversy) at the annual festival in Donaueschingen in October 1953. The opera was not staged, but did include traditional elements of sung aria, live voice, and classical form. There were live soloists and traditional instruments on the stage with the loudspeakers, which caused a blurring of the lines between acoustic and electronic space. In some passages, the taped concrète works as musical accompaniment; in the *Debate d'Orfée*, the tape part serves as a ground bass with a repeating figure in the low register. In other sections, the pre-recorded passages were simply sound effects, as in *The Monsters*, where slowed-down pitches create growls of monsters, loud squawks are underpinned by whispers, and echoing reverberations create an auditory version of Hell. The opera caused an enormous riot among the audience, even though they were well versed in the aesthetics of contemporary music.[11]

Another composer associated with musique concrète pushed the boundaries of opera even further. Michel Chion's *L'Opéra Concret* is a compilation of excerpts from works composed between 1971 and 1997, plus one complete piece, *Étude d'après*

Beethoven. For him, "opera is . . . the scenographical model par excellence, which inspired not only some of these pieces but also the very form of this record: curtain-raisings, entrances and exits, alternation between choruses and solos, conception in scenes and numbers, and so on. With concrete music, we can create an opera for the ear, in which the composer, because he is working on a sound that is fixed, with its own time and space, finds himself with the possibility of providing the music, décors, lighting and also conducting and directing this theatre of loudspeakers."[12]

Whilst we can all accept that a recording of an opera is still an opera, can a recording of excerpts of electroacoustic works be an opera?

Architecture

Gesamtkunstwerk can also refer to architecture. In this context, it indicates that the architect is responsible for the totality of the building, including the structure, landscaping, and furniture. In recent years, architects have also become aware of the sound of the building, although most hire specialists instead of attempting to manipulate the sound of their spaces themselves. An aural architect "selects specific aural attributes of a space based on what is desirable in a particular cultural framework."[13] By drawing from the fields of acoustics, cognitive psychology, and audio engineering, it is possible to completely change the sonic characteristic of a space – you might manipulate building materials, the shapes of rooms, deploy auxiliary playback systems of speakers, and more. The most extreme example of treatment is an anechoic chamber, a silent room which cancels all sonic reflections. Leo Beranek built the first anechoic chamber while designing communications and noise reduction systems for Second World War aircraft at Harvard's electroacoustics laboratory. In 1951, John Cage entered Beranek's room and it profoundly influenced his views on music and silence. Inspired by the experience of becoming aware of the sound of his own body's physiological processes, he wrote that "there is no such thing as empty space or empty time. There is always something to see, something to hear. In fact, try as we may to make silence, we cannot . . . Until I die there will be sounds. And they will continue following my death. One need not fear about the future of music."[14] Robert Ashley believes that "with Silence, Cage wrote, arguably, the most intelligent and influential book on music theory in the second half of the twentieth century."[15]

Music has always been influenced by architecture, and indeed part of the development of the symphony orchestra can be traced to the ability of architects to build larger spaces. Composers have written antiphonal music for millennia, but in the twentieth century, the connection between architecture and music became even more profound. One of the most famous examples of the blending of architecture and sound (at least for electronic musicians) is the 1958 Philips Pavilion, its chief form being the work of the famous architect-composer Iannis Xenakis. As well as 350 speakers, the pavilion included film projections on the interior surfaces. Xenakis went on to create many electronic music works for presentation in unique spaces constructed for his art; his Polytopes incorporated computer-controlled lights and lasers, and he set work on grand scales, such as Persepolis in Iran.[16]

While Xenakis' architectural artworks were often created for a single run and then destroyed, Australian composer David Worrall has developed a transportable structure for electroacoustic perfomance, his Portable Immersive Polymedia Event Spaces (PIPES). Annoyed with concert halls which either had raked seating, over-bearing reverberation, the inability to suspend speakers, or in the worst-case scenario all three, Worrall developed a general-purpose, relatively inexpensive, portable ten-sided geodesic dome for electronic media performances. Loudspeakers are suspended from sixteen equidistant locations and a sub-woofer system on the floor in the center of the dome provides the low-frequency components of the sonic spectrum with a real-time Ambisonic computer system controlling sound spatialization. In addition, there are five screens mounted on each pair of walls, with individual video projectors aimed at each. The domes are transportable by car and can be set up in one day, making them an attractive alternative to traditional venues.[17]

While Worrall decided to create his own acoustic environment, Maryanne Amacher worked deeply with the sonic character of the rooms she chose for her installations. She has been described as "perhaps the first composer whose work has been almost entirely site specific . . . she was interested in structural vibration as opposed to standing waves and air borne sound."[18] She would use multiple and diverse sound sources, mounting speakers outside of the room, in the floor, and aimed at the walls, to create psychoacoustic sound shapes. She had incredible hearing and would spend days or even weeks in a space, not leaving her equipment to even eat or sleep, persistently tweaking the set-up of her speakers and amplifiers. Like a true virtuoso, she would test different DAT machines, even ones by the same manufacturer, to find those which had the sonic quality she sought. Her pieces had to be played back at extreme volumes (over 100dB) to evoke specific otoacoustic emissions (sounds which are generated from within the inner ear). Although there are recordings of her compositions, they cannot compare with the experience of her corporealization of sound in her site-specific installations (see Chapter 11 for further discussion of site-specific art works).

Gaming

Some of the most potent architectures are now virtual rather than physical, as cyberspace and games engines for rendering 3D visuals have come of age.[19] Karen Collins' book *Game Sound* is an introduction to the progression of audio and music in video games, from the 1970s through to the present day.[20] The early and quirky capabilities of 8-bit sound chips in home consoles and computers such as the Atari 2600 or ZX Spectrum have given way to general access to high-quality digital audio. Although much game sound since the late 1980s has been based on playback of pre-recorded samples, perhaps with spatialization as the primary processing, more radical use of live computation of sound is becoming more commonplace again; where *Manic Miner* (1983) cheerfully chirped out a hand-programmed sequence with a time-varying loop that caused the whole game to stutter along, the music to *Spore* (2008) utilizes the Pure Data computer music platform to produce generative music as varied as any of the lifeforms designed and developed in the game. The relationship of music and sound to game mechanics has been explored in many interesting ways, from pop star fantasy fulfillment games such as the 2000s *Guitar Hero* or *Rock Band* series based on simple musical timing tasks to shoot-em-ups and platformers such as *Rez* (2001) and *Sound Shapes* (2012), where game action is intimately tied to musical structure.

Mobile gaming has been one of the massive growth areas for electronic music techniques in the last five years. Apple's iPhone (first released in 2007) has been a particular driver of public access to real-time interactive and generative audio tools. As mentioned in Chapter 6, perhaps the most famous pop star exploiting techniques of electronic music is Björk. Her most recent album *Biophilia* was released in 2011 as both a recording and an iPad application. Each of the ten songs on the album has an associated application within a "mother app." To have the best user experience, fans had to buy the music, the mother app, and also purchase the apps for each song. Each internal app has three elements for varied gameplay: one inspired by nature, one musicological, and one which explores a technological/interactive aspect. Designer Scott Snibe describes one sub-game: "*Virus* is a kind of femme fatale love song between a virus and a cell – she loves him so much, she destroys him. Musically, the app is about generative music, the creation of music that is always different depending on various interactive algorithms and processes. And interactively, we've created a kind of game that you have to lose to win – the only way to hear the whole song is to allow the viruses to kill the cell . . . I think for the moment it sets the bar and will challenge other artists to push music apps beyond music marketing and replicating instruments towards a new 'gesamtkunstwerk' as the Germans say."[21]

In contrast, a game which really focuses in on audition is Somethin' Else's *Papa Sangre*, which they describe as a "video game with no video."[22] It uses a binaural real-time, 3D audio engine implemented on a handheld device to create a first-person thriller horror game which players experience entirely through their headphones. To navigate through the space, players tap on the screen, simulating footsteps. To run, the user simply taps faster; however, this must be done with rhythmic precision or else the avatar will trip, making it likely that zombies will catch and eat the player's character. The game has over 1,500 audio files, fewer than the designers first thought they would need because they "were limited by audio cognition – our ability to perceive the directionality of a sound and space. To imagine ourselves to be in an audio environment we can only understand a number of sound sources at one time – we had to cut that down to three otherwise it was too confusing."[23] Not surprisingly, they found that visually impaired players caught on to the gameplay more quickly than sighted gamers. In the future, the designers want to "fully exploit the sensors on the iPhone including the gyroscope, which would mean players could navigate through real-world movement that might be walking or turning on the spot."[24] The mobile gaming space remains at the time of writing a highly active area for computer musicians, from some more obvious diatonic step sequencer apps to more experimental pursuits.

Sensing and playing

Gaming does not have to imply video games:[25] Lucky Dragons, the duo of Luke Fischbeck and Sarah Rara, describe one of their pieces, *Make a Baby* (2005), as a ritualistic game.[26] The piece centers around a blanket with metal tabs along the edge. The audience is instructed to touch each other and the blanket in order to make sound. What they are not told is they must make a compete circuit, creating a chain of skin-to-skin contact from one tab to another. The piece takes shape as the audience figures out how to perform manipulations of the Nirvana songs *Paper Cuts* and *About a Girl*. As more audience members join the human chain, or change how they are touching each other through the placement and pressure of their hands, the music changes.

In 2007, Joe Paradiso and Mark Feldmeier created a way for even more audience members to influence musical structure, sonic events, and/or lighting and video cues.[27] The system consists of lightweight, inexpensive wireless sensors which are given to audiences. The sensors transmit a radio-frequency pulse whenever they experience an acceleration greater than a pre-determined level. Tomie Hahn wears similar sensors when she performs as Pikapika, an interactive sonic anime character. Hahn and her collaborator Curtis Bahn use robust, easily replaceable elements wherever possible for her costume, which incorporates sensors and body-mounted speakers.[28] Hahn's movements are sonified with clanks, hisses and whirs, mimicking robotic actions. Although she looks, moves, and sounds like a robot, she is a human dancer who controls sound through her movement. However, in 2010, Pikapika shared the stage with actual robots in a completely spontaneous and algorithmically improvised interaction between performer and robotic ensemble. Analysis of

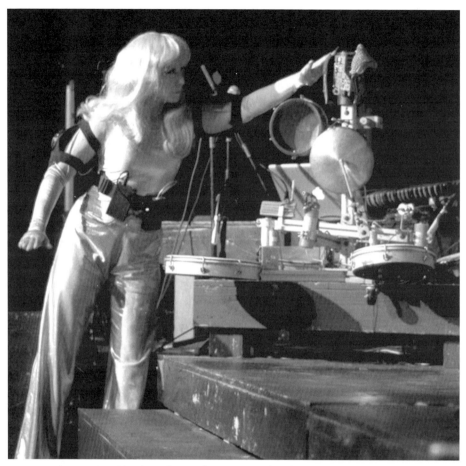

Figure 12.1 Tomie Hahn performing as Pikapika, composed by Curtis Bahn, with robots by Ajay Kapur. Photo: Jim Murphy, 2010 San Jose Biennial. Reproduced by permission

the performer's gestures drove the selection of different sonic palettes, rhythmic generation, dynamics, and large-scale phrasing.[29] The robots Pikapika controlled were Ajay Kapur's percussion robots, including the MahaDeviBot (MDB), a solenoid-based electromechanical robot with an assortment of twelve traditional Indian percussion instruments. MDB can play four frame drums, finger cymbals, a gong, several sets of bells, and wood blocks, and also has a bouncing head it can use to indicate tempo.

Robotic musical instruments perform through motors, solenoids, and gears; there is a long history of mechanical musical instruments and automata before the current era of computer control (see also Chapter 2).[30] Just as the organ can be considered an early synthesizer, the player piano or pianista (1863) can be considered an early musical robot. George Antheil's *Ballet Mécanique* (1926) called for sixteen synchronized player pianos. Unfortunately, the technology did not exist during his lifetime to perform the piece as initially conceived, but in 1999 Paul Lehrman used MIDI player pianos to perform the original score with three xylophones, four bass drums, two pianists, a tam-tam, a set of electric bells, a siren, and three airplane propellers, as well as the aforementioned sixteen synchronized player pianos. In 2006, the National Gallery commissioned an installation version of the piece to correspond with an exhibit on Dadaism. For the installation, the piece was reduced from fourteen to ten minutes and the percussion parts were played by LEMUR (League of Electronic Musical Urban Robots). Eric Singer developed the BeaterBot mechanism, a microprocessor-controlled solenoid and lever mechanism used to move a beater at high velocity to strike a drum surface. The BeaterBot was used more or less directly for the bass drums and tam-tam, and was adapted for use with the xylophones and propellers. For the xylophones, the creators of LEMUR first considered a design using a small number of beaters which could move around to play different keys on each instrument. However, to achieve the playing speeds required by the score, they decided to use a separate beater for each key, 44 beaters per instrument or 132 beaters in total![31] Although the original contract specified seventeen days of operation, soon after the opening, the gallery extended its run by six weeks. The spectacle of sixteen grand pianos playing themselves with a robotic percussion ensemble is indicative of how far automation has come and also how fascinating it can be for humans.

Generating

The composer Conlon Nancarrow is well known for his pieces for player piano, writing pieces far beyond humans' ability to play. Three-quarters of his fifty-one *Studies for Player Piano* use canonic structures. In most of these works, the voices proceed at different, proportionally related speeds, in what are known as tempo canons.[32] *Study 14* is a converging, diverging canon in two compound voices whose rhythms are derived from cyclic presentations of the duration series: $<n, n+1, n+2, n+1>$. In other words, Nancarrow used a mathematical formula to determine the rhythm of his piece, and we may say he thereby created an example of generative art.

The most general definition of generative art is that "the artwork is generated at least in part, by some process that is not under the artist's direct control,"[33] creating a continuum of generated art from pure algorithmic creation (hard) to works where the artist intervenes extensively in the system (soft).[34] As the Nancarrow example shows, generative work does not have to use a digital computer; it can be formed through other methods of calculation. Nancarrow was not the first musician to apply procedures to compose his music; "as early as Guido d'Arezzo's chant generation method through isorhythmic motets to serial techniques and Xenakis' formalized music, interest in processes that produce music has waxed and waned through

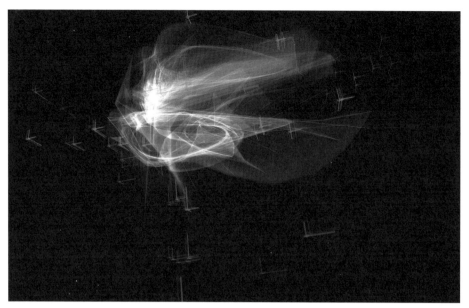

Figure 12.2 Generated visuals from Ryo Ikeshiro's *Construction in Zhuangzi* (2011). Reproduced by permission

several centuries of composition."[35] Computer musicians and digital artists have been especially prevalent in embracing the potential of algorithmic and generative art, from instrumental scores generated by mainframes to electronic dance music created afresh on demand.

A more recent example of a generative work is Ryo Ikeshiro's Max/MSP/Jitter *Construction in Zhuangzi* (2011), a multimedia composition performed in real time based on a modified Lorenz attractor, a three-dimensional dynamical system, and a model of atmospheric convection. As the system is complex, nonlinear, and chaotic, the possibilities to absolutely control the piece are limited and illusory. The two domains of audio and visual are independent, despite being based on the same systems, and emergent phenomena arise from the system's inherent complexity and audiovisualization methods.[36] Although there is a live performer, the piece is more on the "hard" edge of the continuum because the performer cannot predict how the piece will turn out: He or she can only move quickly out of settings he or she doesn't like, or stay on settings that he or she enjoys.

Data

In *Construction in Zhuangzi*, parameters are both sonified and visualized. While most people are familiar with the term "visualization," not as many know the corollary in the auditory domain: *sonification.* Sonification is a subset of a larger field called Auditory Display, which examines how sound can be used as the main conduit for conveying, understanding, and relaying information. "Auditory Display encompasses all aspects of a human–machine interaction system, including the setup, speakers or headphones, modes of interaction with the display system, and any technical solution for the gathering, processing, and computing necessary to obtain sound in response to the data . . . sonification is a core component of an auditory display: the technique of rendering sound in response to data and interactions."[37] Most sonification takes an existing numerical data set, from the stock market, tidal activity, brainwaves, or radio telescope measurements, and translates those numbers into audible sound. This process is called *mapping* – taking the abstract data and mapping it to acoustic variables.

A simple mapping might take the closing index of the stock market and map that to pitch, or take the number of trades and match that to volume. Of course, these mappings are subjective and created by the researcher; another sonification could use the closing price to manipulate frequency modulation and the number of trades could affect the panning; therefore, there is no such thing as *the sound* of the Higgs-Boson particle, no matter what the popular media might report.[38] Lev Manovich, author of the seminal text *The Language of New Media*, calls this the "dark side of mapping and of computer media in general – its built-in existential angst. By allowing us to map anything into anything else, to construct infinite number of different interfaces to a media object, to follow infinite trajectories through the object, and so on, computer media simultaneously makes all these choices appear arbitrary – unless the artist uses special strategies to motivate her or his choices."[39] By selecting perceptually useful mappings, sonifications can be used to understand data sets and/or create music. Bob L. Sturm discovered a new ocean current when he sonified data from ocean buoys, though his original intent was simply to create music from the data.[40] As one can imagine, it is easiest to sonify time-based events (compressing or stretching the data in time as needed), but with mapping, it is possible to change any variable into time, allowing researchers to sonify still images by sweeping through the data over time.

> The next time you are in a room with a florescent light, look up. Does the light flicker or change? You may not see it, but if you were to sonify the light, you would hear a pitch that wavers slightly with the current. The frame rate for film is 24 frames per second, compared with the sampling rate for CD-quality audio, which is 44,100 samples per second. Our ears and eyes function very differently, and sonification allows us to take advantage of the capabilities of auditory processing to understand large data sets. Although humans are often seen as primarily visual creatures (hearing is the "second sense" for everyone but the blind), we do receive a tremendous amount of information through our auditory system.

Multimedia

Composer Garth Paine and dancer Hellen Sky created an immersive multimedia work generated by the movement of the dancer which creates real-time sonification and visualization. In *The Darker Edge of Night* (2008), Sky wears sensors on her head – an EEG for brainwaves, an EOG to track eye movements, and an EMG to capture facial movements. She also has sensors on her arm, her shoulder, and her hand. The bio-data is fed directly to synthesis variables, but these are constrained by a pre-composed range of preferred aesthetics states.[41] Paine developed his own sensor system, and there are commercially available dance controllers such as the DIEM Dance Suit and the Mivuri Suit by Yamaha, but it has become much more common for dancers to control electronic music through video tracking. Such computer vision has also become common in theatrical productions. Meira Asher and Guy Harries' theatrical version of *Infantry* (2002) uses the human voice, electronic processing, camera networks, and pre-recorded film to expose the harsh reality of the life of a child soldier. There is also a purely musical version of the piece which consists of fourteen tracks derived from the theatrical production.[42]

Perhaps the most closely connected art form to electronic music is the moving image; both art forms developed from the later nineteenth century and both started by recording the environment onto a physical medium. One kind of pairing of sound and image is known as "fused" because there is a physical cross-wiring of media signals. The Australian artist Robin Fox plugs audio from a custom-built digital synthesizer into an oscilloscope; in the resulting connection, the cross-wiring of sound to image is immediate, agile, and intense. "Every signal is simultaneously heard and seen; every sound is a form in motion, every form a sound."[43] Composer Bill Alves, who worked with the computer animation pioneer John Whitney, Sr., takes a different approach to his computer music and animation pieces. He creates his soundtracks in tandem with the visual composition, carefully synchronizing movement between points of tension and dissonance and points of stability and tonal consonance. In his 1997 work *Hiway 70*, the harmonies are often direct analogs of the patterns of visual symmetry.[44] Of course, image and sound do not have to relate to each other – they can merely co-exist in time and space – but in general, the most successful pairings of electronic music and other film/video do have an element of Gesamtkunstwerk. Yet another fusion of image and sound is found more often in dance clubs, with the art of VJing (though there are also sit-down festivals of live cinema and other audiovisual combinations; see also the discussion in the next chapter). VJs often mix pre-recorded video and live camera input using specialized software which allows analysis of an audio signal, tap tempo, or other manual control.[45]

Figure 12.3 Drew Daniel from Matmos conducting PLOrk in *Ganzfield in Orange and Black*. Reproduced by permission

The band Matmos often deploy live cinematic elements in their performances, and their work with the Princeton Laptop Orchestra (PLOrk) is no exception. In *Ganzfield in Orange and Black* (2009), they re-enact a famous parapsychological experiment, which is designed to supposedly provide a scientifically verifiable way to test subjects for extrasensory perception (ESP). For the performance, they used a videotaped Ganzfeld session as a graphic score and "lead vocal" while Drew Daniel conducted the orchestra. In the Ganzfeld experiment, subjects undergo a simple state of sensory deprivation, isolated in a dark room, resting on a mattress, listening to white noise on headphones, wearing halved ping-pong balls over their eyes, with a soft red light shining in their faces. In the concert, red lights shine on the orchestra while the image of the subject is projected behind them. During the experiment, the participants are asked to open their minds and try to receive a psychic signal. In Matmos' experiment, they tried to transmit a musical idea: the subjects then describe any sounds they "hear" in their minds, and any objects or actions or events that they seem to see or hear. Responses are divided into three categories: sound-making objects, timbral/textural ideas, and formal musical ideas. These lists were presented to the members of PLOrk, and each member was asked to construct a series of "sonic events" that would realize the images, sounds, and ideas generated during the psychic experiments. The ensemble creates a spontaneous sonic assemblage out of their collective responses to the transcripts of psychic phenomena.[46]

Transmitting and receiving

In *Ganzfeld in Orange and Black,* Matmos explore transmitting data between two individuals through the dubious method of ESP. Maryanne Amacher's *City Links Series* (started in 1967) used the more reliable route of telephone lines to mix together sounds from different locations: This mixture was then transmitted over the radio. Now the Internet makes it possible to transmit a tremendous amount of data around the globe and create *telematic* art. Composer Sarah Weaver works with the UN for her *ResoNations: International Telematic Music Concerts for Peace* series. Concerts take place at the UN and various international sites. The program consists of new compositions for peace by contemporary composers from each participating country for the full telematic ensemble to perform together. The concerts have local audiences in each location and a worldwide webcast. Of course, the concerts all occur at different times (and even different dates!) depending on where in the world the performers and audiences are located. For a November 20, 2009 concert, there were over twenty-five performers involved, including Joan La Barbara, voice, Robert Dick, flute, and Samir Chatterjee, tabla at the UN, Mark Dresser, contrabass at the University of San Diego, Charles Nicols, electric violin, and Chris Chafe, electric cello in Banff Canada, Pedro Rebelo, piano in Belfast, Ireland, and SeungHee Lee, haegeum, with Quartet X, a string quartet in South Korea.[47]

A concert between New York and Nairobi, *Pamoja: Transmissions of Togetherness* (2012), was the first known telematic music concert with a site in Africa. East Africa first acquired fiber optic Internet in the summer of 2009, and one rehearsal had to take place via phone communications since a ship in the Indian Ocean dropped its anchor which broke the only Internet cable, wiping out Internet access for five countries in East Africa that day. Musically and technically, the concert was realized more as a pilot, but the project was memorable, fueled by the dedication to connect for togetherness.[48]

Weaver uses Stanford's Jacktrip software for her telematic concerts. Even using specialized software, network music still has an inherent latency due to the speed of light and any telecommunications equipment, often reaching to hundreds of milliseconds inter-continentally.[49] Threads in JackTrip are scheduled as a real-time priority, but there needs to be some sort of buffer to keep latency constant, and

Figure 12.4 ResoNations, November 20, 2009: International Telematic Music
Concerts for Peace. Reproduced by permission

another method is needed to deal with both under-run and over-run conditions.[50]
Learning to play in an ensemble which is not in the same room or even in the
same time is difficult, though there are precedents, such as the acoustic and visual
spacing of an organist in a church. Pieces must be composed with an awareness of
the challenges. While Jacktrip tries to mitigate the problems of streaming over the
Internet, the Art of Failure's *8 Silences* (2011) uses the very problems of transmission
to generate the audio; the activity of the network and its architecture becomes the
core of the resulting sound performance. *8 Silences* is a live performance made from
mixing together several silent ogg and MP3 stream loops with different quality
settings; error corrections are bypassed which would otherwise attempt to maintain
quality. Each silent loop is emitted to a different location around the globe and
is then sent back to the location of the concert venue and re-transmitted. Due to
transmission errors such as packet loss, the wrong order of reception, and other
artifacts, each initial silent stream slowly produces glitched noise related to its own
route on the network. The sound gets increasingly dense as the loops deteriorate; to
end the performance, the operator turns off the loops one at a time.[51] The piece is
an Internet-era homage to both Cage's *4′33″* and Lucier's "*I am sitting in a room.*"

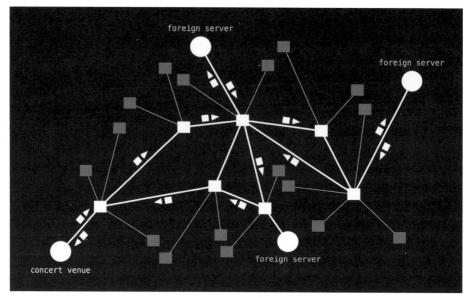

Figure 12.5 *Art of Failure*, diagram of Internet nodes and possible paths for *8 Silences* by Nicolas Maigret. Reproduced by permission

Unbounded futures

The boundaries between categories are permeable. There are pieces which cross many of the sub-headings we articulate above. In *Tweet Dreams* (2010), audience members use their personal mobile devices to tweet messages containing search hash tags, as decided by the performers. These phrases are projected onto one side of the screen, as the tweets from the audience members and the world are sonified and visualized into a dynamic network.[52] This multimedia piece takes in networks and sonification of audience participation.

It seems appropriate, at the close of this chapter, to feature a short story written by Max Mathews about a future where there are two classes of musicians:

> The story, set in 2165, concerns an astronaut wielding a 1704 Stradivarius violin, who returns after nearly two hundred years in hibernation to a planet Earth in which music is very different than it was when he left. On the one hand, there is a monastic society of musicians clad in the formal tails of concert soloists, virtuosi who perform canonized music for "perfect" digital recordings controlled by special stewards within their order. On the other hand, there are participatory mass-improvisations mediated by computers, called "Audances," where players interface with digital machines creating work using all manner of joysticks, knobs and TV screens, all happening inside a specially built room, with no audience and no possibility for error. The story's protagonist reminisces, in his last will and

testament, on the world he left behind, where music was a physical act as well as a social one, involving physical instruments performed from the stage.[53]

While we cannot know what the future will bring, there is no shortage of options for the human race to continue to make music and to extend music's combination with other media. Whether collective composition and an ultimate merging of media is to be part of music's fate, the ubiquity of electronics in the process is pointed to by Laurie Spiegel's prediction of electronic music as folk music: "again, as once upon a time, music can be created and changed at home and directly distributed by an expanding, not contracting, percentage of those who want to, in an expanding variety of ways."[54]

Further reading

Blesser, Barry and Salter, Linda-Ruth (2007) *Spaces Speak, Are You Listening?: Experiencing Aural Architecture* (Cambridge, MA: MIT Press).

Dixon, Steve (2007) *Digital Performance: A History of New Media in Theater, Dance, Performance Art, and Installation* (Cambridge, MA: MIT Press).

Hermann, Thomas, Hunt, Andy, and Neuhoff, John G. (eds.) (2012) *The Sonification Handbook* (Berlin: Logos Publishing House).

Jordan, Ken and Packer, Randall (2002) *Multimedia: From Wagner to Virtual Reality* (New York: W. W. Norton).

Joseph-Hunter, Galen (2011) *Transmission Arts: Artists and Airwaves* (New York: PAJ Publications).

Kahn, Douglas and Whitehead, Gregory (1992) *Wireless Imagination: Sound Radio and the Avant-Garde* (Cambridge, MA: MIT Press).

Michelsen Foy, George (2010) *Zero Decibels: The Quest for Absolute Silence* (New York: Scribner).

Salter, Chris (2010) *Entangled: Technology and the Transformation of Performance* (Cambridge, MA: MIT Press).

Sexton, Jamie (2007) *Music, Sound and Multimedia: From the Live to the Virtual* (Edinburgh University Press).

Chapter 13

Live electronic music

A powerful perspective from which to view the history of electronic music is the role of live performance. The nature of liveness quickly presents dilemmas. When recordings and computers allow the automation of every aspect of music generation and playback, why deal with live human action anymore? Conversely, the traditional human communion of live music making has often felt threatened by new mediating technologies. There remains an irresistible draw to the new just as there is defense of the old: Crowds rushed to witness the first theremin performances, with their seemingly magical action at a distance, and accompanying debates on quite what counts as "musical" or "live" continue to keep theorists occupied.

In electronic music, live control can run on a continuum from a single press of a button to initiate playback, to in-the-moment fine control of all aspects of the music, at a human gestural rate. Because electronic music is so rich with potential complexities of system, its live performance is a negotiation between what is automated and what is left up to human real-time decisions. Various strategies have arisen, including shared control by multiple human musicians, computer artificial intelligences designed for concert situations, mixtures of manual control and autopilot, and other complicated set-ups. Network music even allows action at a distance spanning continents!

Human decision making in live performance also stretches from over-rehearsed scripted actions known well in advance to much looser frameworks within which improvised action can be pursued. Whilst the patterns used in improvisation may themselves have been the subject of intensive rehearsal, decisions on the final form can be deferred to performance time itself, and the shape contingent on performance factors. When other agencies, such as computer programs, are developed to operate in such situations, the devisers of the systems must themselves anticipate the sorts of freedom available. So the manifestation of human agency in electronic music is a complicated business, both for performers and any audience.

Figure 13.1 Laetitia Sonami and the Lady's Glove. Photo by Joker Nies. Reproduced by permission

Live performance examples

To help settle into the concert mood, we describe here three artists and their performance situations in order to establish a sense of the variations within live electronic music. All three have been actively performing internationally within the last decade.

The Japanese performer Atsuhiro Ito has created his own instrument, the Optron, by modifying a fluorescent light into an audiovisual instrument gripped in two hands; when triggered, it acts visually as a strobe, shining suddenly into the darkened performance space, but also contains pickups, blasting out noise via attached guitar effects pedals and amp. In a show at Sonar 2006, the duo Optrum (Optron + drums) performed, making a surreal sort of amplified thrash music.[1]

Laetitia Sonami is one of a number of performers who have worked with adapted clothing; in her case, the Lady's Glove, a chic sensor-laden evening glove on one arm, armed with flex sensors, accelerometers, and more.[2] Movements of this controller, whether graceful or abrupt, are translated through to a computer acting as a sound engine; the actual mapping from sensor data to sound is continually modified throughout the course of performance, renewing and refreshing the experience for an audience on a musical journey.

Powerbooks Unplugged are a laptop ensemble, active since 2004, who slip in amongst the audience to play; they are connected together on a local network and use their laptop speakers as the primary sound in the space.[3] Although they have experimented with a further sub-woofer connected computer on the network, in the main, this means that there are no low-frequency sounds (laptop speakers have issues reproducing anything below around 100Hz); on the other hand, the inherent spatialization of computer music by performer location, and their improvised conversational coding as interface within the environment SuperCollider, makes for a special performance dynamic.

There are many more permutations of humans and their musical machines that have been explored in live performance. These range from the manipulation of pre-existing recordings to suit a particular occasion (as in electroacoustic diffusion and DJing) to new systems of interaction between electronics and humans, whether transforming acoustic inputs or synthesizing from scratch, and showing different degrees of human agency in control. We will now go on to explore some of the options.

Live and recorded music

In Chapter 2, we encountered issues relating to the adoption of recording as a central musical practice. Live music has been particularly threatened by radio and record from the 1920s onward, with the dissolution of much amateur music making for more passive reception. The story is not absolute, given many countermeasures, such as the home popularity of electric guitars or electronic keyboards, the educational (if task delimited) musicianship of computer games like *Rock Band*, continuing hubs of training in many musical styles (including dedicated thereminists!), folk festivals, and more. In economic terms, whilst an essential part of musicians' promotional arsenal is now the recording, in the current world of downloads, monies from touring (concert tickets and merchandise) can provide better revenue than unit sales or radio play.[4] This is especially the case for more experimental acts, who cannot expect to achieve gross shifting of units or a huge amount of streaming.

A recurring issue is modern recording's deceits of skill, such as the chance to re-record takes ad infinitum. Whilst second takes are not available in live shows, prevalent corrective measures such as Auto-Tune[5] may well be. The "falsities" of recording (at least with respect to "in-the-room" acoustic skill) are brought into the greatest stark relief by idealizations of live performance practice. Especially controversial is the prevalence of miming to playback of fixed recordings in concert rather than fresh instantiation: Aside from issues of absent performer skill in some "musicians," a real tension exists between the aspiration to make polished performances at the "impossible" quality standard established by recording trickery and authenticity of portrayal. Taking the side of sampled recordings over live re-enactment, Jon Hassell has claimed that "It's a problem to know what to do with [instrumental virtuosity] in the age of sampling and sleight of hand because the audience is looking for the final results basically. They don't care if it took you twenty years to arrive at it or whether somebody just sampled it off a record and used it."[6]

Hassell may be pushing too far here, since he doesn't account for the joy of live realizations, where imperfect blemishes which would not work for polished recordings only go to show the liveness of the moment. Not all musics are well represented by fixity: Improvised music in particular may hold a reluctance to see recording as much more than incidental documentation, and may reject notions of perfection achieved through countless takes.[7] If music relies on a particular place, if it is dependent on all sensory channels of feedback between participants and if the act of creation in the moment is itself a central part of music making, a fixed file cannot hold all the requisite complexity of a scene and adequately reproduce the full physical experience of being there.[8]

On the other hand, many musics can only exist through recording techniques, and the problem then becomes how to deliver such music in live settings; authentic performance here may necessitate studio equipment at the venue, such as hardware sequencer-driven dance music sets, tracker programs running at raves, a central interface of a mixing desk, turntables, and the like. Certainly, a trend of the later twentieth century is an increasing presence of studio equipment as part of the standard arsenal of a touring band; computers allow the miniaturization and portability of this studio to the extent that a solo laptop artist can tour with only one bag of cabin luggage.[9]

Studio-created music par excellence, such as the beautiful, if seemingly rigid, works of electroacoustic tape music, can still be amenable to a form of live delivery. Electroacoustic performance practice centers on sound diffusion, inspired by the realization that not all acoustic playback environments are the same and that tweaking to individual concert rooms is a pragmatic necessity. Sound projectionists or diffusers explore live mixing for complex arrangements of multiple speakers, working with orchestras of loudspeakers in particular surround sound set-ups; from François Bayle and the Acousmonium to Jonty Harrison and BEAST: see Chapter 9.[10] Even aside from the space-specific challenge of diffusing work, there is a need for a community to have a chance to present work to one another in person that a live public gathering serves beyond home listening.

Recording itself can be a live act: Many works depend on the live capturing of sound, whether through analog tape machines on stage or digital sampling. Pauline Oliveros' works for tape delay, such as *I of IV* (1966), let her perform against delayed copies of herself,[11] a pre-cursor to the work of Robert Fripp, or the use of guitar sample pedals. STEIM's LiSa (Live Sampling), as used as a sound engine by such performers as Michel Waiswisz and Kaffe Matthews, allows live collection and manipulation of sound, now a commonplace technique of digital signal processing environments such as Max/MSP.

Pre-recorded parts provide a fixed background to performance, such as a singer re-enacting his or her vocal live to the original studio backing. Electroacoustic music's investigation of works for tape part and live performer dates back as early as Henry and Schaeffer's mixed-music work *Orphée 51* for voices and tape.[12] This is no different from the case of Les Paul and Mary Ford in the 1950s, appearing live on American television with their tape machine, or Depeche Mode in concert in the 1980s with a tape machine where a drummer might otherwise be. A large number of popular music concerts now depend on partial tape backing in order to get closer to released recordings that the audience are familiar with, typically synchronized via a click track for the drummer (who is very familiar from recording studios with playing to a click!). DJ performance, of course, has never had a problem with presenting slices of ready-made sound for live consumption, though the amount of re-working and re-layering during sets is highly variable. For many musicians, recording technology and live music are now thoroughly intertwined.

Novel interfaces

Electronic music has admitted live performance much more often than sometimes supposed, especially if caricatures of mechanical, robot, and machine music are not adopted too readily. There have been many novel instruments and musical interfaces as sound production has been freed from the scale of mechanical physics into the world of electromagnetism (see Chapters 3 and 5). The Theremin remains an archetype of new possibilities, with its action at a distance, but further alternatives range from touching circuit boards in circuit bending, through domestic appliances turned into musical controllers, to large-scale scaffolding, climbed by multiple people, as in the trio Sensorband's *Soundnet*.[13]

Yet acoustic instruments have often remained a touchstone of developments. Amplification has transformed existing instruments, most prominently seen in the development of the electric guitar, or the change in singing style enabled through microphones.[14] The keyboard interface has remained a familiar sight, even if guiding electrically driven sound, from the Hammond organ through Moog modulars to current generations of hardware synthesizers and MIDI controller keyboards. Some would say that too much comfort and familiarity is to the detriment of new music. Just as John Cage critiqued thereminists for reproducing well-worn classics on their novel instruments, Buchla was uncomfortable with Moog's adoption of an explicit keyboard controller in his systems; Moog won out commercially (see Chapter 5). Yet even with a keyboard front end, the design of the sound engine itself can radically depart from acoustic convention.

New electronic music instruments are often being developed,[15] but more infrequently mass produced. Whether single-person manufacture or company products, the Manta, the Eigenharp, the Monome, the Tenori-On, and their ilk have achieved varying degrees of adoption, and may prove to have lasting appeal to musicians beyond their decade of creation and release. The vast majority of novel instruments presented at the annual New Interfaces of Musical Expression Conference are confined to singular prototypes which will not reach production runs. Yet enthusiasm to build new interfaces remains high, and the sheer customizability of software and hardware often militates against new classic designs; instead, a panoply of ideas is explored and DIY culture embraced. This can be to the detriment of longer-term practice[16] and repertoire development for any one specific instrument, though some dedicated performers, such as the aforementioned Laetitia Sonami and Michel Waiswisz, have put in the practice time through iterations of their interfaces.

Furthermore, hip hop has given rise to intensive practice into the dynamic use of the turntable as instrument, though there are art music precedents to such a capability in live performance from 1930 Grammophonmusik through Cage to Schaeffer.[17] Turntablism includes some more abstract practices from the likes of Christian Marclay as well as the virtuosity of the 1970s Bronx pioneer DJs and later DMC Championship winners. As revealed in the film *Scratch* (2001), many turntablists' first exposure to scratching was the work of Grand Mixer D.ST in Herbie Hancock's single *Rockit* (1983). Turntable crews, such as the Invisibl Skratch Piklz or Scratch Perverts, create edgy and energetic shows, through many decks, many changes of record, and much tight choreography and highly practiced technique. Aside from turntables, in hip hop, drum machine interfaces have also been practiced for live performance; MPC performers such as Arabhram Orellanes (Araabmusik) have achieved some notoriety for their virtuosic skills.[18] The turntable and the drum machine as live instruments again show the close connections of recording technology and new music making. The very materials under control in turntablism, extracts of recorded sound, highlight these tensions.

Some musical interfaces are highly overt. A performer can be involved in full-body motion, perhaps tracked through computer vision, a body suit, or using a huge lever. But the control of electronic music also allows very subtle direction, using little or no clear bodily motion. The EEG interface of Alvin Lucier's *Music for Solo Performer* (1965) is perhaps the most obvious example of a performer avoiding external movement; all the human action, so to speak, is in the brain waves (the sound output is via speaker resonation of acoustic drums, the speakers sonifying the electrically detected and amplified neural signals). In recent times, since around the mid-1990s, laptop computer performance has led to many seemingly ossified people on stage, frozen staring into a screen, and an audience left wondering at the connection between sound and the human supposedly responsible. The gestures are small caresses of a trackpad or nudges of keys, sometimes befitting lower-case sound and sometimes utterly out of proportion in resultant sound energy to the physical impetus.

As David Keane noted in 1979, "Electronic music generation makes possible sonic gestures which are not proportional to the physical bodily force exerted to produce the gesture,"[19] a comment repeated subsequently many times in the literature as worries over the effortlessness of huge sound and loss of physical causality have recurred.[20] Kim Cascone has noted that laptop performance has the same problem as acousmatic music, providing a lack of visual-gestural stimulus clearly related to resultant sound.[21] Dedicated listeners can work past this; unfamiliar interfaces always take time to be accepted, and if the physical gesture/sound engine disconnection will remain problematic for some, it has not stopped whole communities of work forming within the paradigm.[22] Controversies over the theremin's airy interface, or snide comments at Brian Eno playing Battleships with his VCS3 during Roxy Music gigs, did not stop electronic music from being made, nor did it prevent subsequent developments.

Live audiovisuals

Outside of willfully acousmatic settings, the conduct of a performance is not simply about effective aural presence. A whole range of stimuli may be relevant, from physical response to sound waves resonating the body to visual channels of performance action, dance, expression, and other communicative human presence. Live electronics may be deployed as only one component of a grand theatrical production, and pop showmanship has never been entirely about the music. Visual confirmation of the personal presence of an artist, even if inside Deadmau5's LED mouse helmet or the Daft Punk on-stage pyramid, can be an important point of connection between musicians and fans.

Part of concertizing is the sense of danger and occasion. Many performances can, and do, go wrong and many factors can disrupt safety.[23] The Human League, supporting Siouxsie and the Banshees on tour in 1978, had fiberglass shields to protect their synths from thrown beer![24] Laptops have been dented in nightclub shootouts. In the laptop equivalent of burning of guitars, Takeko Akamatsu threw a laptop off a table in 2007: Leif Shackelford created a media performance, *Laptop vs Table-saw* (2009), based around sawing a laptop in half (with it playing, for a while, at least).[25]

Figure 13.2 Lumínico in live performance in 2011, incorporating audio and visual computers, and live acoustic musicians. http://webcache.googleusercontent. com/search?q=cache:eOtHXMecbh4J:www.luminico.org/+http://www.luminico. org/&cd=1&hl=en&ct=clnk&gl=uk. Reproduced by permission

Beyond human presence and spectacle, electronic music performers have investigated the parallel channel of visuals to audio. The visuals may be projected computer graphics and film (paralleling sound synthesis and sampling) or more exotic projections in lights, lasers, and holograms. It should not be thought that this is a new direction as such, though digital technology has made it a common practice. Parallel to electronic music history is a long history of audiovisual experimentation, from the eighteenth-century ocular harpsichord and later "color organs" through experimental film visual music from the 1920s, light shows of the 1960s, video art and hardware visual synthesisers.[26]

MIDI triggering of video clips, so-called audiovisual sampling of joint audio and visual snippets, has been a reality since the 1990s, illuminated by work from pioneers such as Emergency Broadcast Network and Coldcut/Hexstatic. Joint audio and visual action is now commonplace in software, whether through the alliance of multiple programs or within a single multimedia equipped tool such as Max/MSP with Jitter (see also Chapter 12).

Live audiovisuals remain a fast-developing area; for instance, Amon Tobin's recent ISAM shows (2011) have involved projection mapping of computer-generated visuals onto a 3D stage set of boxes, Vocaloid singing voice synthesized anime characters have appeared on stage with live band through holographic projection, and Skrillex has used motion capture technology to control huge virtual body animations which massively amplify his DJing stance.[27] Figure 13.2 is an image of a performance by the Mexican live audiovisual ensemble Lumínico, who manage to reconcile electroacoustic and accessible multimedia performance.

There are new problems with the introduction of other channels. Concentration on multiple modalities can split attention, and a lack of quality in one can undermine the other. Equality of treatment is rare, whether through compositional design or the specifics of venues; not all audio and visual actions have to follow one another precisely, and differences of meaning can arise.[28] On the other hand, opera, theater, dance, and other mixed media art practices have always involved combined presentation, sometimes subservient to a master narrative, sometimes acting in rather more complicated ways (for example, in Merce Cunningham's setting of dance and music as parallel but independent streams). Video operas, such as Steve Reich's *Three Tales* (1998–2002) or JacobTV's reality opera *The News* (2012), synchronize music to video footage, a combination of acoustic ensemble and audiovisual sampling (see also Chapter 12).

Ensembles and roles

An attempt to categorize all kinds of electronic music performance would be doomed to failure, but we can appreciate better the wide scope of performance types by investigating some historic and contemporary trends. We see variation within the fixity of different aspects of the sound world and also in the size of ensemble. Electronic sound may only form part of an ensemble, such as a lone keyboardist in a rock line-up, though in popular music, amplification is a general trend. It may also be the raison d'être of a group, as in a laptop orchestra, or a live electroacoustic ensemble. In some ways, surveying live performance work is to look again over the whole history of electronic music, since the drive to take such music live has been ever present, and even for the avant-garde recorded music movements, the early turntable concerts of musique concrète or experiments in live spatializtion avoid pure one-button playback.

A massive variety of roles are found. Electronic music has its own idiomatic instruments, from the theremin, through the Minimoog, to a mobile phone. Indeed, all of these three examples have appeared in ensembles, as well as solos. Composers have written deliberately for groupings of electronic instruments, such as the scoring of Messiaen's *Oraison* (1937) for six ondes Martenot. Improvisation groups have taken advantage of electronic resources, such as AMM and Musica Elettronica Viva in the 1960s, while more recent performers have adopted unexpected hardware for performance, such as Sachiko M on hardware sampler, Toshimaru Nakamura on no-input feedback mixer, and Ikue Mori on drum machines or laptop. Familiar rock instruments, themselves instances of the impact of amplification on performance, have been combined with live sound processing of a radical degree; for example, in the bass guitar plus processing model of Squarepusher or Boxcutter.[29]

Much of the work of John Cage and his disciples in electronic music, after the Project of Music for Magnetic Tape, was in the creation of live performance situations (as alternative happenings and process music pieces). Live treatments of sound, through amplification, and more complicated sound processing circuitry, pre-figures current live computer processing, but was applied in the 1960s through analog techniques. The audience-displeasing work *Reunion* (1962) controlled the routing of a live electronics ensemble through a rambling wired-up chess game between Cage and Marcel Duchamp.

Whilst computer music took time to gain wider musical adoption, being initially too slow and expensive until the 1980s, real-time analog music synthesizers gained a mass market. Moog synthesizers were played by ensembles, from a 1969 Museum of Modern Art improvisation concert to Mother Mallard's Portable Masterpiece Company and their group performances, in the vein of minimalist pattern pieces.[30] We have seen how synth pop bands arose (see Chapter 7); although sequencers and tape backing were often required, bands often performed a subset of parts live. The synthesizer appears frequently from the 1970s onward as a band instrument, though often in mixed ensembles; a mixture of conventional rock instruments and synth. Whilst the early Yellow Magic Orchestra is a transitional case, and Jean Michel Jarre often admits rock instruments or acoustic instruments into particular performances, Tangerine Dream, Kraftwerk, Telex, and others provide clear touring examples of the all-synthesizer group.

Computer music saw a progression from nonreal-time rendering to live performance, where what was once a seemingly hopelessly slow action of overnight calculation became live rendered sound amenable to in-the-moment decision making. With the 1990s movement toward laptop performance, it was inevitable that situations with more than a lone performer would occur (Kraftwerk themselves toured in 2002 in a laptop-based quartet!). Although PLOrk (founded in 2006) has received the most press,[31] they were not the first organized ensemble of laptopists – earlier precedents include Famers Manual performing as a laptop group in 1995, Tokyo's eponymous "laptop orchestra" performing twenty-strong in 2002, and many laptop jam sessions.

As Simon Emmerson has noted, a single laptopist can produce multiple layers, so a team leads to a "polyphony of polyphonies."[32] Ad hoc laptop jams are often spoilt by the same issues that bedevil inexperienced improvisation groups, with the added danger that the frequency spectrum is so quickly filled up with a struggle for noise supremacy. On the other hand, multiple human participants have the potential to share workload in a way that, if carefully handled, can benefit overall control. In the more autocratic orchestras, human attentional resources are directed toward highly

Figure 13.3 Just another superstar live coding laptop band: Benoît and the Mandelbrots performing live at the SuperCollider Symposium, London, April 2012. Photo by Steve Welburn, available under CC BY-SA 2.0 license

specified strands. In the long-running network computer band the Hub, active in various forms and names since the late 1970s and a strong precedent to much computer teamwork, a more communal ethos is explored, with participants sharing data via a central regulating computer hub.[33] Sergi Jorda sees shared control of an instrument as the most powerful paradigm, instantiated as it is in the Reactable project for a tabletop controller.[34] Mass computation has led to other ultimately computer music-based groups, through more everyday interfaces, such as the mobile phone orchestra MoPho.[35]

With an increasing use of electronic parts in art music, dedicated support for the concert presentation of such works is required. Whilst composers are increasingly ready to deploy processing and parts from their own laptops, even providing stan-dalone programs for performers to take on tour with them – Hans Tutschuku has gone as far as making iPhone apps for specific pieces – some specialist institutions and teams help to support such work, from the new interface hub of STEIM in Amsterdam, through IRCAM's long involvement in live treatments, to the duo Sound Intermedia. The latter have often worked with Jonathan Harvey, as in his *Bird Concerto with Piano Song* (2001); meanwhile, Andrew Gerzso's work with Pierre Boulez on active live computer processing of instruments in *Répons* (first performed 1981) is well known.[36]

The reconciliation of acoustic and electronic parts is a complex matter of sound balance in amplification, of perceived agency in sound treatment, and of real and evoked spatial setting, as discussed by Simon Emmerson in his 2007 book *Living Electronic Music*, amongst other authors (see also the discussion on mixed music in Chapter 9). Although combinations of tape playback and performer can seem inflexible, there are solutions which keep more human-like adaptability of timing and expression, ranging from a human performer cueing electronic parts to artificially intelligent score following systems. Nonetheless, the composer Alejandro Viñao has argued that choices are made on a piece-by-piece basis.[37] As long as the audience perceives a successful piece of music, there is no reason to disregard the click track, whose very rigidity can also be of musical worth.

Computers have empowered many new interaction possibilities. Some of the most exciting, though challenging to effectively design, are in the realm of computerized performers. The dream is of an artificially intelligent (AI) musician able to take part in human music making on an equal footing.[38] For now, humans are still needed as conceptualizers and designers of the AIs, and as audience, human auditory and musical capabilities remaining the essential goldmark. The history of human music making far outweighs the history of mechanization in music by tens of thousands of years and is not ignored in a hurry; however, as a long-term compositional and research aim, virtual musicianship is only increasing as a possibility in electronic music. Given how much electronic music is actually performed live, across so many different models of activity, we need have no fear that the lifeblood of live music is being cut off.

Further reading

Emmerson, Simon (2007) *Living Electronic Music* (Aldershot: Ashgate).
Lewis, George (ed.) (2012) *Oxford Handbook of Critical Improvisation Studies* (2 vols.) (New York: Oxford University Press).
Peters, Deniz, Eckel, Gerhard, and Dorschel, Andreas (2012) *Bodily Expression in Electronic Music: Perspectives on Reclaiming Performativity* (New York: Routledge).
Pressing, Jeff (1992) *Synthesizer Performance and Real-Time Techniques* (Oxford University Press).

Chapter 14

Conclusions

We hope you've found much to engage you in this introduction to electronic music. We could hardly explore every path, but have pointed out a few routes; the further reading and listening suggestions in the chapters will lead you on many interesting musical journeys. The final suggestions for this chapter are a collection of some further alternative histories, theories, ideas, and music to pursue. We'd like to take the opportunity in the paragraphs remaining to us to point to a few further trends and movements in electronic music, perhaps because they were given less attention elsewhere in the book or are worth acknowledging as ongoing sites of scholarship and musical activity.

There is certainly a mass interest in electronic music history, evidenced by articles and programs on electronic music in popular media, and often associated with the avid technology-rich cultures of the present. Retro movements pore over the inspiring examples, and missed opportunities, of the past, spending more time with, say, 8-bit music, than the accelerating technology curve allowed in the 1980s. Enthusiasts collect and restore old equipment; Phil Cirocco describes in great detail a loving restoration of a 1940 Novachord, a romantic adventure in electronics, metal, and wood, set against a peril of "black tar" contamination of the unit by old capacitors.[1] There is a continuing use of legacy equipment, such as in the analog studio room at The Hague's Institute of Sonology, amongst many other institutions keeping alive tape and analog synthesizer tradition. Long-term maintenance is an active issue in the fast-paced technology world, especially for software; open source software has a potentially greater chance of survival, as seen by the long existence of the Music 1 descendant Csound. Propellerheads' proprietary *Rebirth* software, originally released in 1997, has been discontinued and is now given tribute in an online museum (www.rebirthmuseum.com), though it has also recently re-appeared in the form of an iPhone app.

The legacies of creators are being constantly re-appraised, and whilst there can be no promise that everyone will get their ultimate due, with so many historic, active and future practitioners to credit, figures like Daphne Oram have received much retrospective coverage. A 2011–12 exhibit at London's Science Museum, *Oramics to Electronica*, makes her experimental synthesis work (based on sonification of

192

drawn control shapes) a center piece. The popular press also picked up on the finding amongst Delia Derbyshire's own archives of a late 1960s tape experiment that anticipates much 1990s electronica.[2] Interest in Russian electronic music pioneers is being advanced with the publication of Andrei Smirnov's new book *Sound in Z – Experiments in Sound and Electronic Music in Early 20th Century Russia*. Much remains to be discovered.

The international headlong rush of online activity makes documenting cultural movement an exhausting process (as part of real life, the Internet is perhaps its own best document, though some sort of information guide can be crucial to manage exploration).[3] Mass access to content creation software has brought about a new age of the amateur, with human efforts split over a multitude of parallel creative threads. It is a joyous state of affairs that so many people can now be involved in electronic music making and that so many minority interests can co-exist and innovate. Yet Utopian tendencies remain tempered by the realization that mass success is still at the mercy of narrow promotional channels and limited mass-media attention. But this is not to stop anyone's DIY projects and the formation of independent communities – in music, the viral success of charming self-released pop videos can break past commercial sluggishness and critical cynicism. To point to one example, a fan cover of Depeche Mode's *Everything Counts* by the Colombian DMK trio (a father and two children) has been viewed by over a million people.[4] They re-create the electronic original live with a home keyboard, a mix of miked-up acoustic instruments and voices, and multiple video cameras.

Attitudes to machines have been mixed, with waves of technology promoting greater efficiency of means and new opportunities, often acting at the expense of people's investment in older mechanisms. The economic pressure to keep changing has social consequences, and the rapid pace of technological development is often mirrored in the music produced, with accompanying rapid shifts in style commensurate with an age of mass communication. The exhausting proliferation of sub-genres and social-technical-stylistic developments are not going to freeze whilst this book is in press. Brostep may be sisstep by publication, or a retro movement for mainframe computer music may have gripped the popular imagination post-Raspberry Pi. It's a fascinating time to live, with so much going on, and so much that could happen next!

Further reading

Duckworth, William (2005) *Virtual Music: How the Web Got Wired for Sound* (New York: Routledge).

Norman, Katharine (2004) *Sounding Art: Eight Literary Excursions Through Electronic Music* (Aldershot: Ashgate).

Oram, Daphne (1972) *An Individual Note of Music, Sound and Electronics* (London: Galliard Ltd.).

Smirnov, Andrei (2010) *Sound in Z – Experiments in Sound and Electronic Music in Early 20th Century Russia* (Cologne: Buchhandlung Walther König GmbH & Co. KG).

Tompkins, Dave (2010) *How to Wreck a Nice Beach: The Vocoder from World War II to Hip-Hop, The Machine Speaks* (Brooklyn, NY: Melville House Publishing).

Notes

1 Introduction

1. Which is not to say the weak, strong, and gravitational forces can't have roles in music, whether in quantum computer music or sonifications of black hole dynamics.
2. Paul Théberge (2007) *Any Sound You Can Imagine: Making Music/Consuming Technology* (Hanover, NH: Wesleyan University Press).
3. Joel Ryan (1991) "Some remarks on musical instrument design at STEIM," *Contemporary Music Review*, 6(1): 3–17.
4. It is not that you can't conceive of this being possible in ancient history – think of a boulder precariously balanced on a cliff edge, waiting for the human prod to fall with a huge crash – but the sheer repeatability of the act, armed only with a laptop and a massive sound system, is the novelty in evolutionary time.
5. Alvin Toffler (1970) *Future Shock* (London: Pan Books Ltd.).
6. Timothy D. Taylor (2001) *Strange Sounds: Music, Technology, and Culture* (New York: Routledge).
7. Mike Rubin (2000) "Techno: Days of future past" in Peter Shapiro (ed.), *Modulations. A History of Electronic Music: Throbbing Words on Sound* (New York: Distributed Art Publishers Inc.), pp. 108–27.
8. And the robot references go on, from Flight of the Conchords' *Robot Song* and the synth punk band Robots in Disguise, to fascinating work in real life musical robotics.
9. Geoffrey C. Bowker and Susan Leigh Star (2000) *Sorting Things Out: Classification and its Consequences* (Cambridge, MA: MIT Press).
10. Roy Shuker (2008) *Understanding Popular Music Culture*, 3rd edn. (Abingdon: Routledge), pp. 5–7.
11. Scott Johnson (2000) "The counterpoint of species" in John Zorn (ed.), *Arcana: Musicians on Music* (New York: Granary Books, Inc.), pp. 18–58.
12. Trevor Wishart has argued forcibly against the autocractic impositions of "lattice" music based on discrete scale and time position systems, and eulogized the infinity of points in between. See Trevor Wishart (1996) *On Sonic Art*, revised edn., edited by Simon Emmerson (New York: Routledge).
13. Thomas Licata (ed.) (2002) *Electroacoustic Music: Analytical Perspectives* (Westport, CT: Greenwood Press). Mary Simoni (ed.) (2006) *Analytical Methods of Electroacoustic Music* (New York: Routledge).

14. Our only chance may be automated computer systems to collect and categorize vast music databases, as explored in the field of music information retrieval. Pending the creation of an artificial ear of the same perceptual abilities as the human mind, such attempts still have a huge distance to cover, but it is a great research challenge of the age.
15. Simon Reynolds (2005) *Rip It Up and Start Again* (London: Faber & Faber).
16. Louis Nieber (2010) *Special Sound: The Creation and Legacy of the BBC Radiophonic Workshop* (New York: Oxford University Press), p. 73.
17. Tara Rodgers (ed.) (2010) *Pink Noises: Women on Electronic Music and Sound* (Durham, NC: Duke University Press). See also Elizabeth Hinkle-Turner (2006) *Women Composers and Music Technology in the United States* (Aldershot: Ashgate). A more open scene for women in Berlin is discussed in Tony Naylor (2008) "The female techno takeover," *The Guardian*, May 24, www.guardian.co.uk/music/2008/may/24/features16.theguide.
18. For the record, Nick wrote Chapters 1, 2, 5, 6, 7, 8, 10, 13, and 14, Meg wrote 11 and 12, and Scott wrote 3, 4, and 9.
19. Dave Henderson (2010) *Journey to a Plugged In State of Mind* (London: Cherry Red Books).
20. Simon Reynolds (2010) "CREEL PONE," http://reynoldsretro.blogspot.co.uk/2010/12/creel-pone-wire-2010-by-simon-reynolds.html.

2 Recording technologies and music

1. Christoph Cox and Daniel Warner (eds.) (2004) *Audio Culture: Readings in Modern Music* (London; New York: Continuum).
2. Exceptions include the full records of 1930 Grammophonmusik, the Telharmonium, and Russolo's original intonorumori.
3. Vaucanson went on to be involved in the development of automatic loom technology, which in turn led to computing!
4. Piano rolls for automated pianos provide very important historical documents of the playing of Grieg, Scriabin, Gershwin, and Prokofiev, amongst others. The earliest born pianist so recorded is Reinecke, who had heard Chopin play as a youth: see www.pianola.org/reproducing/reproducing_welte.cfm.
5. Hugh Davies (1996) "A history of sampling," *Organised Sound*, 1(1): 3–11.
6. Sarah Angliss (2011) *The Bird Fancyer's Delight*. BBC Radio 4, July 5.
7. Recent scanning techniques have allowed reconstruction from the early plates to create the earliest surviving recordings post hoc. The story is told with sound examples at http://firstsounds.org/sounds.
8. Charles Cros in Paris co-invented a phonograph in 1877, but did not receive the same publicity and did not create a successful business from the invention. Andrew Hugill (2007) "The origins of electronic music" in Nick Collins and Julio d'Escriván (eds.), *The Cambridge Companion to Electronic Music* (Cambridge University Press), pp. 7–23, at p. 14.

9. George Brock-Nannestad (2009) "The development of recording technologies" in Nicholas Cook, Eric Clarke, Daniel Leech-Wilkinson, and John Rink (eds.), *The Cambridge Companion to Recorded Music* (Cambridge University Press), pp. 149–76.

10. An art interest in the player piano continued as an early acoustic sequencer; the music of Conlon Nancarrow is worth exploring here. George Antheil's *Ballet Mécanique* (1926) uses the player piano as a central agent of mechanization.

11. There are a variety of early designs and patent battles here, characteristic of the entrepreneurial inventors of the times. The standard carbon microphone design measures a varying voltage via carbon granules between the diaphragm and a fixed plate; when incident air pressure is higher, they are more densely packed together, reducing resistance and increasing the measured voltage.

12. John Eargle (2005) *The Microphone Book* (Oxford: Focal Press).

13. Greg Milner (2009) *Perfecting Sound Forever: The Story of Recorded Music* (London: Granta Publications).

14. Early phonograph cylinders and gramophone discs would only last for tens of playbacks. Vinyl records can still wear out over hundreds of plays. The action at a distance of magnetic tape avoids this physical wear from the playback and recording heads, but has its own dangers from reel-to-reel winding, rogue magnets, and splicing. An MP3 file may seem most impermeable, but all digital media suffer a (very low) rate of bit error over time that requires periodic review, and digital backup is a convoluted topic including hard-drive lifetime expectancies of three years and returns to such media as tape storage.

15. Ownership of the music itself is an interesting issue here, since streaming does not necessarily imply that the receiver can keep a copy.

16. Thom Holmes (2012) *Electronic and Experimental Music*, 4th edn. (New York: Routledge), pp. 48–9.

17. Julio d'Escriván (2009) "Sound art (?) on/in film," *Organised Sound*, 14(1): 65–73.

18. Spencer Sundell (2006) "The pre-history of sound cinema, part 1: Thomas Edison and W. K. L. Dickson," www.spencersundell.com/blog/2006/04/10/the_pre-history_of_sound_cinema_part_1.

19. Though there are synthesis experiments based around such mechanisms as acoustical ridges in doorways, and the organ has been around in various forms across millennia. Alexander Dillmann in 1910 deliberately cut his own record grooves for synthesis: Mark Katz (2004) *Capturing Sound: How Technology Has Changed Music* (Berkeley, CA: University of California Press), p. 104.

20. Neil Lerner (2010) "The strange case of Rouben Mamoulian's sound stew: The uncanny soundtrack in Dr. Jekyll and Mr. Hyde (1931)" in Neil Lerner (ed.), *Music in the Horror Film: Listening to Fear* (New York: Routledge), pp. 55–79.

21. Thomas Y. Levin (2003) "'Tones from out of nowhere': Rudolph Pfenninger and the archaeology of synthetic sound," *Grey Room*, 12: 32–79.

22. William Moritz (2004) *Optical Poetry: The Life and Work of Oskar Fischinger* (Bloomington: Indiana University Press).

23. Another example is provided by the work of the Australian Jack Ellitt, many of whose experimental works have not survived, but include sound collage experiments as well as 1930s drawn film sound. *Journey #1* (probably early 1930s) is an impressively early document of recorded sound manipulation and drawn sound techniques. See Peter Manning (2005) "The influence of recording technologies on the early development of electroacoustic music," *Leonardo Music Journal*, 13: 5–10 and the release of existing recordings on Shame File Music: Clinton Green (2011) "Jack Ellitt – Sound Constructions (sham066)," www.shamefilemusic.com/ellitt.html.

24. See László Moholy-Nagy (2004, originally 1922/3) "Production-reproduction: potentialities of the phonograph" in Cox and Warner (eds.), *Audio Culture*, pp. 331–3.

25. Katz, *Capturing Sound*.

26. Holmes, *Electronic and Experimental Music*, p. 195. Les Paul was not the only North American to explore multitrack machines ahead of commercial products; both Hugh Le Caine and Raymond Scott created their own multiple recording and playback head tape machines.

27. Brian Kane (2011) "Acousmatic fabrications: Les Paul and the 'Les Paulverizer'," *Journal of Visual Culture*, 10(2): 212–31.

28. John Dack (2009) "From sound to music, from recording to theory," in Amanda Bayley (ed.), *Recorded Music: Performance, Culture and Technology* (Cambridge University Press), pp. 271–90.

29. Carlos Palombini (1993) "Machine songs V: Pierre Schaeffer. From research into noises to experimental music," *Computer Music Journal*, 17(3): 14–19.

30. Milner, *Perfecting Sound Forever*.

31. *Ibid.*, p. 129.

32. *Ibid.*, p. 333.

33. In some cases, ostensible remixes turn out as covers, as when the KLF remixed the Pet Shop Boys' *So Hard* (1990), re-made all parts and got Neil Tennant to sing the vocal again! There are also remixes which are entirely new tracks, as in the urban myth of the courier turning up at Aphex Twin's residence to collect a remix on deadline day and Richard James handing over a randomly selected DAT; the record company loved the work.

34. Reynolds, *Rip It Up and Start Again*, p. 341.

35. Joseph Grobelny (2008) "Mashups, sampling, and authorship: A mashupsampliography," *Music Reference Services Quarterly*, 11(3–4): 229–39.

36. Katz, *Capturing Sound*, pp. 3, 74.

37. A mania shown to good dramatic effect in Woody Allen's imaginary jazz guitarist biopic *Sweet and Lowdown* (1999).

38. Daniel Leech-Wilkinson (2009) *The Changing Sound of Music: Approaches to Studying Recorded Musical Performance* (London: CHARM), Chapter 1.2.1, para. 22, www.charm.rhul.ac.uk/studies/chapters/intro.html. Michael Chanan (1995) *Repeated Takes: A Short History of Recording and its Effects on Music* (London: Verso).

39. Virgil Moorefield (2005) *The Producer as Composer: Shaping the Sounds of Popular Music* (Cambridge, MA: MIT Press), p. 3, discusses the dishonesty of editing versus the purity of performance.
40. Milner, *Perfecting Sound Forever*, p. 67.
41. Andy Harrower (2005) "Copyright issues in digital music," *Contemporary Music Review*, 24(6): 483–8.
42. Paul D. Miller (ed.) (2008) *Sound Unbound: Sampling Digital Music and Culture* (Cambridge, MA: MIT Press).
43. John P. Murphy (1990) "Jazz improvisation: The joy of influence," *The Black Perspective in Music*, 18(1–2): 7–19.
44. *Scratch* (2001), directed by Doug Pray.
45. As the jazz guitarist Howard Roberts notably said (probably quoting someone else): "If you steal from only one guy it's plagiarism; if you steal from two or more it's research!"
46. Jeremy J. Beadle (1993) *Will Pop Eat Itself? Pop Music in the Soundbite Era* (London: Faber & Faber).
47. See two chapters in Cox and Warner (eds.), *Audio Culture*: Chris Cutler, "Plunderphonia" (pp. 138–56) and John Oswald, "Bettered by the borrower: The ethics of musical debt" (pp. 131–7).

3 New sounds and new instruments: Electronic music up until 1948

1. A practice which continues to this day with the New Instruments for Musical Expression conference (www.nime.org). However, exotic instruments are not all recent: some early developments were equally quixotic.
2. Hugh Davies (2012) "Denis d'or," *Grove Music Online. Oxford Music Online*, www.oxfordmusiconline.com/subscriber/article/grove/music/47638.
3. Michael B. Schiffer, Kacy L. Hollenback, and Carrie L. Bell (2003) *Draw the Lightning Down: Benjamin Franklin and Electrical Technology in the Age of Enlightenment* (Berkeley, CA: University of California Press), p. 172.
4. Letter from Benjamin Franklin to Peter Collinson dated September 1753. Leonard W. Labaree (ed.) (1962) *The Papers of Benjamin Franklin* (New Haven, CT: Yale University Press), vol. 5, p. 69.
5. Charles Herbermann (ed.) (1913) "Andrew Gordon" in *Catholic Encyclopedia* (New York: Robert Appleton Company), p. 649.
6. Schiffer, Hollenback, and Bell, *Draw the Lightning Down*, pp. 244–6.
7. C. G. Page (1837) "The production of galvanic music," *American Journal of Science*, 32: 396–7. See also the discussion at www.ilt.columbia.edu/projects/bluetelephone/html/page.html.
8. Helmholtz's synthesizer is currently in the Whipple Museum of the History of Science at the University of Cambridge. Information on the instrument (including photographs) and Helmholtz himself can be found on its website: www.hps.cam.ac.uk/whipple/explore/acoustics/hermanvonhelmholtz.

9. For detailed discussion, see Edward Evenson (2000) *The Telephone Patent Conspiracy of 1876: The Elisha Gray–Alexander Bell Controversy* (Jefferson, NC: McFarland).

10. Helen M. Fessenden (1940) *Fessenden: Builder of Tomorrows* (New York: Coward-McCann, Inc.), p. 153.

11. Joel Chadabe (1997) *Electric Sound* (Upper Saddle River, NJ: Prentice Hall), p. 6.

12. Lee de Forest (1950) *Father of Radio: The Autobiography of Lee de Forest* (Chicago: Wilcox & Follett), pp. 306–7.

13. Brian Winston (1998) *Media Technology and Society: A History: From the Telegraph to the Internet* (London: Routledge), p. 44.

14. Holmes, *Electronic and Experimental Music*, p. 44.

15. Anonymous (1900) "December 20, 1900: Nature reports on William Duddell's 'musical arcs'," *APS News*, 19(11): 2.

16. The definitive study on the Telharmonium remains Reynold Weidenaar (1995) *Magic Music from the Telharmonium* (London: Scarecrow Press, Inc.).

17. Edwin Hall Pierce (1924) "A colossal experiment in 'just intonation'," *Musical Quarterly*, 10(3): 326–32.

18. *Ibid.*, 328.

19. Anonymous (1906) "Twain and the telephone," *New York Times*, December 23.

20. *Ibid.*

21. Ray Stannard Baker (1906) "New music for an old world," *McClure's Magazine*, 27(3): 291–301.

22. *Ibid.*, 301.

23. Ferruccio Busoni (1907) *Sketch of a New Esthetic of Music*. Translated by Dr. Th. Baker (New York: Schirmer). Available online from Project Gutenberg: www.gutenberg.org/files/31799/31799-h/31799-h.htm.

24. There is an interesting discussion of some of the lines of thinking which anticipated and fed into ideas about electronic music in Hugill, "The origins of electronic music."

25. Anonymous (1907) "Music on wires," *New York Globe and Commercial Advertiser*, January 31, p. 4. Quoted in Weidenaar, *Magic Music from the Telharmonium*, p. 136.

26. Edith Borroff (1982) "The Choralcelo: One uniquely American instrument," *College Music Symposium*, 22(1): 46–54.

27. Rahma Khazam (2009) "Nikolay Obukhov and the Croix Sonore," *Leonardo Music Journal*, 19: 11–12.

28. Albert Glinsky (2000). *Theremin: Ether Music and Espionage* (Urbana, IL: University of Illinois Press).

29. Khazam, "Nikolay Obukhov."

30. Anonymous (1934) "TITTERS GREET MUSIC OF OBOUHOFF IN PARIS; singers' strange performance, accompanied by electrical instrument, causes stir," *New York Times*, May 16.

31. Joachim Stange-Elbe (1994) "Elektrische Musikinstrumente: Ein historischer Rückblick mit zeitgenössischen Dokumenten. 5.Teil: Sphärenklänge," *ZeM Mitteilungsheft*, 14: 6–10. Reproduced online at www.zem.de/heft/14_emu5.htm.

32. Joachim Stange-Elbe (1994) "Elektrische Musikinstrumente: Ein historischer Rückblick mit zeitgenössischen Dokumenten. 6.Teil: Saitenspiele (1)," *ZeM Mitteilungsheft*, 15: 6–10. Reproduced online at www.zem.de/heft/15_emu6_1.htm.

33. www.thomasbloch.net/en_ondes-martenot.html.

34. Holmes, *Electronic and Experimental Music*, pp. 25–8.

35. www.cslevine.com/ondea.

36. While a significant development, De Forrest's particular approach was not the one adopted in the end by the film industry for talkies.

37. For discussion of this and other optical instruments, see Derek Holzer (2010) "A brief history of optical synthesis," *Tonewheels: Audiovisual Performance*, www.umatic.nl/ tonewheels_historical.html.

38. Hugh Davies and Peter Donhauser (2011) "Superpiano," *Grove Music Online. Oxford Music Online*, www.oxfordmusiconline.com/subscriber/article/grove/music/ L2214975.

39. Holzer, "A brief history."

40. Benjamin F. Miessner (1936) "Electronic music and instruments," *Proceedings of the Institute of Radio Engineers*, 24(11), reproduced at www.discretesynthesizers.com/ archives/miessner/em1936.htm.

41. Holzer, "A brief history."

42. Miessner, "Electronic music."

43. Holzer, "A brief history," 490.

44. Holzer, "A brief history."

45. An interesting discussion of the history of art works and instruments combining light and sound can be found in Jiři Heřman (2006) "Sons & lumières" in *Disk II/2006 – Selections from the Czech Journal for the Study of Dramatic Art* (Prague: Nakladatelstvi), pp. 138–52. This consists largely of a discussion of a number of works presented at a retrospective exhibition at the Centre Pompidou in Paris in 2004.

46. A detailed historical overview is available at www.hammond-organ.com/html/history. htm (while this was formerly used as the official website of Hammond in the UK, it is not the website of Hammond-Suzuki).

47. For full technical detail of the original design, see Laurens Hammond (1934) "Electrical musical instrument," *US Patent* 1956350.

48. Anonymous (1938) "ORGAN COMPANY CITED: FTC orders Hammond makers to cease representations," *New York Times*, July 12. See also the discussion at www. 1377731.com/hammond/index.html.

49. www.hammond-organ.com/History/hammond_accomplishments.htm.

50. Holmes, *Electronic and Experimental Music*, pp. 31–2.

51. The Clavioline had true vibrato, i.e., variation in pitch rather than amplitude. See Gordon Reid (2007) "The story of the Clavioline," *Sound on Sound*, March, www. soundonsound.com/sos/mar07/articles/clavioline.htm.

52. See again Hugill, "The origins of electronic music."

53. Benjamin Grosbayne (1931) "ELECTRICITY, ETHER AND INSTRUMENTS: Some considerations, reflections, and inferences on the modern cult of vitamineless art and the synthetic aesthetic," *New York Times*, September 6.

4 The post-war sonic boom

1. When the radio service to London was introduced in 1927, a three-minute call cost $75 (about $950 in 2012 terms). Information from AT&T's history website: www.corp.att.com/history/history2.html.

2. Pierre Schaeffer (1952) *A la Recherche d'une Musique Concrète* (Paris: Éditions du Seuil).

3. Palombini, "Machine songs V".

4. John Cage had explored the idea of "found sound" in the past of course and had been influenced by Duchamp's ready-mades. What is sometimes called "bottom-up" composition, or allowing the form to emerge gradually out of the musical material and its implications, was also not unprecedented.

5. Jérôme Peignot (1960) "De la musique concrète à l'acousmatique," *Esprit*, 280: 111–23.

6. Based on sources in Iamblichus, amongst others. See, for example, the discussion in E. L. Minar (1944) "Pythagorean communism," *Transactions and Proceedings of the American Philological Association*, 75: 34–46, at 39.

7. Pierre Schaeffer (1966) *Traité des objets musicaux* (Paris: Le Seuil), p. 91.

8. Michel Chion (1983) *Guide des objets sonores, Pierre Schaeffer et la recherche musicale* (Paris: Ina-GRM/Buchet-Chastel). John Dack and Christine North provide an English translation at www.ears.dmu.ac.uk/spip.php?page=articleEars&id_article=3597.

9. Note that Schaeffer's usage is somewhat distinct from common parlance. In colloquial usage, *entendre* usually denotes a passive activity. Chion notes that Schaeffer's usage is consistent with the word's etymology (*Guide des objets sonores*, p. 25). See also the discussion in Brian Kane (2007) "L'Objet Sonore Maintenant: Pierre Schaeffer, sound objects and the phenomenological reduction," *Organised Sound*, 12(1): 15–24.

10. Schaeffer, *Traité des objets musicaux*, pp. 270–2.

11. Chadabe, *Electric Sound*, p. 34.

12. Note that while the parametric understanding of music that underlies this approach provides some insights, it is not the only way to view music. We do not necessarily listen to music as a collection of discrete parameter streams!

13. See, for example, the discussion in Holmes, *Electronic and Experimental Music*, p. 59; and Peter Manning (2004) *Electronic and Computer Music* (Oxford University Press), pp. 19 and 28.

14. Luciano Berio (1956) "Studio di Fonologia Musicale," *The Score*, 15: 86.

15. Karlheinz Stockhausen (1964) *Texte zur Musik* 2, Dieter Schnebel (ed.) (Cologne: Verlag M. DuMont Schauberg), p. 23.

16. See Stockhausen's discussion in Karlheinz Stockhausen (1961) "Two lectures," *Die Reihe* 5 (Bryn Mawr: Theodore Presse), p. 59.

17. Palombini, "Machine songs V," 18.

18. Interview with Konrad Boehmer at www.furious.com/perfect/ohm/eimert.html.

19. Ibid.

20. See the discussion in Manning, *Electronic and Computer Music*, p. 68; and Chadabe, *Electric Sound*, p. 48.

21. Holmes, *Electronic and Experimental Music*, p. 82.

22. Sophie Fuller. "Oram, Daphne Blake," *Grove Music Online. Oxford Music Online*, www.oxfordmusiconline.com/subscriber/article/grove/music/45636.

23. The piece was submitted for the BBC for the Italia Prize, but Oram was told over the phone that "Still Point could only be judged as a 'straight score' – so apparently adjudicators didn't understand the acoustic variations or the manipulated pre-recording techniques." See http://daphneoram.org/oramarchive/bbc.

24. Hugh Davies (2003) "Obituary: Daphne Oram," *The Guardian*, January 24, www.guardian.co.uk/news/2003/jan/24/guardianobituaries.artsobituaries.

25. Holmes, *Electronic and Experimental Music* has a useful chart of early European studios on p. 92, as well as additional material on worldwide studio developments.

26. Information on Le Caine is available at www.thecanadianencyclopedia.com/articles/emc/hugh-le-caine and at www.hughlecaine.com. The definitive study of his life and instruments remains Gayle Young (1989) *The Sackbut Blues: Hugh Le Caine, Pioneer in Electronic Music* (Ottawa: National Museum of Science and Technology).

27. Hugh Le Caine (1964) "Recherches au temps perdu" typescript auto-biography, quoted in Gayle Young (1984) "Hugh Le Caine: Pioneer of electronic music in Canada," *HSTC Bulletin: Journal of the History of Canadian Science, Technology and Medecine / HSTC Bulletin : revue d'histoire des sciences, des techniques et de la médecine au Canada*, 8(1): 20–31.

28. Le Caine used the famous glissando in the clarinet solo from *Rhapsody in Blue* as a demonstration. See Chadabe, *Electric Sound*, p. 14.

29. www.sciencetech.technomuses.ca/english/collection/music7.cfm.

30. Chadabe, *Electric Sound*, p. 14.

31. www.thecanadianencyclopedia.com/articles/emc/hugh-le-caine.

32. Hugh Le Caine (1953) "Short presentation of the 1948 Sackbut: The Sackbut Blues." Republished in *An Anthology of Noise and Electronic Music, Vol. 4*. Sub Rosa (2006).

33. www.inagrm.com/accueil/outils/acousmographe.

34. The software developer David Zicarelli refers to this sort of effect as "machines breaking down." This is one of his three tongue-in-cheek categories of electronic music, the others being "machines operating properly" (which might apply to the opening of *Dripsody*) and "sword-fighting" (which might apply to the middle). See David Zicarelli (2001) "Keynote speech for the 2001 International Computer Music Conference in Havana, Cuba," http://finearts.uvic.ca/icmc2001/after/keynote.php3.

35. Manning, *Electronic and Computer Music*, p. 77.

36. See some discussion of the CPEMC and the RCA Mark II in the OHM+ interview with Babbitt, available at http://cec.sonus.ca/econtact/12_2/interviews_chasalow_cassidy.html.

37. Chadabe, *Electric Sound*, p. 52.

38. *Ibid.*, p. 53.

39. Warren Bourne (2008) "Cary, Tristram," *Grove Music Online. Oxford Music Online*, www.oxfordmusiconline.com/subscriber/article/grove/music/05052.

40. Holmes, *Electronic and Experimental Music*, p. 83.

41. For discussion, see Barry Schrader (2008) "Barron, Bebe," *Grove Music Online. Oxford Music Online*, www.oxfordmusiconline.com/subscriber/article/grove/music/47066; and Barry Schrader (2008) "Barron, Louis," *Grove Music Online. Oxford Music Online*, www.oxfordmusiconline.com/subscriber/article/grove/music/47067.

42. Holmes, *Electronic and Experimental Music*, p. 98.

43. For some discussion, see J. Brockman (1992) "The first electronic filmscore: *Forbidden Planet*," *The Score*, 7(3): 5–13.

44. See Chadabe, *Electric Sound*, p. 55; and James Pritchett (1996) *The Music of John Cage* (Cambridge University Press), p. 91.

45. Richard Bayly (1983) "Ussachevsky on Varèse: An interview April 24, 1979 at Goucher College," *Perspectives of New Music* 21(1–2): 145–51.

46. *New York Telegraph*, March 16, 1916.

47. Larry Sitsky (2002) *Music of the Twentieth-Century Avant-Garde: A Biocritical Sourcebook* (Westport, CT: Greenwood Press), p. 533, emphasis in original.

48. Felix Meyer and Heidi Zimmerman (eds.) (2006) *Edgard Varèse – Composer, Sound Sculpture, Visionary* (Woodbridge: Boydell Press), p. 340.

49. There is some discrepancy of the number of loudspeakers included. See, for example, the discussion in Olivia Mattis (2006) "From Bebop to Poo-wip: Jazz influences in Varèse's *Poème électronique*" in Meyer and Zimmerman (eds.), *Edgard Varèse*, pp. 309–17.

50. Mauricio Kagel (2006) "Edgard Varèse: Years later" in Meyer and Zimmerman (eds.), *Edgard Varèse*, pp. 476–8.

51. See the discussion in Mattis, "From Bebop to Poo-wip."

52. Manning, *Electronic and Computer Music*, p. 82.

53. Paul Bernays (producer) (2009) "1959: The Year that Changed Jazz." BBC Four http://www.bbc.co.uk/programmes/b00jf64y.

5 From analog to digital

1. Julius Edgar Lilienfeld has a US patent ("Method and apparatus for controlling electric currents," US 1745175 (A)) for a field-effect transistor component, filed in 1925 and granted in 1930, though he did not publish further on or build such devices. See, for example, http://en.wikipedia.org/wiki/History_of_the_transistor.

2. To some degree, this was a historical quirk of the early 1950s with the commitment of elektronische Musik to absolutely precise serialist experiments, and the musique concrète avoidance of synthesis, and we should acknowledge those like Raymond Scott who kept active on other paths.

3. Reid, "The story of the Clavioline."

4. Seven modular systems were sold at around $15,000 each in one afternoon to rock groups: Trevor Pinch and Frank Trocco (2002) *Analog Days: The Invention and Impact of the Moog Synthesizer* (Cambridge, MA: Harvard University Press), p. 118.

5. Mark Vail (2000) *Vintage Synthesizers* (San Francisco, CA: Backbeat Books), p. 26; Pinch and Trocco (*Analog Days*, p. 216) note that 12,000 were made.

6. Pinch and Trocco, *Analog Days*, p. 11.

7. For example, see Museum of Soviet synthesizers at www.ruskeys.net/eng/synths.php; and Gordon Reid (2010) "Formanta Polivoks Synthesizer: the story of the Polivoks," *Sound on Sound*, July, www.soundonsound.com/sos/jul10/articles/polivoks.htm.

8. Dates and details herein are drawn from Chapter 1 of Walt Kester (ed.) (2005) *The Data Conversion Handbook* (Burlington, MA: Newnes).

9. Nick Collins (2010) *Introduction to Computer Music* (Chichester: Wiley), p. 36. Paul Doornbusch provides an extract from his book on the first Australian computer music online: "The music of CSIRAC," available at www.csse.unimelb.edu.au/dept/about/csirac/music.

10. Lejaren Hiller and Leonard Isaacson (1959) *Experimental Music: Composition with an Electronic Computer* (Westport, CT: Greenwood Press).

11. Max V. Mathews (1963) "The digital computer as a musical instrument," *Science*, 142 (3592): 553–7.

12. A similar role, as MIDI data workstations, would be one mode of computer music activity in the 1980s alongside early sound editing and 8-bit sample tracker programs.

13. Excellent material on the RCA Synthesizer(s) appears in Holmes, *Electronic and Experimental Music*, pp. 176–90.

14. Manning, *Electronic and Computer Music*, p. 207.

15. *Ibid.*, p. 210.

16. Laurie Spiegel (1998) "Graphical GROOVE: memorial for the VAMPIRE, a visual music system," *Organised Sound*, 3(3): 187–91.

17. Vail, *Vintage Synthesizers*, pp. 143, 220.

18. Mikko Ojanen, Jari Suominen, Titti Kallio, and Kai Lassfolk (2007) "Design principles and user interfaces of Erkki Kurenniemi's electronic musical instruments of the 1960s and 1970s," *Proceedings of the 2007 Conference on New Interfaces for Musical Expression (NIME07)*, New York. There is also a movie glorifying Erkki Kurenniemi's circuits, *The Future Is Not What It Used to Be* (2002), directed by Mika Taanila.

19. Four generations of these would go up to the famous 4X (completed by 1984), empowering such works as Pierre Boulez's *Répons* (1984). See Pierre Boulez and Andrew Gerzso (1988) "Computers in music," *Scientific American*, 258(4): 44–50, also available at http://articles.ircam.fr/textes/Boulez88c.

20. Holmes, *Electronic and Experimental Music*, p. 281. See also Julius O. Smith's personal recollections: https://ccrma.stanford.edu/~jos/kna/Experiences_Samson_Box.html.

21. Vail, *Vintage Synthesizers*, p. 68; see also pp. 201–5.

22. Ian Peel (2005) "Trevor Horn: 25 years of hits," *Sound on Sound*, March, www.soundonsound.com/sos/mar05/articles/trevorhorn.htm.

6 Into the mainstream

1. Holmes, *Electronic and Experimental Music.*
2. Hugill, "The origins of electronic music."
3. Vincenzo Lombardo, Andrea Valle, John Fitch, Kees Tazelaar, Stefan Weinzierl, and Wojciech Borczyk (2009) "A virtual-reality reconstruction of *Poème électronique* based on philological research," *Computer Music Journal,* 33(2): 24–47.
4. James Wierzbicki (2005) *Louis and Bebe Barron's Forbidden Planet: A Film Score Guide* (Lanham, MD: Scarecrow Press, Inc.).
5. The Theremin might have achieved better mass production if the Great Depression hadn't hit; 1929 is when RCA received its license to produce the instrument on a factory production line, but no more than 500 were made (Albert Glinsky (2005) *Theremin: Ether Music and Espionage* (Urbana and Chicago, IL: University of Illinois Press)). The Hammond Company had more economic success by positioning itself as saving money compared to traditional acoustic organs.
6. Burtt began work on the film two years in advance of its release. See Pinch and Trocco, *Analog Days,* p. 274.
7. Taylor, *Strange Sounds.*
8. A list of "Films with significant electroacoustic content" compiled by Jef Chippewa from multiple contributors, appears at http://cec.sonus.ca/econtact/8_4/films.html. See also Wierzbicki, *Louis and Bebe Barron's Forbidden Planet;* and Julio d'Escriván (2007) "Electronic music and the moving image" in Collins and d'Escriván (eds.), *The Cambridge Companion to Electronic Music,* pp. 156–70.
9. William Möritz (2004) *Optical Poetry: The Life and Work of Oskar Fischinger* (Bloomington, IN: Indiana University Press); Thomas Y. Levin (2003) "'Tones from out of nowhere': Rudolph Pfenninger and the archaeology of synthetic sound," *Grey Room,* 12: 32–79.
10. Russell Lack (1997) "Electronic film music and musical understanding" in *Twenty Four Frames Under: A Buried History of Film Music* (London: Quartet Books Ltd.), pp. 310–21, at p. 314.
11. *Ibid.,* pp. 318–19.
12. Wierzbicki, *Louis and Bebe Barron's Forbidden Planet.*
13. "ORAL HISTORY PROJECT: The video archive of the electroacoustic music," curators Eric Chasalow and Barbara Cassidy. Babe Barron interview available at http://ericchasalow.com/video/BebeForbidden.mov.
14. More were missed out; you might investigate sound design in *THX 1138* (1971), for example.
15. It would be ironic if the aliens, rather than recognizing the structure of diatonic music as representing intelligence, had taken it as sign of a lack of high art principles and retaliated with planetary destruction.
16. Lack, "Electronic film music," p. 316.

17. For a discussion of Carpenter's scoring and the role of synthesizers, see K. J. Donnelly (2010) "Hearing deep seated fears: John Carpenter's *The Fog* (1980)" in Neil Lerner (ed.), *Music in the Horror Film: Listening to Fear* (New York: Routledge), pp. 152–67.

18. Or at least simulacra of acoustic instruments through large sample databases. Lack ("Electronic film music," p. 315) points to Hans Zimmer as very successfully blurring the line between acoustic and electronic in *Black Rain* (1990).

19. Interestingly, a notable book on film music is by electroacoustic composer Michel Chion, a disciple of Pierre Schaeffer. Michel Chion (1994) *Audio-vision* (New York: Columbia University Press). Originally published in 1990, translated by C. Gorbman.

20. Lack, "Electronic film music," pp. 106–7.

21. *Ibid.*, p. 165.

22. *Ibid.*, p. 163.

23. D'Escriván, "Electronic music and the moving image," p. 161.

24. One interesting example is the original theme tune to *The Green Hornet* (1936–52) radio show on Detroit WXYZ, which used a theremin for a buzzing sound. See Wierzbicki, *Louis and Bebe Barron's Forbidden Planet*, p. 21.

25. Nieber, *Special Sound*, p. 5.

26. *Ibid.*, p. 155.

27. A further footnote here is to the fate of one of Maddalena Fagandini's popular 1960 interval signals, which became grafted onto the *Time Beat* (1962) single pushed out by George Martin under the male cover name Ray Cathode, obscuring her role. See *ibid.*, pp. 84–5.

28. Ron Rodman (2011) "'Coperettas,' 'Detecterns,' and space operas: Music and genre hybridization in American television' in James Deaville (ed.), *Music in Television: Channels of Listening* (New York: Routledge), pp 35–56, at p. 50.

29. Though stadium rock had a revenge of sorts on MTV in the mid-1980s, diversification of coverage to hip hop offset this somewhat, as did general trends in popular music production.

30. Raymond Scott (2000) *Manhattan Research Inc.* BASTA Audio/Visuals, Holland, CD liner notes, p. 50.

31. *Ibid.*, p. 48.

32. Holmes, *Electronic and Experimental Music*, p. 194.

33. Pinch and Trocco, *Analog Days*, pp. 55–6.

34. *Ibid.*, p. 163.

35. Ethan Smith (2002) "Organization Moby," *Wired*, 10.05, www.wired.com/wired/archive/10.05/moby.html.

36. Karen Collins (2008) *Game Sound* (Cambridge, MA: MIT Press).

37. Early uses of synthesizers in 1960s rock and pop are explored in Walter Everett (2009) *The Foundations of Rock: From Blue Suede Shoes to Suite: Judy Blue Eyes* (New York: Oxford University Press), particularly pp. 78–81. See also Henderson, *Journey to a Plugged In State of Mind*; and Pinch and Trocco, *Analog Days*.

38. From the back cover notes of Kid Baltan, Electronic Music 7" single, Philips 315 538. Images are available at www.discogs.com/viewimages?release=384969.

39. Taylor, *Strange Sounds*, p. 106.
40. Morton Subotnick's commission to produce *Silver Apples of the Moon* (1967) is a companion piece, of modest success, showcasing Don Buchla's synthesizer. Indicative of the Moog–Buchla split on keyboard versus alternative controllers, Carlos re-works Bach for a greater mass success, and Buchla uses sequencers for some accessibility, but is much more abstract in general approach.
41. It's a recurring theme of popular music, such as with David Bowie's not-so-electronic *Space Oddity* (1969) tapping into the Moon landing mania.
42. Taylor, *Strange Sounds*, p. 83.
43. It is worth acknowledging the commercial musicians working on their own record releases as well as sessions, commercials, and movies; Beaver and Krause's *The Nonesuch Guide to Electronic Music* (1966), for instance, stayed on the Billboard chart for 26 weeks (Henderson, *Journey to a Plugged In State of Mind*, p. 74).
44. Pinch and Trocco, *Analog* Days, p. 125.
45. David Toop (2000) *Rap Attack 3: African Rap to Global Hip Hop* (London: Serpent's Tail), p. 126.
46. Pinch and Trocco, *Analog* Days, p. 183.
47. Nicola Dibben (2009) *Björk* (London: Equinox Publishing Ltd.).
48. *Ibid.*, p. 98.
49. *Ibid.*, p. 53.
50. *Ibid.*, p. 75.
51. *Ibid.*, p. 59.
52. *Ibid.*, p. 78.
53. *Ibid.*, p. 33.
54. *Ibid.*, p. 130.

7 Synth pop

1. Tangerine Dream arose in the same free improv milieu as Kraftwerk and also transformed into an all-synthesizer outfit. However, their pop impact was not substantial, though they had some success in progressive and ambient work.
2. Whilst not directly synth pop but a sort of eclectic mix from soul to hip hop ("cybersoul"), a more recent manifestation of *Metropolis*' far-reaching influence is Janelle Monáe's Cindi Mayweather alias and backstory to her *Metropolis: Suite I (The Chase)* E.P. (2007) and *The ArchAndroid (Suites II and III)* album (2010).
3. As for so many acts within living memory, YouTube and other video sites can be a great source of vintage footage.
4. *Autobahn* reached No. 25 in the US charts in a cut-down single version and bankrolled their first US tour, no doubt fueled as much by the American love of driving as the novelty of the synthesizer instrumentation.
5. Simon Reynolds (1999) *Generation Ecstasy: Into the World of Techno and Rave Culture* (New York: Routledge), p. 14.

6. Pascal Bussy (2005) *Kraftwerk: Man, Machine and Music*, 3rd edn. (London: SAF Publishing Ltd.), p. 190.
7. In this same era, Throbbing Gristle began their industrial experiments, growing out of performance art scenes. Though known more for their weirder side in noise and industrial music, they produced the odd subversive sickly and repetitive synth pop track, such as *United* (1978).
8. *Synth Britannia* documentary, BBC, aired October 16, 2009.
9. Also a big US hit, no doubt the automobile link making synthesizers palatable again!
10. Gary Numan with Steve Malins (1979) *Praying to the Aliens: An Autobiography* (London: Andre Deutsch); Paul Goodwin (2004) *Electric Pioneer: An Armchair Guide to Gary Numan* (London: Helter Skelter Publishing).
11. Courtney Sanders interviews Gary Numan, May 9, 2011, www.undertheradar.co.nz/utr/interviewMore/CID/302/N/Gary-Numan.utr.
12. Dave Thompson (1994) *Depeche Mode: Some Great Reward* (New York: St. Martin's Press), p. 6.
13. Reynolds, *Rip It Up and Start Again*.
14. The duo model has been used recently by Hurts, a Manchester synth-pop act who came to prominence in the UK in 2010.
15. As Reynolds, *Rip It Up and Start Again* notes, there was an American backlash against British acts who promoted what we might endearingly call "synth fop": "synths and rhythm programming being insufficiently strenuous, white-collar work" (p. 534). This extended to some original US acts too associated with 1970s–1980s innovation: "As American rockers grabbed hold of videos and synths, Devo – the original home-grown pioneers of synth-rock and video pop – found it harder to get on to MTV" (p. 536).
16. If this has never happened to you, try this link: www.youtube.com/watch?v=dQw4w9WgXcQ.
17. Peel, "Trevor Horn."
18. Another source is the hip hop production-influenced trends in so-called "R&B" or "urban" music. A single artist often crosses many genre allusions: Beyoncé's *Sweet Dreams* is more synth pop, while *Single Ladies* is a harder post-Timbaland hip hop and Jamaican dancehall-tinged production, inasmuch as these labels help rather than hinder the freedom to take influence from any preceding music.
19. One representative directory listing just of Swedish synth-pop acts is www.student.nada.kth.se/~f95-msv/artistsABC.html.
20. "World is Mine Live in HD," www.youtube.com/watch?v=DTXO7KGHtjI.
21. *Synth Britannia* documentary.
22. The synthesizer was a "Transcendent 2000" advertised in the magazine *Electronics Today*: *Synth Britannia* documentary.
23. Peter Hook (2009) *The Haçienda: How Not to Run a Club* (London: Simon & Schuster).
24. *Synth Britannia* documentary.
25. Richard Witts (2011) "Vorsprung durch Technik: Kraftwerk and the British fixation with Germany" in Sean Albiez and David Pattie (eds.) (2011) *Kraftwerk: Music Non-Stop* (New York: Continuum), p. 172.

26. David Pattie (2011) "Introduction: The (Ger)man machines" in Albiez and Pattie (eds.), *Kraftwerk: Music Non-Stop*, p. 8.

27. Witts ("Vorsprung durch Technik," p. 175) notes the link to Schubertian harmony, and claims a link with OMD, although through the track *Electricity*'s four-chord sequence rather than the much more direct use of Aeolian i bVI in *Almost*.

28. Such has been the take-up of rigidly controlled backbeats that even with rock bands working to a click, producers these days often replace drum-kit parts with synthesized (and consistently controlled) events, and tighten all the timing in the digital audio workstation!

8 Electronic dance music

1. Ian Cross (2001) "Music, cognition, culture and evolution," *Annals of the New York Academy of Sciences*, 930: 28–42.

2. Will Straw (2007) "Dance music" in Simon Frith, Will Straw and John Street (eds.), *The Cambridge Companion to Pop and Rock* (Cambridge University Press), pp. 158–77.

3. David Toop (2000) *Rap Attack 3: African Rap to Global Hip Hop* (London: Serpent's Tail), p. 143.

4. Kembrew McLeod (2001) "Genres, subgenres, sub-subgenres and more: Musical and social differentiation within electronic/dance music communities," *Journal of Popular Music Studies*, 13: 59–75.

5. Before proceeding further through the chapter, you may want to try and write down as many electronic dance music genres as you can name. You might also consider the following list: Skweee, shallow house, suburban garage, crack house, UK merengue, common groove, hip techno, and hip house. Which are real sub-genre terms and which are invented?

6. Bill Brewster and Frank Broughton (2006) *Last Night a DJ Saved My Life* (London: Headline Book Publishing), p. 307.

7. *Ibid.*

8. Moog engineer Robbie Wedel is credited with the synthesizer programming and sync in Richard Buskin (2009) "Donna Summer 'I Feel Love': Classic tracks," *Sound on Sound*, October, www.soundonsound.com/sos/oct09/articles/classictracks_1009.htm.

9. Toop, *Rap Attack 3*; Peter Shapiro (2005) *Turn the Beat Around: The Secret History of Disco* (London: Faber & Faber).

10. Brewster and Broughton, *Last Night a DJ Saved My Life*, p. 292.

11. There is controversy over what the first house record release actually is, a fact that is in clear evidence in comments about this record at the discogs website, for instance: www.discogs.com/Jesse-Saunders-On-And-On/release/176575. Nonetheless, most authors acknowledge Saunders' importance to the scene, if only to inspire other producers to get involved.

12. Brewster and Broughton, *Last Night a DJ Saved My Life*, p. 330.

13. Gordon Reid (2004) "The history of Roland part 2: 1979–1985," *Sound on Sound*, December, www.soundonsound.com/sos/dec04/articles/roland.htm#3.

14. Discussion of the first acid house track takes us down a familiarly difficult road of attribution. As Roland had originally hoped, the TB-303 was used in all sorts of places, from Italo-disco (Alexander Robotnick's *Problèmes D'Amour* (1983)), through indie pop (Orange Juice's No. 8 UK hit *Rip It Up* (1983)) to an obscure at the time work created by composer Charanjit Singh in Mumbai: *Synthesizing: Ten Ragas to a Disco Beat* (1982). See "The primer on the Roland TB-303" *The Wire*, 303 (May 2009) and Stuart Aitken (2011) "Charanjit Singh on how he invented acid house… by mistake," *The* Guardian, May 10, 2011, www.guardian.co.uk/music/2011/may/10/charanjit-singh-acid-house-ten-ragas.

15. Reynolds, *Generation Ecstasy*, p. 27.

16. *Ibid.*, p. 34.

17. Heiko Hoffmann (2005) "From the Autobahn to I-94: The origins of Detroit techno and Chicago house," http://pitchfork.com/features/articles/6204-from-the-autobahn-to-i-94.

18. "*techno-* from Gk. tekhno-, combining form of tekhne 'art, skill, craft, method, system'," www.etymonline.com/index.php?search=Techno.

19. Bussy, *Kraftwerk*, p. 149. The original title of Kraftwerk's 1986 album *Techno Pop* was actually going to be *Technicolor*!

20. Reynolds, *Generation Ecstasy*.

21. Dan Sicko (2010) *Techno Rebels: The Renegades of Electronic Funk*, 2nd edn. (Detroit, MI: Wayne State University Press).

22. Andy Thomas (2011) "ELECTRONIC ENIGMA: The myths and messages of Detroit techno," *Wax Poetics*, 45. Reproduced with additional discussion at http://createdigitalmusic.com/2011/06/future-shock-the-emergence-of-detroit-techno-told-by-wax-poetics.

23. Liner notes, *Techno! The New Dance Sound of Detroit.* 10 Records, 1988.

24. Simon Reynolds (2009) "THE HARDCORE CONTINUUM, or, (a) theory and its discontents," February 27, http://energyflashbysimonreynolds.blogspot.com/2009/02/hardcore-continuum-or-theory-and-its.html.

25. Birgit Richard and Heinz Hermann Kruger (1998) "RAVERS' PARADISE?: German youth cultures in the 1990s" in Tracey Skelton and Gill Valentine (eds.), *Cool Places: Geographies of Youth Cultures* (London: Routledge), pp. 162–75.

26. Quoted in Dave Haslam (2001) *Adventures on the Wheels of Steel: The Rise of the Superstar DJs* (London: Fourth Estate), p. 8.

27. Gavin Steingo (2005) "South African music after Apartheid: Kwaito, the 'party politic,' and the appropriation of gold as a sign of success," *Popular Music and Society*, 28(3): 333–57.

28. A number of other family trees are available online, from "Ishkur's guide to electronic music" website (http://techno.org/electronic-music-guide) explicitly mentioned later in this chapter to the Distilled agency's (not altogether accurate) 2011 animation of style progression and geographic location over time for the Thomson holiday company ("The evolution of Western dance music!" www.thomson.co.uk/blog/wp-content/uploads/infographic/interactive-music-map/index.html). *The Guardian* has an online interactive timeline of key moments in popular music, with tracks

for dance and R&B/hip hop (www.guardian.co.uk/music/interactive/2011/jun/11/history-modern-music-timeline) See also Peter Kirn (ed.) (2011). *Keyboard Presents the Evolution of Electronic Dance Music* (Montclair, NJ: Backbeat Books).

29. Simon Reynolds (2007) *Bring the Noise: 20 Years of Writing About Hip Rock and Hip Hop* (London: Faber & Faber), pp. 312–29.
30. www.discogs.com/Lil-Louis-French-Kiss/master/9593.
31. Shapiro (ed.), *Modulations*.
32. Brewster and Broughton, *Last Night a DJ Saved My Life*, p. 182.
33. Mark J. Butler (2006) *Unlocking the Groove* (Bloomington, IN: Indiana University Press), p. 137.
34. "Juke and footwork – from Chicago to the world," October 8, 2010, http://ripitup.co.nz/contentitem/feature-juke-and-footwork-from-chicago-to-the-world/1107. See also www.planet.mu/discography/ZIQ290 and www.planet.mu/reviews/ZIQ290?review=902.

9 Continuing the classical?

1. As we mentioned in the Introduction, the word "electroacoustic" is a great example of this. In 1982 Chion wrote: "The term Electroacoustic Music has expanded to such a degree that it has become a meaningless catch-all." In the original: "Musique électroacoustique a pris en se répandant une extension très grande, au point de devenir un fourre-tout sans signification précise." M. Chion (1982) *La musique électroacoustique* (Paris: PUF), p. 9.
2. See the discussion in Margaret Schedel (2007) "Electronic music and the studio" in Collins and d'Escriván (eds.), *The Cambridge Companion to Electronic Music*, pp. 24–37.
3. There are of course free and open source DAWs, for example, Ardour: http://ardour.org.
4. http://supercollider.sourceforge.net.
5. www.ircam.fr. For a fascinating and not uncritical discussion of IRCAM's culture through to the mid-1990s and issues of institutionalization, see Georgina Born (1995) *Rationalizing Culture: Boulez, IRCAM, and the Instituionalization of the Musical Avant-Garde* (Berkeley, CA: University of California Press).
6. www.zkm.de.
7. http://steim.org.
8. http://cnmat.berkeley.edu.
9. https://ccrma.stanford.edu.
10. www.cmmas.org.
11. www.cirmmt.mcgill.ca.
12. www.sarc.qub.ac.uk.
13. http://en.ccom.edu.cn/academics/cemc/introduction/200803240043.shtml.
14. Kees Tazelaar (2009) "The Institute of Sonology," *Leonardo Music Journal*, 19: 69–70.
15. Any resemblance to the 1950s fictional composer Hilda Tablet's *musique concrète reinforcée* is entirely coincidental.
16. www.inagrm.com.

17. www.agitateur.org/spip.php?page=imprimer&id_article=1248.

18. www.imeb.net/IMEB_v2/index.php?option=com_content&view=frontpage&Itemid= 100021.

19. Dhomont had independently begun experiments in musique concrète using a wire recorder around the same time as Schaeffer's early work: www. thecanadianencyclopedia.com/articles/emc/francis-dhomont. In the context of the theme of this chapter, it is also worth reading his artists' statement: Francis Dhomont (2007) "For classicism," in Collins and d'Escriván (eds.), *The Cambridge Companion to Electronic Music*, pp. 194–5.

20. The composer Kevin Austin, who teaches at Concordia, once described the program as "electroacoustics with options in music, rather than the other way around." Private conversation with the author, Montréal, 2000.

21. www.electrocd.com/en/bio/vandegorne_an. See also Eric de Visscher (2001) "Vande Gorne, Annette" in Stanley Sadie and John Tyrrell (eds.), *The New Grove Dictionary of Music and Musicians*, 2nd edn. (London: Macmillan).

22. Jonty Harrison (1989) "Denis Smalley, EMAS and (electro-acoustic) music," *Musical Times*, 130(1759): 528–9, 531.

23. www.electrocd.com/en/bio/harrison_jo.

24. For more information on Latin American electroacoustic music, see Ricardo del Farra's "Latin American electroacoustic music collection" on the Daniel Langlois Foundation website: www.fondation-langlois.org/html/e/page.php?NumPage=556.

25. Although the Acousmonium is rightly emphasized in the literature as an influential early example of such a system, it is worth noting that the Bourges group inaugurated its loudspeaker orchestra, the Gmebaphone, slightly earlier in the summer of 1973. See Christian Clozier (2001) "The Gmebaphone concept and the cybernéphone Instrument," *Computer Music Journal*, 25(4): 81–90.

26. François Bayle (2007) "Space, and more," *Organised Sound*, 12(3): 241–9. Multichannel systems established on the French model are often referred to as "loudspeaker orchestras."

27. *Ibid.*, p. 242.

28. Jonty Harrison (1999) "Diffusion: Theories and practices, with particular reference to the BEAST system," *eContact*, 2(4), http://cec.sonus.ca/econtact/Diffusion/Beast.htm.

29. Whether or not this should be considered performance is a matter of some disagreement.

30. The Gmebaphone is notable for its "spectral splitting" approach, dividing the sound into different frequency ranges and routing them to different speakers: Clozier, "The Gmebaphone concept."

31. For an overview, see David G. Malham and Anthony Myatt (1995) "3-D sound spatialization using ambisonic techniques," *Computer Music Journal*, 19(4): 58–70.

32. Ville Pulkki (2001) "Spatial sound generation and perception by amplitude panning techniques," Sc.D. dissertation, Sibelius Academy, Helsinki.

33. Chandrasekhar Ramakrishnan, Joachim Goßmann, and Ludger Brümmer (2006) "The ZKM Klangdom," *Proceedings of the 2006 International Conference on New Interfaces for Musical Expression (NIME06), Paris, France*, pp. 140–3.

34. Scott Wilson and Jonty Harrison (2010) "Rethinking the BEAST: Recent developments in multichannel composition at Birmingham ElectroAcoustic Sound Theatre," *Organised Sound*, 15: 239–50.

35. W. Matthew McFarlane (2003) "The development of acousmatics in Montréal," *eContact*, 6(2), http://cec.sonus.ca/econtact/6_2/mcfarlane_acousmatics.html.

36. Francis Dhomont (1995) "Acousmatic update / Rappel acousmatiques," *eContact*, 8(2), http://cec.sonus.ca/contact/contact82Dhom.html.

37. Jonty Harrison (2006) "Dilemmas, dichotomies and definitions: Acousmatic music and its precarious situation in the arts," keynote address to the *SoundAsArt* conference. Available online at: www.urbannovember.org/conference/viewpaper.php?id=31&cf=2.

38. Harrison, "Diffusion."

39. Nicolas Collins (2004) "Composers Inside Electronics: Music after David Tudor," *Leonardo Music Journal*, 14(1): 1–3.

40. Ron Kuivila (2004) "Open sources: Words, circuits and the notation-realization relation in the music of David Tudor," *Leonardo Music Journal*, 14: 17–23, at 20.

41. www.paristransatlantic.com/magazine/monthly2006/02feb_text.html#10.

42. Personal conversation with Scott Wilson, September 1999.

43. Alvin Lucier (1995) "'Every room has its own melody'" in *Reflections/Reflexionen* (Cologne: Musiktexte), pp. 94–103.

44. Alvin Lucier (1995) "'I am sitting in a room'" in *Reflections/Reflexionen*, pp. 322–35.

45. Chadabe, *Electric Sound*, pp. 101–3.

46. The Wikipedia article on experimental music provides an interesting overview of the history of the term, its various definitions, and the advocates thereof: http://en.wikipedia.org/wiki/Experimental_music.

47. For example, this is a central argument in Michael Nyman (1999) *Experimental Music: Cage and Beyond*, 2nd edn. (Cambridge University Press).

48. The fact that an experimental practice can even be said to comprise a "tradition" illustrates the etymological inconsistencies and politics involved!

49. www.nicolascollins.com/aboutpeasoup.htm.

50. Barry Truax (1996) "Soundscape, acoustic communication and environmental sound composition," *Contemporary Music Review*, 15(1–2): 49–65.

51. Barry Truax (2001) *Handbook for Acoustic Ecology* [CD-ROM] (Vancouver: Cambridge Street Publishing).

52. It is interesting to note that the WSP and acoustic ecology were born in the same city, and at about the same time, as Greenpeace.

53. http://wfae.proscenia.net.

54. www.chriswatson.net.

55. www.resoundings.org.

56. Noel B. Zahler (2012) "Davidovsky, Mario," *Grove Music Online. Oxford Music Online*, www.oxfordmusiconline.com/subscriber/article/grove/music/07281.

57. Eric Chasalow, liner notes to *The Music of Mario Davidovsky, Vol. 3.*

58. http://bangonacan.org.

59. Holmes, *Electronic and Experimental Music*, p. 368.

60. Julian Anderson (2000) "A provisional history of spectral music," *Contemporary Music Review*, 19(2): 7–22.

61. Diana Young (2002) "The Hyperbow controller: Real-time dynamics measurement of violin performance," *Proceedings of the 2002 Conference on New Instruments for Musical Expression (NIME-02)*, Dublin, Ireland.

62. See George Lewis (2000) "Too many notes: Computers, complexity and culture in Voyager," *Leonardo Music Journal*, 19: 33–9. For an interesting discussion of broader issues of interactivity in computer music, see George Lewis (1999) "Interacting with latter day musical automata," *Contemporary Music Review*, 18(3): 99–112.

63. For further discussion of Ferrari's use of ambient recordings, see Luc Ferrari (1996) "I was running in so many different directions," *Contemporary Music Review*, 15(1–2): 95–104.

64. http://magazine.concordia.ca/2006/Fall/features/rockers.shtml.

65. Prokofiev refers to his style as "nonclassical" and runs a record label of the same name. See http://gabrielprokofiev.com.

66. www.djspooky.com.

10 Experimental electronica

1. For more discussion of this and some overlapping themes, see Nick Collins (2009) "Electronica" in Roger Dean (ed.), *The Oxford Handbook to Computer Music* (New York: Oxford University Press), pp. 334–53.

2. Brian Eno (2004) "Ambient music" in Cox and Warner (eds.), *Audio Culture*, pp. 94–7.

3. William Duckworth (2005) *Virtual Music: How the Web Got Wired for Sound* (New York: Routledge), p. 5.

4. Amusingly, for the Residents are masters of dark humour, they released a disco dance beat version of *Eskimo* called *Diskomo* (1980)!

5. Rob Young (2005) *Warp Labels Unlimited* (London: Black Dog Publishing), p. 56.

6. *Ibid.*

7. Makis Solomis (1997) (Sharon Kanach (trans.)) Liner notes to *Xenakis: Electronic Music*, Electronic Music Foundation Ltd.

8. James Harley (2004) *Xenakis: His Life in Music* (New York: Routledge).

9. Umbro Apollono (ed.), Robert Brain, R. W. Flint, J. C. Higgitt, and Caroline Tisdall (translations) (1973) *Futurist Manifestos* (London: Thames & Hudson), pp. 86–7.

10. Carter was a frequent reader of the magazine *Practical Electronics*, as reported in the *Synth Britannia* documentary, BBC, aired October 16, 2009.

11. Hook, *The Haçienda*, p. 92.

12. Mick Sinclair (1984) "CONCERTO FOR VOICE AND MACHINERY," *Sounds*, January, http://micksinclair.com/sounds/einica.html.

13. Reynolds, *Rip It Up and Start Again*, p. 484.

14. *Ibid.*, p. 485.

15. *Ibid.*, p. 339.

16. Reynolds, *Bring the Noise*, p. xii.

17. Kim Cascone (2000) "The aesthetics of failure: 'Post-digital' tendencies in computer music," *Computer Music Journal*, 24(4): 12–18; Caleb Stuart (2003) "Damaged sound: Glitching and skipping compact discs in the audio of Yasunao Tone, Nicolas Collins and Oval," *Leonardo Music Journal*, 13: 47–52; Rob Young (2002) "Worship the glitch" in Rob Young (ed.), *Undercurrents: The Hidden Wiring of Modern Music* (London: Continuum), pp. 45–55; Janne Vanhanen (2003) "Virtual sound: Examining glitch and production," *Contemporary Music Review*, 22(4): 45–52; Phil Thomson (2004) "Atoms and errors: Towards a history and aesthetics of microsound," *Organised Sound*, 9(2): 207–18.

18. Kevin Concannon (1990) "CUT AND PASTE: COLLAGE AND THE ART OF SOUND," from Sound by Artists, Art Metropole and Walter Phillips Gallery. Available at www.ubu.com/papers/concannon.html

19. Shapiro (ed.), *Modulations*, p. 36.

20. Cascone, "The aesthetics of failure," 15–17.

21. *Ibid.*, 16.

22. Reed Ghazala (2005) *Circuit-Bending: Build Your Own Alien Instruments* (Indianapolis, IN: Wiley Publishing, Inc.); Nicolas Collins (2006) *Handmade Electronic Music: The Art of Hardware Hacking* (New York: Routledge).

23. Worms Making Music II, www.youtube.com/watch?v=Lb4jOCAr8ow.

24. John Latartara (2011) "Laptop composition at the turn of the millennium: Repetition and noise in the music of Oval, Merzbow, and Kid606," *Twentieth-Century Music*, 7(1): 91–115.

25. Karlheinz Stockhausen *et al.* (2004) "Stockhausen vs. the 'technocrats'" in Cox and Warner (eds.), *Audio Culture*, pp. 381–5.

26. Written on the actual CD of Autechre, *Anti EP* (1994), Warp Records.

27. See Latartara, "Laptop composition" for another three works analyzed through spectrograms.

28. "Kristin Grace Erickson >> Blectum from Blechdom," available at www.kevyb.com/portfolio/?page_id=51.

29. The Prix Ars electronica entry on their Distinction is a good insight into their humor and varied musical procedures: http://90.146.8.18/en/archives/prix_archive/prix_projekt.asp?iProjectID=11010.

30. http://en.wikipedia.org/wiki/The_Tuss.

11 Sound art

1. Though even here, an artist such as Francisco Lopez might straddle some people's classifications.

2. Satie and Picasso's collaboration on *Parade* in 1917, or Andy Warhol's work with the Velvet Underground, might also be worth mentioning in this regard.

3. Christoph Cox (2003) "Return to form: Christoph Cox on neo-modernist sound art," *Artforum International*, XLII(3).

4. Alan Licht (2007) *Sound Art: Beyond Music, Between Categories* (New York: Rizzoli), p. 221. Further discussion can be found in Joanna Demers (2010) *Listening Through the Noise: The Aesthetics of Experimental Electronic Music* (Oxford University Press), p. 70.

5. As Joanna Demers notes in her own discussion of the problems of definition, Alan Licht has changed his definitions from his 2007 book to a 2009 journal introduction: "a universal definition and definitive history of sound art may not be likely . . . but ultimately it is better to honour sound pieces created in a non-time-based, non-programmatic way as being sound art." Demers, *Listening Through the Noise*, p. 146.

6. www.annealockwood.com/compositions/pianotransplants.htm.

7. Christian Marclay (2012) *Cyanotypes* (Zurich: Ringier).

8. Licht, *Sound Art* calls out the austere CD packaging of the likes of Francisco Lopez and Ryoji Ikeka, claiming that the lack of image *is* the image.

9. Demers, *Listening Through the Noise*.

10. George Lewis, quoted in Jeanne Schinto (2001) "Raptured," www.sandiegoreader.com/news/2001/apr/19/cover-raptured.

11. William Furlong (2011, original 1994) in Caleb Kelly (ed.), *Sound* (Cambridge, MA: MIT Press/London: Whitechapel Gallery), p. 67.

12. Max Neuhaus (2000) "Sound art?" Liner notes for *Volume: Bed of Sound* (New York: P.S.1).

13. Demers, *Listening Through the Noise*, p. 42.

14. Licht, *Sound Art*, p. 274.

15. "Turner Prize: Susan Philipsz wins with Lowlands Away," *BBC News*, December 7, 2010, www.bbc.co.uk/news/entertainment-arts-11928557.

16. http://oliverranchfoundation.org/towerperformances.

17. www.max-neuhaus.info/drawings.

18. Max Neuhaus (1993), letter provided by Silvia Neuhaus.

19. Max Neuhaus, quoted in Alicia Zuckerman (2002) "Max Neuhaus' 'Times Square'," *Arts Electric*, www.artselectric.org/articles0203/020530.neuhaus.html.

20. www.max-neuhaus.info/soundworks/vectors/invention/sirens/Sirens.pdf.

21. www.musicweb-international.com/SandH/2000/may00/SonicBoom.htm.

22. Christian Marclay, quoted in Philip Sherburne (2005) "This artist makes music like you've never seen before, and art like you've never heard before," *Interview*, March: 162–7.

23. Alan Licht (2009) "Organizing the unpredictable: Tim Knowles and Pe Lang + Zimoun at bitforms gallery," http://rhizome.org/editorial/2009/feb/18/organizing-the-unpredictable.

24. Collins, "Electronica," p. 344.

25. www.christinakubisch.de/english/klangundlicht_frs.htm.

26. R. Murray Schafer (1994) *The Soundscape: Our Sonic Environment and the Tuning of the World* (Rochester, VT: Destiny Books), p. 212.

27. Janet Cardiff, quoted in Mirjam Schaub (2005) *Janet Cardiff: The Walk Book* (Vienna: ThyssenBornemisza Art Contemporary), p. 79.

28. Greg Tate (2007) *Black Light White Noise* (Houston: Contemporary Arts Museum), p. 42.
29. Paul Hegarty (2007) *Noise Music: A History* (New York: Continuum), p. 175.
30. Ryoji Ikeda (1997) +/− TO: 30 Touch, liner notes.
31. Charles Stankievech (2007) "From stethoscopes to headphones: An acoustic spatialization of subjectivity," *Leonardo Music Journal*, 17: 55–9.
32. Gascia Ouzounian (2008) "Sound art and spatial practices: Situating sound installation art since 1958," Ph.D. thesis, University of California, San Diego, p. 280.
33. This is the secondary title of Alan Licht's book *Sound Art*.

12 Further connections

1. Richard Wagner (1849) "Outlines of the artwork of the future" in Randall Packer and Ken Jordan (eds.) (2001), *Multimedia: From Wagner to Virtual Reality* (New York: W.W. Norton), p. 3.
2. Tay Vaughan (2006) *Multimedia: Making it Work* (New York: McGraw-Hill), p. 13.
3. Ken Friedman (2005) in Hans Breder and Klaus-Peter Busse (eds.), *Intermedia: Enacting the Liminal* (Dortmund: Schriften Zur Kunst), p. 51.
4. Coleridge wrote "Narrative allegory is distinguished from mythology as reality from symbol; it is, in short, the proper intermedium between person and personification." Albert Charles Hamilton (1990) *The Spenser Encyclopedia* (University of Toronto Press), p. 171.
5. Friedman in Breder and Busse (eds.), *Intermedia*, p. 14.
6. http://beagleboard.org/static/flyer_latest.pdf.
7. Edgar Berdahl and Wendy Ju (2011) "Satellite CCRMA: A musical interaction and sound synthesis platform," *Proceedings of the New Interfaces for Musical Expression Conference*, Oslo, Norway.
8. Larry L. Lash (2003) *Financial Times*, November 12.
9. www.olganeuwirth.com/fset1.html.
10. www.artnet.com/artwork/426086674/424400297/olga-neuwirth-miramondo-multiplo.html.
11. Barbara Fox (2005) "Schaeffer stands his ground: Orfée 53 and evocative sound," *EMS: Electroacoustic Music Studies Network*, Montréal.
12. Michael Chion (1998) *L'Opéra Concret: Musiques Concrètes 1971–1997* MCE, liner notes.
13. Barry Blesser and Linda-Ruth Salter (2006 *Spaces Speak, Are You Listening?: Experiencing Aural Architecture* (Cambridge, MA: MIT Press), p. 5.
14. John Cage (2011) *Silence: Lectures and Writings, 50th Anniversary Edition.* (Middletown, CT: Wesleyan University Press), p. 8.
15. Robert Ashley (2011) "The influence of John Cage," http://johncagetrust.blogspot.com/2012/02/robert-ashleys-influence-of-john-cage.html.
16. Sven Sterken (2001) "Towards a space-time art: Iannis Xenakis's polytopes," *Perspectives of New Music*, 39(2): 262–73. See also Harley, *Xenakis*.

17. David Worrall (1996) "A multichannel performance space for presenting experimental polymedia compositions," *MediaMix '96*, University of York.

18. Licht, *Sound Art*, p. 271.

19. Combinations of virtual and physical state in augmented reality are now fast growing as we seek fluid interfaces between the two.

20. Collins, *Game Sound*.

21. Scott Snibbe (2011) "With Biophilia, Björk creates album art for the 21st century (it's an app!)," www.fastcodesign.com/1664720/with-biophilia-bj-rk-creates-album-art-for-the-21st-century-its-an-app#1.

22. www.papasangre.com.

23. Nick Ryan in Jemima Kiss (2010) "Papa Sangre: The sonic iPhone horror game you've been looking for," *The Guardian*, December 20, www.guardian.co.uk/technology/pda/2010/dec/20/papa-sangre-game-audio.

24. *Ibid.*

25. There are also musical uses of game theory, which is the study of strategic decision making used famously by Iannis Xenakis in his compositions *Duel* (1959), *Stratégie* (1962), and *Linaia Agon* (1972).

26. Beverly Bryan (2008) "Lucky Dragons 'Make a Baby' with electricity and audience participation," *VenusZine*, http://ollestadresearch.blogspot.com/2010/10/one-word-joy.html.

27. Mark Feldmeier and Joseph. A. Paradiso (2007) "An interactive music environment for large groups with giveaway wireless motion sensors," *Computer Music Journal*, 31(1): 50–67.

28. Tomie Hahn and Curtis Bahn (2002) "Pikapika – the collaborative composition of an interactive sonic character," *Organised Sound*, 7(3): 229–38.

29. Ajay Kapur, Michael Darling, Dimitri Diakopoulos, Jim Murphy, Jordan Hochenbaum, Owen Vallis, and Curtis Bahn (2011) "The machine orchestra: An ensemble of human laptop performers and robotic musical instruments," *Computer Music Journal*, 25(4): 49–63.

30. Ajay Kapur (2005) "A history of robotic musical instruments," *Proceedings of the International Computer Music Conference*, Barcelona.

31. Paul D. Lehrman and Eric Singer (2006) "A 'Ballet mécanique' for the 21st century: Performing George Antheil's Dadaist masterpiece with robots," *Proceedings of the New Interfaces for Musical Expression Conference*, Paris.

32. Margaret E. Thomas (2000) "Nancarrow's canons: Projections of temporal and formal structures," *Perspectives of New Music*, 38(2): 106–33.

33. Margaret Boden and Ernest Edmonds (2009) "What is generative art?" *Digital Creativity*, 20(1–2): 21–46.

34. Personal conversation with Marius Watz, April 2008.

35. Robert Rowe (2001) *Machine Musicianship* (Cambridge, MA: MIT Press), p. 6.

36. Ryo Ikeshiro (2012) "Audiovisual harmony: The realtime audiovisualisation of a single data source in *Construction in Zhuangzi*," *Organised Sound*, 17(2): 148–55.

37. Thomas Hermann, Andy Hunt, and John G. Neuhoff (2011) "Introduction" in Thomas Hermann, Andy Hunt, and John G. Neuhoff (eds.), *The Sonification Handbook* (Berlin: Logos Publishing House), p. 21.

38. Archil Kobakhidze (2012) "Higgs the musical: The sound of the 'God particle'," *The Conversation*, July 19, 2012, http://theconversation.edu.au/higgs-the-musical-the-sound-of-the-god-particle-8252.

39. Lev Manovich (2002) "The anti-sublime ideal in data art," www.manovich.net/DOCS/data_art.doc.

40. Bob Sturm (2005) "Pulse of an ocean: Sonification of ocean buoy data," *Leonardo Music Journal*, 38(2): 143–9.

41. Garth Paine (2009) "Pools, pixies and potentials," *Proceedings of the 2009 International Symposium on Electronic Arts*, Singapore.

42. M. Asher and Guy Harries (2004) *Infantry*. Sub Rosa 186.

43. Mitchell Whitelaw (2008) "Synaesthesia and cross-modality in contemporary audiovisuals," *Senses and Society*, 3(3): 259–76, at 261.

44. Bill Alves (2005) "Digital harmony of sound and light," *Computer Music Journal*, 29(4): 45–54.

45. Amy Alexander and Nick Collins (2008) "Live audiovisuals" in Collins and d'Escriván (eds.), *The Cambridge Companion to Electronic Music*, pp. 126–39.

46. http://music.princeton.edu/PLOrk-Spring2009.

47. http://sarahweaver.org/resonations_international_telematic_music_concerts_for_peace.

48. Personal correspondence with Sarah Weaver, July 2012.

49. Chris Chafe and Michael Gurevich (2004) "Network time delay and ensemble accuracy: Effects of latency, asymmetry," *Proceedings of the AES 117th Convention*, San Francisco, CA

50. Juan-Pablo Caceres and Chris Chafe (2009) "JackTrip: Under the hood of an engine for network audio," *Proceedings of the International Computer Music Conference*, Montréal.

51. Personal correspondence with Nicolas Maigret.

52. Luke Dahl, Jorge Herrera, and Carr Wilkerson (2011) "TweetDreams: Making music with the audience and the world using real-time Twitter data," *Proceedings of the New Interfaces for Musical Expression Conference*, Oslo, Norway.

53. Luke DuBois (2011) "The first computer musician," http://opinionator.blogs.nytimes.com/2011/06/08/the-first-computer-musician.

54. Laurie Spiegel (1992) "Music: Who makes it? Who just takes it?" "Backpage" guest editorial in *Electronic Musician*, 8(1): 114.

13 Live electronic music

1. A search for Optron or Optrum on YouTube will reveal a number of videos of performances, including publicity for the Sony Walkman.

2. Laetitia Sonami. "The Lady's glove, a brief history," www.sonami.net/works/ladys-glove. See also Bert Bongers (2000) "Physical interfaces in the electronic arts:

Interaction theory and interfacing techniques for real-time performance" in Marcelo M. Wanderley and Marc Battier (eds.), *Trends in Gestural Control of Music* (Paris: IRCAM).

3. Julian Rohrhuber, Alberto de Campo, Renate Wieser, Jan-Kees van Kampen, Echo Ho, and Hannes Hölzl (2007) "Purloined letters and distributed persons," *Music in the Global Village Conference*, http://globalvillagemusic.net/2007/purloined-letters-and-distributed-persons.

4. Though concert income is by no means guaranteed. Many tours and shows have been loss leaders, or just losses, such as Rick Wakeman's extravagant *King Arthur on Ice* Wembley shows of 1975 or OMD's (highly unprofitable) support slots for Depeche Mode's (highly profitable) *101* tour in 1988.

5. Auto-Tune use has become ubiquitous. It has even been used to doctor talent show auditions, as in a 2010 scandal on the UK show *X Factor*. See Mark Savage (2010) "How commonplace is auto-tune?" *BBC News*, August 23, 2010, www.bbc.co.uk/news/entertainment-arts-11056840. Auto-Tune and other pitch-correction technologies have appeared in many popular music and music gaming contexts: One of the most amusing uses of Auto-Tune is in the YouTube series "Auto-Tune the news," which mixes up news footage with auto-tuned speech and music production.

6. Shapiro (ed.), *Modulations*, p. 96.

7. Derek Bailey (1980) *Improvisation: Its Nature and Practice in Music* (Ashbourne: Moorland Publishing).

8. Future recording formats may seek much more all-consuming reproductions beyond (typically stereo) sound alone and can attempt to simulate interactivity of experience in augmented reality following current-generation music video games.

9. An engaging discussion of this and related issues appears in reflections by Robert Henke (2007, 2009) "Live performance in the age of supercomputing. Parts 1 and II," www.monolake.de/interviews/supercomputing.html.

10. Jonty Harrison (1998) "Sound, space, sculpture: Some thoughts on the 'what', 'how' and 'why' of sound diffusion," *Organised Sound*, 3(2): 117–27.

11. Nicolas Collins (2007) "Live electronic music" in Collins and d'Escriván (eds.), *The Cambridge Companion to Electronic Music*, pp. 38–54, at pp. 43–5.

12. Simon Emmerson (2009) "Combining the acoustic and the digital: Music for instruments and computers or prerecorded sound" in Roger T. Dean (ed.), *The Oxford Handbook of Computer Music* (New York: Oxford University Press), pp. 167–88, at p. 168.

13. www.sensorband.com/soundnet/index.html.

14. Arguably, not all electronic music uses microphones and loudspeakers, as for instance in musical robotics, with computer-controlled acoustic synthesis (electrically triggered solenoids and motors physically strike, pluck, and energize acoustic instruments).

15. Eduardo R. Miranda and Marcelo M. Wanderley (2006) *New Digital Musical Instruments: Control and Interaction Beyond the Keyboard* (Middleton, WI: A-R Editions, Inc.).

16. Sageev Oore (2005) "Learning advanced skills on new instruments (or practising scales and arpeggios on your NIME," *Proceedings of NIME 2005*, Vancouver, Canada, pp. 60–5.

17. Sophy Smith (2000) "Compositional strategies of the hip-hop turntablist," *Organised Sound*, 5: 75–9.

18. Jon Caramanica (2011) "Lots of beats, but no drum in sight," *New York Times*, February 11, www.nytimes.com/2011/02/13/arts/music/13beatmachine.html?_r=2.

19. David Keane (1979) "Some practical aesthetic problems of electronic music composition," *Interface*, 8: 193–205, at 197.

20. See also Joel Ryan (1991) "Some remarks on musical instrument design at STEIM," *Contemporary Music Review*, 6(1): 3–17; Julio d'Escriván (2006) "To sing the body electric: Instruments and effort in the performance of electronic music," *Contemporary Music Review*, 25(1–2): 183–91; John Croft (2007) "Theses on liveness," *Organised Sound*, 12(1): 59–66.

21. These issues are discussed in the whole issue of Kim Cascone (ed.) (2003) "The laptop and electronic music," *Contemporary Music Review*, 22(4).

22. The trope of computer music performance inadequacy also appears in Andrew W. Schloss (2003) "Using contemporary technology in live performance: The dilemma of the performer," *Journal of New Music Research*, 32(3): 239–42.

23. Transporting electronic equipment to gigs can bring its own problems, from theft to overheating in desert festivals.

24. Reynolds, *Rip It Up and Start Again*, p. 165.

25. As another example, Bill Thompson's *dismantle* (2010) amplifies the sounds of laptop destruction against a backdrop of London's cathartically destructive Scrap Club. Bill Thompson (2010) "Scrapyard aesthetics and the swansong of the Inspiron," *eContact!*, 12(3), http://cec.sonus.ca/econtact/12_3/thompson_dismantle.html.

26. Amy Alexander and Nick Collins (2007) "Live audiovisuals" in Collins and d'Escriván (eds.), *The Cambridge Companion to Electronic Music*, pp. 126–39.

27. www.xsens.com/en/entertainment/live-entertainment/skrillex-live-on-stage.

28. Nicholas Cook (1998) *Analyzing Musical Multimedia* (Oxford University Press).

29. Ben Neill (2002) "Pleasure beats: Rhythm and the aesthetics of current electronic music," *Leonardo Music Journal*, 12: 3–6.

30. Pinch and Trocco, *Analog Days*.

31. Dan Trueman (2007) "Why a laptop orchestra?" *Organised Sound*, 12(2): 171–9.

32. Simon Emmerson (2007) *Living Electronic Music* (Aldershot: Ashgate), p. 114.

33. Chris Brown and John Bischoff (2002) "Indigenous to the Net: Early network music bands in the San Francisco Bay area," http://crossfade.walkerart.org/brownbischoff/IndigenoustotheNetPrint.html.

34. Sergi Jordà (2007) "Interactivity and live computer music" in Collins and d'Escriván (eds.), *The Cambridge Companion to Electronic Music*, pp. 89–106.

35. Ge Wang, Georg Essl, and Henri Penttinen (2012) "The mobile phone orchestra" in Sumanth Gopinath and Jason Stanyek (eds.), *The Oxford Handbook of Mobile Music Studies* (New York: Oxford University Press).

36. Boulez and Gerzso, "Computers in music."
37. Sean Bellaviti (2007) "Perception, reception, and all that popular music: An interview with Alejandro Viñao," *Discourses in Music*, 6(2) (Spring–Summer), available at www.discourses.ca/v6n2a1.html.
38. Rowe, *Machine Musicianship*.

14 Conclusions

1. Phil Cirocco (2006) "The Novachord restoration project," www.discretesynthesizers.com/nova/intro.htm.
2. Nigel Wrench (2008) "Lost tapes of the Dr Who composer," *BBC News*, July 18, http://news.bbc.co.uk/1/hi/entertainment/7512072.stm.
3. Future authors may have to defer to information assistants rather than hope to survey things themselves!
4. www.youtube.com/watch?v=BxQSEvHdyjQ.

Index

Cambridge Introductions to Music

'Cambridge University Press is to be congratulated for formulating the idea of an "Introductions to Music" series.' Nicholas Jones, *The Musical Times*

Each book in this series focuses on a topic fundamental to the study of music at undergraduate and graduate level. The introductions will also appeal to readers who want to broaden their understanding of the music they enjoy.

- Contain textboxes which highlight and summarise key information.
- Provide helpful guidance on specialised musical terminology.
- Thorough guides to further reading assist the reader in investigating the topic in more depth.

Books in the series

Electronic Music   Nick Collins, Margaret Schedel, and Scott Wilson

Gregorian Chant   David Hiley

Music Technology   Julio d'Escrivan

Opera   Robert Cannon

Postmodernism in Music   Kenneth Gloag

Serialism   Arnold Whittall

The Sonata   Thomas Schmidt-Beste

The Song Cycle   Laura Tunbridge